D1127552

The New Politics of Food

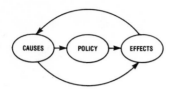

Policy Studies
Organization Series

The New Politics of Food

Edited by

Don F. Hadwiger
Iowa State University

William P. Browne
Central Michigan University

Lexington Books
D.C. Heath and Company
Lexington, Massachusetts
Toronto

Library of Congress Cataloging in Publication Data

Main entry under title:
  The new politics of food.

  (Policy Studies Organization series ; 19)
  1. Agriculture and state—United States—Addresses, essays, lectures.
I. Hadwiger, Don Frank, 1930-   II. Browne, William Paul, 1945-
III. Series: Policy Studies Organization. Policy Studies Organization series ;
19.
HD1765 1978.N48   338.1'873   77-11574
ISBN 0-669-01986-0

Published simultaneously in Canada.

Printed in the United States of America.

International Standard Book Number: 0-669-01986-0

Library of Congress Catalog Card Number: 77-11574

Contents

v

Acknowledgments

The editors very much appreciate the encouragement and support of Jim Hildreth and Neill Schaller (formerly) of Farm Foundation; J.B. Penn, John Lee, and Lynn Rader of the USDA Economic Research Service; and Stuart Nagel, Executive Secretary of the Policy Studies Organization, who provided vital help at every stage. We also wish to thank Risë Pennell, Sherry Smay, and Fran Dehn all of whom, as expert stenographers, were helpful in many editorial tasks. Don Hadwiger expresses appreciation to the USDA's Agricultural Research Service and the Iowa Agricultural Experiment Station, which provided him time and facilities needed for this undertaking.

The Policy Studies Organization gratefully thanks the United States Department of Agriculture for its aid to the symposium on which this book is based. Thanks are particularly owed to John Lee, J.B. Penn, and Lynn Rader of the USDA Economic Research Service. However, no one other than the individual authors is responsible for the ideas advocated here.

List of Abbreviations

AAA	Agricultural Adjustment Administration
AAM	American Agriculture Movement
AFBF	American Farm Bureau Federation
AMS	Agricultural Marketing Service
APHIS	Animal and Plant Health Inspection Service
ARPAC	Agricultural Research Policy Advisory Committee
ARS	Agricultural Research Service
ASCS	Agricultural Stabilization and Conservation Service
CBO	Congressional Budget Office
CCC	Commodity Credit Corporation
CEA/CFTC	Commodity Exchange Authority/Commodity Futures Trading Commission
CFA	Consumer Federation of America
CSRS	Cooperative State Research Service
DSG	Democratic Study Group
ERS	Economic Research Service
FAS	Foreign Agricultural Service
FCIC	Federal Crop Insurance Corporation
FCS	Farmers Cooperative Service
FES	Federal Extension Service
FmHA	Farmers Home Administration
FNS	Food and Nutrition Service
FS	Forest Service
NASULGC	National Association of State Universities and Land-Grant Colleges
NFO	National Farmers Organization
NFU	National Farmers Union
OMB	Office of Management and Budget
PMA	Production and Marketing Administration
PSA	Packers and Stockyards Administration
RDS	Rural Development Service
REA	Rural Electrication Administration
SCS	Soil Conservation Service
SRS	Statistical Reporting Service
USDA	U.S. Department of Agriculture

Part I
Agricultural Policy Changes and American Political Institutions

Introduction to Part I

William P. Browne

The lessons of American political history teach that changes in the policy process portend policy-related changes. And nowhere are process changes of potentially greater consequence than within the institutions responsible for policy making. The politics of American agriculture in the 1970s demonstrates vividly the relationship between institutional change and policy change, as well as how one limits the other.

From the depression of the 1930s until the passage of the 1973 farm bill, the general theme of agricultural policy was maintenance of farm incomes. To this end, specific agricultural programs emphasized production efficiency, economy of farm scale, soil conservation, and a battery of price supports. However, 1973 marked a decided turning point in general policy. Because the prospects for foreign food exports appeared attractive, supply control programs were deemphasized. Farmers were encouraged to plant every available acre and to maximize yield. Restraints on production were labeled as antiquated, and producers were urged to plow profits back into capital investments to ensure continuing increases in future years.

Then, according to the nation's farmers, disaster occurred. Supply outstripped demand as foreign markets demonstrated their unreliability. Farm prices fell below the cost of production. Once again, there were policy changes as the 1977 farm bill reincorporated many income maintenance measures of the past. The 1977 bill was not a simple return to prior practices though. Much of the production maximization spirit of 1973 was still manifest, and a new concern with budgetary responsibility permeated the bill's deliberations.

What caused these changes? Was the foreign market the sole explanatory variable? The first question is complex in its answer, but in large part it relates to institutional changes in American politics. The answer to the second question is emphatically "no." Foreign trade, like the issues of economy and budgeting, was only one factor in convincing the new alignment of participants in the agricultural policy process that basic policy change was in order. Accordingly, there was experimentation with ideas that were not really all new to 1973—the Farm Bureau had, after all, long championed many of the principles of that year's act. And 1977 was, in part, a reaction to the experiment.

The chapters in the first half of this book are about institutional changes as they explain what happened in 1973 and 1977. As the careful reader will note, change is tempered with continuity in the agricultural policy arena.

Most of the chapters in Part I focus on the subsystem concept of American politics—and for good reason. The "agriculture establishment," most observers have long agreed, has comprised one of the most closely knit, impenetrable cadres of political decision makers in the whole of American government. Since

3

the 1930s, whenever policies and programs have been enacted, they have been determined by a small cast of key members of Congress, U.S. Department of Agriculture (USDA) bureaucrats, interest group representatives, and research specialists. The subsystem has not been without conflict, but most of the conflict has been confined internally and arbitrated by the participants themselves.

In Chapter 1, Charles Hardin, one of the most prominent agricultural policy analysts for several decades, presents an overview of the changing agricultural subsystem as it relates to the price support issue. Of all the chapters, Hardin's contains the most information about Presidential leadership and its limits vis-à-vis the institutionalized powers in agricultural policy. After Hardin, and expanding on his comments, Laurellen Porter and John G. Peters explain changes within Congress. Porter's chapter deals with legislative reforms and their impact on the 1977 farm bill. Peters' analysis builds on Porter's research and examines logrolling, vote tradeoffs, and coalition building in the bill's final construction. Following those chapters, Alan S. Walter, a participant in the 1977 congressional budgeting negotiations, picks up on the reform comments of Professor Porter and draws conclusions about the future role of the Congressional Budget Office in agricultural appropriations.

Several aspects of bureaucracy are covered by Jan Mabie, Kenneth Meier, Alex McCalla, and Heather Johnston Nicholson. Mabie's analytical chapter demonstrates changes in the bureaucratic ranks and nicely relates those personnel moves to the funding of USDA bureaus. Similarly, Meier looks at USDA bureaus and the impact of their interest group support. McCalla's chapter is of special significance because it examines the presumed foundation of the modern agricultural establishment research. Professor Nicholson looks at one component of research in her case study of the science of agriculture versus the politics of agriculture. As per McCalla's warnings, Nicholson finds important policy results because of the demands made on science by the agricultural subsystem. Jonathan Lurie, with bureaucracy in mind, writes critically of the regulatory and self-regulatory features of the commodity exchanges.

Interest groups are a recurring subject in several of the chapters. Meier asks—in a quantitative study—what organizational support provides. Hardin and McCalla both take note of the fragmentation of interests and their support within the subsystems. A separate chapter by Charles Wiggins and myself examines the behavior of general farm organizations. Finally, James Guth examines consumer interests in terms of their strategies, strengths, and relationships to the agricultural subsystem.

What do we learn from these chapters? In terms of impact, the authors seem to agree that the agricultural subsystem, as a whole, is alive and well. The 1977 farm bill is used as the best example. Consensus exists, however, that the influence of agricultural institutions has been eroded by the accelerating competition for budgetary resources. But no one sees the agricultural establishment as out of control, contextually antiquated, or about to be toppled by new or old political forces. The change of greatest consequence appears to be the need for and the success of new coalition building with such "new" forces as labor, consumers, and even environmentalists.

Another notable point from this collection is the tremendous fragmentation of the subsystem itself. Perhaps, as the McCalla piece suggests, it would be better to speak of a set of agricultural subsystems rather than one. Unfortunately, no research exists to confirm the presence of multiple subsystems in Congress or to explain how they might operate within USDA. In fact, the Mabie and Meier chapters make it difficult to determine how multiple subsystems could maintain themselves.

Of course, not all the important changes in the institutions of American agriculture are dealt with in this book of readings. Only the Porter chapter deals sufficiently with changes in institutional personnel, and much current discussion suggests that Congress is not the only institution where such changes are of consequence.

Recent changes at the secretarial and directorship levels within the Department of Agriculture, for example, have drawn plaudits from groups outside the establishment. And, as noted in Chapter 10, new staff lobbyists are being added to the general farm organizations. These new faces and the perspectives they bring with them to the agricultural policy subsystem merit the attention of political researchers.

Finally, farmers themselves are neglected in most of Part I. The emergence of the American Agriculture Movement and its national farm strike indicates that this should not be so. As the article on the general farm groups suggests, farmers will stress economic demands prior to any of their other political concerns; and political institutions will respond to them. To what extent will the rest of the agricultural subsystem adjust? As a result, how much will agricultural subsystem participants intensify their conflict with the rest of the political system on issues of resource scarcity?

Those questions are not answered here. In that sense, this book is but a beginning. What we do have in Part I, while insufficient to answer each of the important questions about agricultural policy changes in the 1970s, is a series of chapters that provide an integrated view of a number of political institutions reacting together within a common environment. Their individual and collective adjustment to new conditions, as well as the importance of this adjustment to policy outcomes, is strikingly revealed. Thus these chapters, as a collection, are important because they demonstrate the explanatory value of a detailed, systematic inquiry into the specifics of one area of public policy. Careful readers will, I believe, know what limits on change to expect from the politics of agriculture.

1

Agricultural Price Policy: The Political Role of Bureaucracy

Charles M. Hardin

The Nature of Bureaucracy and Its Historical Role

Like much other American policy, agricultural price policy has been strongly influenced by what I shall call "bureaucracy" and others call "the triangle of power," or "political subsystems," or still other names—but like Stein and Shakespeare's roses, they are all the same.[1] Bureaucracies are found in centers of semi-independent power that arise in certain agencies and strategic legislators, committee chairmen usually, plus the affected and organized interests. Bureaucracies arise when clever politicians learn to use the stresses within our constitutional system to neutralize, to a significant extent at least, the ability of either the executive or Congress as a whole to supervise them. The bureaucracy then escapes control by either.

I shall cite the agricultural price support bureaucracy, first called the Agricultural Adjustment Administration (AAA), later the Production and Marketing Administration (PMA), then the Commodity Stabilization Service, and eventually the Agricultural Stabilization and Conservation Service (ASCS).

During its heyday, which lasted at least until the middle 1960s, the ASCS had considerable influence on policy. In World War II, in the face of the need for all-out food production, the AAA, concerned about the threat of surpluses to farmers, was a drag on the policy of expansion. Through the War Food Administration also and for the same reason—fear of surpluses—the bureaucracy pressed for the "bare shelf" policy toward the war's end when a disastrous famine in Western Europe was narrowly avoided. Then, too, the PMA was a considerable factor in maintaining high price supports in the postwar period until the late 1950s. These price supports helped pile up surpluses of feed grains, wheat, and cotton that prompted a huge surplus disposal program under P.L. 480, frequently including dumping. The surpluses and the need to sell them or get rid of them abroad also prompted Congress to shackle American efforts at technical assistance in agriculture. The concessional exports often hampered agricultural development in less developed countries.

Among many readers of a longer paper from which this is abstracted and with the proper absolutions, I wish to thank Professor James T. Bonnen and Ross B. Talbot for helpful criticisms of the material contained here.

Changes in the Structure of Policy Making

The 1960s brought changes in agricultural policies and politics. Farmers declined in numbers. The Supreme Court nullified the rural advantages in legislative apportionment. The vested position of agriculture, especially cotton, in the leadership of Congress was considerably weakened, and new interests—consumers, environmentalists, and organized labor—elbowed their way into farm policy making. Later, also, the executive began to preempt agricultural policy, for example, by imposing embargoes.

The agricultural political establishment, sometimes imprecisely called "the farm bloc," was often said to be nearing extinction. And yet its presence was still significantly felt, especially in cotton and wheat, in the Agricultural Act of 1965—and after that, too, even into the 1970s, judging by the way agricultural benefit payments bulked in the budget, considering the small numbers of farmers and producers who got the lions' shares.

In 1973, however, the long-heralded collapse of the "farm bloc" seemed to occur. The politics of agriculture had become so chaotic that the passage of any act seemed fortuitous. Nevertheless, Weldon V. Barton discerned an example of intricate coalition building in the House of Representatives that made the Agriculture and Consumer Protection Act appear more than accidental.[2] A coalition within agriculture including wheat, feed grains, and cotton—but with cotton no longer dominant—then achieved a logrolling deal with organized labor's representatives, backing minimum wage and food stamps for strikers in return for labor's backing of farm price supports and subsidies. Barton considered that the farm-labor coalition, although its durability is problematic, is essential to the retention of an effective farm price support policy.

James T. Bonnen also found coalition building among labor, consumers, and agriculture contributing much to the passage of the 1973 Agriculture and Consumer Protection Act. But his analysis suggests somewhat different interpretations from Barton. Bonnen believes that Presidential leadership is essential in agricultural price support legislation. Barton downplays the role of leadership in political analysis generally and in coalition building in particular. A second important difference is suggested by Bonnen, although the inference requires some violation of his intention, namely, that making a coalition between agricultural and consumer representatives would require bargaining on a price level that will appear neither too low to farmers nor too high to consumers—in short, the achievement of a workable compromise.[3] Barton views the coalition between agriculture and labor as operating through logrolling: neither agriculture nor labor worries about the other's piece of pie as long as it gets what it wants.

Changes in Price Policy

Before an evaluation is made of these differing conceptions of price policy making, a review of changes since 1961 is in order. These began in the feed grains program of 1961 and were marked in the Wheat-Cotton Act of 1964 and again in the Agricultural Act of 1965. They were continued with some adjustments in 1970 and with more fundamental shifts in 1973. At the heart of the changes is the move from price supports essentially through Commodity Credit Corporation (CCC) loans without recourse (although the CCC is still the engine of the price support program) to a policy of farm prices determined by the market with the government making up the difference between market prices and supported prices to cooperating farmers by means of "production payments." By the late 1960s, the new program, though expensive, was working well enough to please some economists and to appease political claimants.

The act of 1973, passed in a political climate conditioned by rapidly rising agricultural prices that reflected shortages occasioned by widespread droughts and crop failures, promised target prices to cooperating farmers. Cost of production, the bugbear of 1933, was substituted for parity. According to the USDA, the act was "designed to require few controls—to actually encourage production while including low product floor prices."

Market-Oriented Agricultural Price Policy: Portents of Durability

What, if any, are the portents of durability of a market-oriented price policy? One may be found in the memory of what happened under the price support programs of the 1940s and 1950s, namely, the surpluses that mounted ever higher despite the P.L. 480 program to peddle them on attractive, sometimes virtually give-away, terms abroad. The surpluses impelled a shift in policy to embrace an idea advocated by many agricultural economists, to let prices go to the market level and use production payments to give farmers parity or whatever.

A second portent favoring a market-oriented policy lies in the shift to production payments which, in contrast to the obscurities of the earlier method of supporting prices and subsidizing cooperating farmers through loans without recourse, are open and easily calculable. Government subsidies could then be readily linked to statistics on farm sizes and incomes, long a rather occult subject, that were being published. What the price support program cost and who got the benefits became much clearer. Those righteously indignant about the regressive income effects of farm price policy now had more ammunition. The complainants included Midwestern farm politicians, long chafing under the high costs of subsidies that went mainly to cotton and other Southern and Western crops but gave the Corn Belt a bad name. In 1973 Congress limited subsidy payments to $20,000 a year per farmer.

A third portent, perhaps the most important, lies in the political decline of agriculture. Loss of numbers, loss of overrepresentation, and loss of strategic congressional leverage were combined with the emergence of other interests— consumers and environmentalists—and the activation of labor's interest in farm policy. Also potentially significant may be the political awakening of taxpayers, those propelled by inflation into higher income tax brackets and increasingly fearful, and resentful, of inflation that they blame on governmental spending.

Such are the portents favoring a market-oriented farm price policy as against a policy of costly price supports in a country ordinarily blessed by an abundance of food—and one unvexed by the historical memory of famines or grinding food scarcities, the typical European experience that engenders support for policies protective of agriculture.

A Revival of High Price Supports

Nevertheless, agricultural politicians are prepared to show that reports of their death are greatly exaggerated. The target prices set by the act of 1973, if subsequent market forces outpaced them, were still generous when viewed by historical standards. The act also incorporated cost of production which was to provide an indexing feature designed to boost price supports. Then, too, Congress passed agricultural legislation in 1975, ultimately endorsed by organized labor as well as by consumer groups, considerably boosting price supports, only to have it vetoed by President Ford. In 1977 the Senate passed a bill raising price supports to a level that the administration first said was unacceptable and that set support levels markedly higher than those proposed by President Carter and Secretary Bergland. But the administration quite promptly raised its own proposals much closer to those of the Senate. The House bill was a bit lower than the Senate's, but the ultimate measure provided supports estimated to cost the Treasury $4 billion in fiscal 1978—twice the sum Carter had set for the upper limit. The administration's acquiescence had already been forecast in the announcement of dairy price supports at 85 percent of parity in order, according to Secretary Bergland, to avoid an even higher increase by Congress.

Policy Making for Agriculture: An Evaluation

Returning to the classic tensions between President and Congress, we may ask whether the executive is showing skill in using its instruments of governance, including liaison with members of Congress, consolidation of support among the public, and persuasion of the agencies, as well as a sense of timing and an appreciation of the virtues of consistency that, all together, add up to effective leadership. With regard to agricultural policy, at least a feeling grew in 1977 of vacillation and uncertainty in the Carter White House.

Congress, however, has strengthened its struggle for ascendancy by organizing itself to attain what might be called its own presidential perspective. The agency to achieve the degree of hierarchy necessary to effective congressional government under modern conditions, the Budget Committee, tends to agree with the President. But then the hopes of both are undermined by the traditional group, committee, and bureaucratic orientation of Congress. It is an interesting question whether congressional coalition building will support Presidential or traditional congressional perspectives. To oversimplify somewhat, a coalition between consumers and farmers, negotiating out their divergent interests on food price levels, should attain more of an aggregating policy, more of a "presidential" perspective. By contrast, a coalition between agriculture and labor would likely be based on more traditional logrolling.

Which of these alternatives, if they are real, would more nearly provide and maintain a market-oriented farm price policy? Such a policy requires an aggregative approach to agriculture rather than one composed of an amalgamation of commodity policies, many of which are designed with a view to serving commodity interests nearly exclusively. This statement becomes more convincing when we consider foreign policy in the economic aspects of which agriculture is heavily involved. Negotiating tariffs, persuading foreign countries to rationalize their agricultural policies, dealing with international cartels—all are, by nature, executive matters, as are the more dangerous defense policies. They call for a synchronizing and integrating approach. The fact that a number of recent Presidents have committed grave mistakes in foreign affairs does not mean that congressional foreign policy with, potentially at least, 535 Secretaries of State is a viable alternative.

Domestically, too, we find agricultural price policy often "picked to pieces" by "local and special interests."[4] Tobacco, dairy, rice, peanuts, wool, sugar, and cotton programs provide examples. The trend seems to favor commodity approaches, and differentiations within commodities, as the Flanigan report of 1972 suggested when it found that commodity organizations are more effective politically than general farm organizations. "They can zero in on legislation. . . . They are more sophisticated . . . better organized, and . . . have better access to power than many other special interest groups."[5]

The fragmentation of farm policy promises to be promoted further by the shift from parity to cost of production as a rationale, a slogan, a goal, and a moral purpose of agricultural policy. Parity was an aggregating concept in principle, at least, whereas cost of production makes no sense unless it is broken down by commodities and even by farms. As the Congressional Budget Office (CBO) put it, "Production costs are highly variable among farms and regions. Differences in farm sizes and management skills affect production costs importantly."[6]

The fragmenting trend in the agricultural political establishment may be countered by tendencies, exemplified in the budget committees and the CBO, for Congress to consolidate itself and to develop its own hierarchy, its own capacity for centralized leadership. Within Congress, however, the indigenous fragmenting tendencies that contributed vitally to the growth of bureaucratic power are still alive. If these tendencies are weakened somewhat in committees, they are strengthened in individual members of Congress, each enjoying vastly expanded resources and increasing advantages as an incumbent in obtaining reelection. As the position is enhanced in attractiveness, each member of Congress is all the more motivated to hang on to it—"running scared" in the time-honored tradition. In districts with considerable agriculture, the situation will be ripe for mutual assistance between members of Congress and commodity organizations who form, between them, two legs of the bureaucratic triangle. The dairy cooperatives have shown the way.

No inexorable forces seem to coincide in order to compel agricultural policy to aggregate, for example, on the principle of market orientation or, contrarily, to strengthen and perpetuate the traditional congressional tendency to fragment policy. Willard Cochrane and Mary E. Ryan cite three factors that may maintain the "essential integrity and internal consistency of farm policy"[7] against the tendency for local and special interests to pick it to pieces, namely, program costs, party discipline, or Presidential leadership. Program costs may become more urgent factors in congressional actions as middle-income constituents become increasingly conscious of the growth of their tax burdens. The argument for Presidential leadership has been adumbrated above. Elsewhere, I have argued for party government, not just with regard to agricultural policy, but to cope with more fundamental defects of the American political system.[8]

Notes

1. Richard E. Neustadt, "Politicians and Bureaucrats," in David B. Truman (ed.), *The Congress and America's Future* (Englewood Cliffs, N.J.: Prentice-Hall 1955); applied to agriculture in my *Food and Fiber in the Nation's Politics* (Washington: GPO, 1967). See also my *Presidential Power and Accountability* (Chicago: University of Chicago Press, 1974), chaps. 4 to 6. James T. Bonnen, "Observations on the Changing Nature of National Agricultural Policy Decisions," Department of Agricultural Economics, Michigan State University, 1977. Ivan Garth Youngberg, "U.S. Agriculture in the 1970's: Policy and Prospects," in James E. Anderson (ed.), *Economic Regulatory Policies* (Lexington, Mass.: D.C. Heath, 1975).

2. See his "Coalition-building in the U.S. House of Representatives: Agricultural Legislation in 1973" American Political Science Association Convention, Chicago, 1974.

3. See note 1 for the reference. Professor Bonnen objected to an earlier draft that sharpened the distinction between him and Barton (letter to the author, Sept. 13, 1977). The real strength of "consumer groups" he said, lies in their allies, organized labor (this accords with the stress on the importance of formally organized groups in interest group politics); cf. Edward C. Banfield,

Political Influence (New York: The Free Press, 1961), and James Q. Wilson, *Political Organizations* (New York: Basic Books, 1973). Nevertheless, the distinction between logrolling and compromise is vital, and the function of compromise must operate somewhere if government is to achieve fiscal responsibility. See Lewis Froman, *The Congressional Process* (Boston: Little Brown, 1967).

4. Willard Cochrane and Mary E. Ryan, *American Farm Policy, 1948-1973* (Minneapolis: University of Minnesota Press, 1976), p. 114.

5. *The Congressional Record*, April 12, 1973, S 7201 ff.

6. Congressional Budget Office, "Food and Agriculture Policy Options," February 1977, Congress of the United States, Washington, p. 29.

7. Cochrane and Ryan, *American Farm Policy*.

8. Hardin, *Presidential Power and Accountability*.

2 Congress and Agricultural Policy, 1977

Laurellen Porter

Introduction

In short term and for the short term, the dynamic agricultural commodity tail appears to wag the dog of congressional food and fiber policies. For the long term, basic, comprehensive decision rules and practices within these rules are contextually more important in shaping policy outcomes than are problems with current-year crops. Process is policy; it is also context for the substantively policy-oriented. Procedural changes alter the opportunities of various actors to influence government programs.

A Reformed House of Representatives

Since 1950, the rapid decline in the number of individuals engaged in agriculture and associated rural occupations, coupled with the constitutional requirements for reapportionment and redistricting after each national census, altered both the geographical constituencies and the composition of the House parties. From within the Congress in the 1970s, representatives of farming areas and spokesmen for agricultural concerns spoke of an urban Congress lacking basic understanding of farm and other rural issues. They pursued a number of strategies, and the legislative record contained numerous references, both negative and positive, to farm-labor, rural-urban, rural-suburban, and urban-cotton coalitions. Jamie Whitten, chairman of the Subcommittee on Appropriations for Agriculture and Related Agencies, championed urban 4-H clubs, urban gardens, farmers' markets, and improved wholesale facilities for farm produce as he sought to educate and enlarge the constituency for agricultural programs. House members from rural districts organized and staffed the Congressional Rural Caucus to support funding at adequate levels authorized programs for rural development, including housing, sanitation, water projects, and economic development.

A secular change in the composition of the majority party of the House of Representatives, particularly from 1958 on, provided the conditions for institutional change within Congress. Most noteworthy, the House Democratic Party became much more Northern, urban, and liberal. In the decade following World War II, Southern Democrats had constituted a majority of the House Democratic Party and acquired the seniority on committees by which they were able to

15

dominate policy decisions long after the Northern Democrats had become numerically the dominant wing of the House Party. Liberal Democrats organized in 1959 to affect policy outcomes and sought to develop alternatives to conservative positions. Their mechanism was the Democratic Study Group (DSG) with its own staff and whip system.[1] By the late 1960s, DSG was convinced of the need for reorganizing the House Democratic Party, for revising and formalizing the procedures of House standing committees so often dominated by elderly and Southern chairmen, and for upgrading the support systems and reforming the rules of the House of Representatives. DSG pressures bore fruit in the Legislative Reorganization Act of 1970 and in House rule changes and party reforms in the 92d, 93d, 94th, and 95th Congresses. House Republicans actively supported House rule changes which would enhance their positions and at times upstaged and pressured the Democrats with their own party reforms. As a consequence, the House of Representatives is a much different legislative assembly from what it was a few Congresses ago.

In the early 1970s the Democratic Caucus became the instrument of the House party's majority for influencing committee assignments, selecting committee chairmen, reorganizing the party's instruments of leadership, and, to a lesser extent, asserting its right to have caucus-supported amendments to tax bills considered on the House floor.[2]

Personnel decisions within the caucus in 1975 caught public attention as they demonstrated a new majority and a new will. The caucus unseated three chairmen of standing committees; all were Southerners, and all were elderly. Representative W.R. Poage of Texas, first elected to the House in 1937, lost his chairmanship of the House Agriculture Commiteee by a very narrow margin. He was replaced by Representative Thomas S. Foley of Washington, second-ranking Democrat on the committee and, at the time, chairman of the Democratic Study Group. In 1977 the House Democrats selected all committee chairmen on the basis of seniority; however, they ousted one scandal-riddened chairman of an Appropriations subcommittee, and several voted against Jamie L. Whitten (D-Miss.), the dominating chairman of the Subcommittee on Agriculture Appropriations. Representative Whitten in 1975 had saved his chairmanship by relinquishing jurisdiction over consumer and environmental matters. By 1977, Southern Democrats constituted 30 percent of the House Democratic Party and held 5 of 22 chairmanships of standing committees.

The quality and style of leadership may be as important as the composition of the Congress. Discretionary leadership choices provide clues to the direction in which important elements wish to move an institution. One recent study of the motivations of freshman Democrats in supporting the unseating of senior chairmen emphasized the criterion of fairness to all sides in the committees.[3] Chairmen were unseated if their committee performances were judged unfair and if suitable alternatives by this same standard were available. If this were the standard, Chairman Foley fully qualified. The House debate on the farm bill in

1977 was replete with encomiums attesting to the chairman's patience, fairness, and legislative skills.

Caucus efforts to strengthen the Speaker were as important as its actions on personnel. In 1973, the caucus created a new Steering and Policy Committee, chaired by the Speaker. Its 24 members included all party leaders; the whip hierarchy; 4 members appointed by the Speaker to represent such disadvantaged groups as women, blacks, and freshmen; and 12 members chosen by the regional caucuses. The committee's major function in weekly meetings is to develop policy and oversee the party's legislative strategies.[4] In 1975 the Steering and Policy Committee was also assigned the committee-on-committee functions, formerly exercised by Democrats on the Ways and Means Committee. The Speaker's powers to move legislation were further strengthened by the caucus's decision that the Speaker should appoint all Democratic members of the Rules Committee, subject to reappointment with each new Congress. The enlargement of the whip organization and an increase in its professional staff further enhanced the leadership's ability to inform and advise the membership and to be informed of member concerns—but without displacing DSGs.

Democrats disputed a major reorganization of the House standing committee jurisdictions in the fall of 1974 and settled on a modest committee reform and on House rule changes to legitimate innovation in bill assignments to committees. The House's failure in 1974 to enact a more comprehensive reform of its committee jurisdictions contributed to a new emphasis in the rules and in practice on leadership "ad hocracy," itself a powerful tool for a knowledgeable leader.

The 1974 reform of the committee jurisdictions did transfer the nontariff aspects of international trade from the Ways and Means Committee and the foreign policy aspects of the Food for Peace programs from the Committee on Agriculture to the House Committee on International Relations, formerly the House Foreign Affairs Committee. Both transfers affected agricultural interests. Both were executed not for policy purposes but rather to upgrade the House standing committee on foreign policy relative to its Senate counterpart.

As noted above, since the early 1970s Democrats have moved toward majority party and leadership control of the policy processes of the House of Representatives. Other forces made for decentralization in the House Democratic Party. One such force was the size of the majority party. In 1977 the political needs and goals of 290 members had to be accommodated within a single party. The House Agriculture Committee experienced some typical problems of size and turnover.

By House rules, adopted in 1974, Democrats and Republicans are to be assigned to committees at a ratio approximating that of the two parties in the House of Representatives: 5:4 in the 93d Congress; 2:1 in the 94th Congress; and 2:1 plus 1 in the 95th Congress. The House Agriculture Committee during the 93d Congress had 20 Democrats and 16 Republicans. Rather than drop

Republicans, the Agriculture Committee was expanded to 38 Democrats and 14 Republicans in 1975 and to 31 Democrats and 15 Republicans in 1977. Of the 46, 11 were new to the committee, 10 new to Congress, and 18 in their second congressional term. Regional representation had also shifted; in 1973, half of the Democrats on the committee, including its chairman, were from 13 Southern states; in 1977, only 10 of 31 represented these states. Most of the Republicans were Midwesterners. In 1977 passing a major farm and food bill through the House of Representatives proved to be easier for the committee and House leadership than integrating the efforts of the large and inexperienced membership of the Committee on Agriculture.

Other developments increased the problems of coordination. Committees fragmented at the subcommittee level. Standing committee chairmen lost their perquisites: subcommittee assignments, control of staff, bill assignment to subcommittees, and resources to mobilize external support from other chairmen and members. Subcommittees proliferated in response to member goals, specialization, increased workloads, and recent rule changes requiring committees to organize subcommittees. In 1977 almost half of all Democrats, including many juniors, headed subcommittees. Subcommittee chairmen often processed legislation from the initial stages of consideration on through a full committee, the House Rules Committee, floor consideration, a conference committee, and back to the floor. At times problems developed with poorly crafted bills, jurisdictional disputes, inadequate floor preparation, unanticipated floor reactions, and a shortfall of the political wallop needed to deliver votes from busy members of Congress.[5] Many members without much legislative experience had a "stake in the action" but in a way that fragmented the whole.

The House Agriculture Committee operated in the mid-1970s with six commodity subcommittees and four operational subcommittees. Two second-term Democrats became subcommittee chairmen in January 1977. Frederick Richmond, a wealthy representative from a predominantly black and Spanish district of New York City, headed the Domestic Marketing, Consumer Relations, and Nutrition Subcommittee with jurisdiction over food stamps. Farm district Congressman Richard Nolan of Minnesota, at 33 an intense advocate of the family farm and a vocal opponent of corporate agriculture, headed the Subcommittee on the Family Farm, Rural Development, and Special Studies. In 1977, subcommittee chairmen made the case for the title or titles of the agriculture bill under the jurisdictions of their respective subcommittees. Several of these chairmen proposed amendments previously defeated in the full committee. Often they were opposed by Chairman Foley, who insisted on hearings, adequate study, and more concern for the aggregate implications of the proposals for the farm program.

A tendency toward fragmentation and decentralization in the House of Representatives is also a latent consequence of reforms meant to enhance responsiveness and accountability to the public: recorded teller votes, open markups, open conference committee sessions, and a myriad of bill reporting requirements, including committee votes.

Congressional support agencies, especially following their staff explosions of the 1960s, enhance the influence of those who have both access to them and the skill to utilize their products. It seems that in recent years many of those specifically recruited to congressional policy and leadership positions, and many of their colleagues, organize themselves in terms of explicit conceptual frameworks differing in degree at least from those of the generation they are replacing. Congresspersons speak of inputs, outputs, feedback, systemwide effects, trade-offs, subsystems, interdependencies, data bases, computerized models and analyses, etc. Not surprisingly, in a Congress designed as a key element of a national system, this mode of analysis easily adapts to an emphasis on national and international perspectives which support a rationale for system dominance of subsystems. Excellent examples of the modern congressman at work and the utilization of support services can be found in Representative Foley's account in 1976 of the investigations of the food stamp program by the Agriculture Committee.[6] Foley's brief comments on proposed amendments during the debate on the agriculture bill in 1977 exemplified a national perspective on food and agriculture issues.

The Senate

The Senate, less directly and dramatically impacted by population changes and shifts and less organized than the larger House, lagged the House in its internal reforms, participated with the House in increasing the number and quality of staff and congressional support agencies, and followed the House in opening its committee meetings to the public. It modified its cloture rule. In early 1977, the Senate adopted a major reform of its standing committees, reducing their number, rationalizing jurisdictions, and limiting the number of committee, subcommittee, and chairmanship assignments of any one senator. The reform also included provisions for improving scheduling of committee floor activities, mandated public notice of committee hearings, and procedures to speed the flow of work on the Senate floor.[7]

The 1977 Senate committee reform renamed the Agriculture Committee as the Agriculture, Nutrition, and Forestry Committee. The resolution brought to the Senate floor abolished outright the Select Committee on Nutrition and Human Needs and transferred its functions to the agriculture panel as of December 31, 1977. Existing subcommittees were continued, and a new Subcommittee on Nutrition was added. As before, the whole committee handled food stamps.

Committee assignment decisions in 1977 increased the size of the Agriculture, Nutrition, and Forestry Committee from 14 to 18; 11 were Democrats, and 7 Republicans. Three of the four newcomers were from the Midwest; the fourth was a California Republican. The committee in 1977 included among its ranks a former Vice President, two former major party candidates for the United States Presidency, and a recent candidate for Vice President.

Budgeting for the Agriculture Function

The Budget and Impoundment Act of 1974 (P.L. 93-344), more than most congressional reforms discussed, affects directly and generally the substantive policy outcomes of Congress. The act created a new budget process with an awesome timetable structuring all legislative efforts—authorizations, appropriations, and taxation. It established a budget committee with staff in each house. Several consequences followed. First, the CBO, the budget committees, and the standing committees in required reports to the budget committees provide additional and alternative sources of information to that of the executive branch and conventional sources. Second, the process affects issue definitions. Third, there is a new explicitness about goals and value choices.[8]

For the committees of Congress, budget considerations are pervasive. Programs and policies that are relatively low-cost or which require less Treasury "exposure" have survival advantages. Monitoring activities by the budget committees and the CBO throughout the legislative year inform committees of cost estimates of current programs and of proposals being considered.

FY 1978 budgeting for the agriculture function, the smallest of the budget categories, may have been the exception that proved a rule of some sort. Agricultural expenditures for the short term were the least manageable of all budget functions.

The Carter administration in February requested $2.3 billion for agriculture for the 1978 fiscal year. The Senate recommended an allocation of $3.7 billion. Senate conferees agreed to the "higher House outlay levels for agriculture to reflect the high cost of new farm bills being drafted by the House and Senate Agriculture Committees and the lack of detailed estimates for those bills from the Agriculture Department."[9] The agreed target ceiling was $4.35 billion.

Less than a week after Congress adopted its first budget resolution for fiscal 1978, the Senate Agriculture Committee brought its food and agriculture bill before the Senate. Projected costs for commodity price support programs exceeded those allocated to such programs in the budget resolution. Senator Muskie, chairman of the Budget Committee, doggedly defined the major issue of the commodity portions of the bill as a budget issue both for fiscal 1978 and for later years. His views did not prevail on the Senate bill. Budget Chairman Giaimo reminded his colleagues throughout the spring and summer that

the pressures on the Federal Budget are enormous, and deserving as the American farmer is of every consideration by Government, other sectors of the economy have equally pressing needs—cities, states, the poor, minorities, older Americans—all can lay claim to a portion of the Nation's resources. To be fair to all, we must make hard choices in every budget category.[10]

Like Senator Muskie, Representative Giaimo appeared to have little influence on budgeting for agriculture—at least for the immediate future.

In early August, CBO estimated costs of the Senate version of the farm bill at \$5.6 billion for the 1978 fiscal year. It later projected the costs of the conference bill at \$6.3 billion. In the debate on the conference report, it was claimed that USDA estimates in mid-September, based on new crop reports and administrative decisions made under the pending legislation, put the 1978 costs at \$7.7 billion.[11]

The Senate Budget Committee in September reported a second budget resolution with a ceiling of \$5.6 billion for the agriculture function. The resolution included language in the nature of a reconciliation instruction directing the Agriculture Committee to limit the spending under its direction to an amount not to exceed \$5.6 billion. Senator Talmadge, chairman of the Committee on Agriculture, Nutrition, and Forestry, offered an amendment for himself and 37 cosponsors to increase the resolutions ceiling to \$6.3 billion. The amendment, thoroughly debated, passed the Senate 64-27. The House Budget Committee accepted the House Agriculture Committee's August estimate for the House bill at \$6.102 billion. An amendment offered by Representative Foley and accepted by the House increased the ceiling by \$200,000. The conference and both houses accepted a \$6.3 billion target for agricultural spending in the 1978 fiscal year.

Attention given to the farm bill and the budget resolution for the 1978 fiscal year was focused on short-run or even immediate outlays as deficiency payments for producers of corn, wheat, rice, and perhaps sugar. For the long term, other provisions of the bill were important. In many respects, the Food and Agriculture Act of 1977, as passed, was much more oriented to a national management of agricultural decisions and activities in the aggregate than earlier programs had been. The act authorized adjusting commodity programs comprehensively, taking into account the interdependencies among crops as these relate to prices, production, acreage set-asides, and supply management. Several provisions promoted market adjustments of supply and price. The Senate cost of production guarantee in its bill was dropped in favor of a House formula for adjusting target prices to changes in production costs. Compliance with the national farm program was encouraged by increased payment ceilings and more stringent requirements for payment eligibility, including participation in USDA set-aside acreage programs. From a national perspective, the bill sought to balance the interests of consumers and producers and to control program costs to the federal government.

Notes

1. Norman J. Ornstein, "Causes and Consequences of Congressional Change: Subcommittee Reforms in the House of Representatives, 1970-1973," in Norman J. Ornstein (ed.), *Congress in Change: Evolution and Reform* (New York: Praeger, 1975), pp. 90-91.

2. Larry Dodd, "Emergence of Party Government in the House of Representatives," *DEA News Supplement*, no. 10, a publication of the Division of Educational Affairs, American Political Science Association, Washington, Summer 1976, p. S1.

3. Burdett A. Loomis, "Freshman Democrats in the 94th Congress: Actions and Reactions to a Changing House," a paper presented at the meeting of the Midwest Political Science Association, Chicago, April 21-23, 1977, p. 11.

4. Bruce I. Oppenheimer, "The Rules Committee in the New House," a paper presented at the annual meeting of the Midwest Political Science Association, Chicago, April 21-23, 1977.

6. U.S. Cong., House of Representatives, Committee on Agriculture, *Food Stamp Program: Hearings before the Committee on Agriculture*, 94th Cong., 2d Sess., Washington, 1976, pp. 13-14.

7. "Senate Approves Committee Changes," *Congressional Quarterly Weekly Report*, 35, no. 7 (February 12, 1977):279-284.

8. Catherine Rudder, "Changes in Congress: The Budgetary Process and Finance Policy," *DEA News Supplement*, no. 10, a publication of the Division of Educational Affairs, American Political Science Association, Washington, Summer 1976. Also see Catherine Rudder, "The Impact of the Budget and Impoundment Control Act of 1974 on the Revenue Committees of the U.S. Congress," a paper presented at the annual meeting of the Midwest Political Science Association, Chicago, April 21-23, 1977.

9. "Conference Agrees on Defense Targets," *Congressional Quarterly Weekly Report*, 35, no. 20 (May 14, 1977):900.

10. Cong. Rec., 26 April, 1977, p. H3554.

11. Cong. Rec., 8 Sept., 1977, p. S14334.

3

The 1977 Farm Bill: Coalitions in Congress

John G. Peters

Introduction

On September 15, 1977 the U.S. House of Representatives voted 283-107 to adopt the 1977 farm-food bill. When the chair announced the final vote, House members, Democrats, and Republicans alike honored Agricultural Committee Chairman Thomas Foley (D-Wash.) with a rare standing ovation for his skillful handling of a controversial and complex piece of legislation.[1] The vote culminated months of technical and tedious committee hearings and markup sessions, two full weeks of arduous and delicate floor debate including consideration of over 40 amendments, followed by a week of tough bargaining in the House-Senate Conference Committee. The bill itself was one of the most technical and varied pieces of legislation considered by Congress for some time. The final version consisted of 18 separate titles ranging from the traditional commodity support programs on wheat, corn, and other feed grains, cotton, dairy, rice, peanuts, soybeans, and sugar to food stamps, Food for Peace (P.L. 480), rural development, federal grain inspection, and wheat research and nutrition education.[2]

The ovation for Chairman Foley was well deserved. A combination of depressed prices for farm commodities, a general "drying up" of farm credit (especially in the Great Plains region), the prospect of bumper wheat and corn crops added to the already burgeoning stocks on hand, and the general difficulties which rural representatives have in obtaining needed agricultural legislation coalesced in 1977 to produce a situation requiring the development of intricate legislative strategies if passage of the new farm bill was to be ensured. Chairman Foley, then, had to pursue a legislative strategy which resulted in a farm bill that was capable of securing enough votes for passage on the House floor, that provided sound programs to satisfy the demands of farmers and consumers, and that allowed new members of the Agriculture Committee opportunities to build reelection records, all with a price tag acceptable to a President who threatened to veto any "budget busting" farm program.

This study is based on research conducted by the author during the spring and summer of 1977. Many of the findings reported here are derived from interviews conducted with 25 members of the U.S. House Agriculture Committee and many congressional staff members. The author acknowledges the financial support of the University of Nebraska Fund for the Study of Congress administered by Professor Adam C. Breckenridge, and thanks Representative Charles Thone (R-Neb.) and his Washington staff for their help on this project.

Some Old and New Strategies

Every congressional committee faces problems in overcoming the obstacles standing in the way of achieving member and committee goals.[3] In the past twenty years, primarily the House Agriculture Committee has faced the difficulty of finding enough votes to secure passage of agricultural legislation.[4] The dimensions of this problem can be better understood when one considers that in 1976 out of 435 congressional districts, perhaps only 80 could truly be labeled as rural. In practical terms, this means that approximately 150 urban and suburban members have to be convinced to vote for agricultural legislation. Over the past thirty years, the committee has employed three basic strategies to achieve its goals.

The traditional strategy utilized has been referred to as "intra-agricultural commodity trading."[5] Under this strategy the various agricultural commodities recognized the mutual advantage of putting their price support programs into one "omnibus" farm bill rather than having each "go it alone." The wheat and feed grains representatives could then support cotton, tobacco, peanuts, and rice, and vice versa. This situation worked very well in the 1950s and the 1960s, but in 1973 there were signs that cotton might pull out of the agricultural coalition rather than go along with proposed changes in the 1973 Agriculture and Consumer Protection Act which were damaging to cotton growers—particularly the $20,000 price support payment limitation to individual producers.[6]

By 1977, such intracommodity trading had become automatic. As usual, the various commodity subcommittees had responsibility for markup of their own sections of the new farm bill. For instance, the Subcommittee on Oilseeds and Rice prepared the cotton, peanuts, and rice titles. When each section was introduced and debated in the full committee markup sessions, rules of "equity" and "fair share" for commodities prevailed. One committee member observed that "When a [farm] bill is written, equity among the ... [commodity] programs is stressed. ... There are many weak programs supported because of the historical factor ... and the need for agriculture to 'hang together.' "

So in 1977 the newer, more expensive programs such as wheat and feed grains implicitly supported the existence of the older and weaker programs such as cotton, rice, and tobacco in exchange for support for increasing the levels of wheat and feed grains loan rates and price supports. Interestingly, this strategy began to backfire on Chairman Foley, for the wheat representatives were able to secure from cotton, tobacco, sugar, peanuts, and rice the loan and price support levels for wheat and corn far in excess of those recommended by Foley.

A second strategy that has been used to secure the passage of agricultural legislation emerged in 1964 when the food stamp program was first incorporated into farm legislation.[7] Initially a very limited program for dispensing surplus agricultural commodities to the needy, the food stamp program soon burgeoned into a full-scale "welfare" program with estimated expenditures for 1977 at over

$5.4 billion—approximately one-half of the total authorization for the entire agriculture bill! This inclusion of food stamps, however, provided rural representatives with a ready-made issue on which to trade rural votes on food stamps for urban votes on the commodity portions of the bill. This trading characterized the passage of the omnibus farm bills of the 1960s, and it was in evidence in 1973. There has always been some uneasiness on the part of rural members of Congress, particularly Republicans and Southerners, about having a welfare program contained in a farm bill. As one committee member put it:

It seems that every time we [write] a farm bill the Republicans and a few of the Southern [members] want to vote it [food stamps] out of the bill. Now I'll tell you, its *absolutely essential* . . . to have it . . . or we'd never pass a farm bill.[8]

For the 1977 bill this general state of "uneasiness" was exacerbated when the Carter administration announced its plans to eliminate that part of the food stamp program which required recipients to purchase a portion of their stamps. Under the new program, an individual would receive a full allotment of food stamps if eligibility requirements were met. Strong opposition to elimination of the "purchase requirement" surfaced especially among Republicans. Many who opposed the change began referring to the program as "free stamps."

A third strategy that has been used to secure passage of farm legislation might be called "urban-rural trader politics." Although throughout the 1960s rural and urban representatives vote-traded on several legislative measures, this relationship was rather ad hoc. During consideration of the 1973 Agriculture and Consumer Protection Act, a wheat and feed grains-labor alliance emerged as potentially the most stable cluster of interests in agricultural policy making.[9] Weldon Barton describes the trading in 1973 as urban-labor representatives voting for the agriculture bill and rural members of Congress voting for the "minimum wage" bill. He maintained that this alliance of labor and wheat and feed grains was significant for it rendered the participation of cotton in the agricultural coalition more marginal. Whether the new rural-labor alliance would emerge in 1977 was a matter of some speculation when the bill was at the committee stage in the spring. There certainly were any number of urban labor-oriented bills to trade for, particularly the minimum wage bill and the proposed consumer protection agency.

Whatever traditional or new coalition strategies Chairman Foley advocated for 1977, he did operate under one strategic premise. During the course of the House Agriculture Committee hearings and the markup sessions, Foley continually urged the members to report a farm bill to the House of Representatives that had a considerably lower price tag than the Senate-passed version (S. 275). Foley's reasoning was that adopting the price levels advocated in the Senate bill would risk a certain veto by President Carter. Rather, the House should pass a much "leaner" bill and then once it was in the House-Senate Conference

Committee, they could split the difference with the Senate—the result being satisfactory to all parties, particularly the President. While most of the commodities went along with this game plan, the representatives of the hard-pressed wheat regions tried unsuccessfully (by a 32-22 vote) in the full committee markup session to raise the levels on loans and price supports.

On May 15, the Agriculture Committee reported the 1977 farm food bill (H.R. 7171) to the full House of Representatives.[10] Chairman Foley and the ranking minority member, Representative William Wampler (R-Va.), along with the other members of the committee then began the process of finding support for the new bill among their House colleagues, particularly the urban members.

Consideration by the House of Representatives

In late July 1977, the House took up consideration of the 1977 farm food bill. The debate over the farm bill proved to be long and difficult. Foley's hopes to hold together the delicate bill put together by the committee were soon in jeopardy. Throughout the course of the floor debate, several amendments were introduced by members of the Agriculture Committee which had the potential for unraveling the entire farm bill. In other words, a series of amendments were introduced which threatened the cohesiveness of the "intracommodity" trading strategy.

The first such amendment was introduced by Representative Richard Nolan (D-Minn.) which would have prohibited federal farm subsidy payments to corporations in which those holding majority interest were not solely engaged in farming. Ordinarily, such controversial amendments are "worked out" at the committee stage. It is a reflection of Chairman Foley's democratic style of leadership that he permitted amendments which were rejected in commmittee to be brought up on the floor. As one senior committee member stated,

That [Nolan] amendment would not have seen the light of day when Poage was chairman. . . . Such amendments not only damage the bill, but lower the prestige of the committee in the eyes of [nonmembers].

But this amendment offered by Richard Nolan to deny payments to corporate farms was also a reflection of a spirit of agricultural reform displayed by several new members of the committee deeply committed to the notion of the "family farm" and the "rural way of life." For instance, a substitute amendment was offered by Representative Paul Findley (R-Ill.) to an original amendment of Floyd Fithian (D-Ind.) which would have limited payments to sugar producers to $50,000 annually. Such a limitation would have the effect of virtually wiping out large sugar producers. Similarly, another Findley amendment sought to put a ceiling of $30,000 on the total amount of government payments to individual producers, no matter how many commodities they produced. Although these three amendments were defeated, they all drew substantial support.

In Table 3-1 a vote analysis for these "reform" amendments, several other amendments, and the final vote is presented. It is apparent from the breakdown that these amendments garnered many votes from the Eastern and Midwestern regions of the United States, urban and suburban members of Congress, and particularly support from those members elected in 1974 to the 94th "reform" Congress and to a lesser extent the 95th. The Nolan corporate farm pay limitation in particular was supported by this group: over 75 percent of the "reformers" voted in favor of it. Paul Findley, being a respected member of House Republican leadership, was able to gain the support of a substantial proportion of Republicans for his two amendments. Chairman Foley did not support any of these amendments basically because they jeopardized the passage of the entire farm bill. One committee member who supported all three amendments stated that

Foley vigorously objected to the Fithian [Findley] Sugar Amendment because he [Foley] . . . did not want any major unraveling amendments. If one goes, they all go. . . . in such a delicately balanced bill as the Farm Bill it has to remain pretty much intact . . . as the committee reported it.

After the debate and defeat of the Nolan and Findley amendments, Foley called the "reform" members together and warned them that it was not beneficial to the Agriculture Committee or to the 1977 farm food bill to "play out" these controversies in front of the whole House.

A much more damaging issue to the solidarity of the intra-agricultural commodity coalition was an amendment introduced by Agriculture Committee member Margaret Heckler (R-Mass.) to drastically reduce the price supports for peanuts. Price supports for peanuts historically have been set well above the cost of production, in effect setting the market price. Heckler argued that such "favoritism" was not fair to the other commodities and that it was not fair to consumers to drive up the price of peanut products such as peanut butter with extravagant government subsidies. Other committee members argued that even though this was a "weak" program, it was necessary to hold the agriculture commodity coalition together. As one Midwestern committee member representing a wheat district stated before a vote on the amendment, "If peanuts go, there will be a domino effect . . . cotton, tobacco, rice, corn, wheat . . . all will fall one by one."

The final vote on the Heckler peanut amendment was too close for comfort—as time ran out on the roll call, the vote tally was 208-202 for passage of the amendment. After the chair called for late votes and changes, the final vote read 207 for the amendment, 210 against—the peanut amendment was rejected. Table 3-1 indicates that support came from the same sources as the

Table 3-1
1977 Farm Food Bill: Vote Breakdown

Attribute	N	Agriculture Reform					Food Stamps				Final Passage	
		Nolan[a]	Findley 1	Findley 2	Heckler	Symms	Kelly	Junk-Food	Work	Sugar	H.R. 7171	Farm Bill
Region[b]												
East	(106)	72[c]	68	56	72	8	17	37	24	23	58	65
South	(108)	19	29	18	11	35	69	50	48	68	79	80
Border	(35)	56	40	31	35	20	31	32	40	77	80	81
Midwest	(110)	60	60	69	68	25	38	47	45	61	75	77
Far West	(70)	36	32	11	49	31	36	43	30	83	68	63
Party												
Democrats	(290)	54	40	33	37	10	22	24	17	58	82	84
Republicans	(139)	35	63	54	72	54	78	85	81	60	48	48
District Composition												
Urban	(137)	67	60	43	59	13	19	31	19	45	61	70
Suburban	(114)	48	60	48	58	24	41	49	42	46	60	59
Urban/Rural	(92)	34	39	41	43	27	57	59	59	67	77	74
Rural	(86)	35	23	25	27	28	44	41	40	87	92	91
Seniority												
94th Congress (elected 1974)	(90)	75	60	48	61	14	26	36	19	57	72	75
95th Congress (elected 1976)	(70)	52	45	35	54	22	38	34	35	57	72	79
All Others	(209)	38	45	39	34	28	46	49	45	59	70	70
Final Vote		199-207	201-210	167-241	207-210	102-317	170-249	185-227	159-255	246-165	294-114	283-107

[a]*Nolan:* Payment limitation to corporate farms; *Findley 1:* Limit federal payments to corporate farms; *Findley 2:* Limit payments to sugar producers; *Heckler:* Peanut program reduction; *Symms:* Eliminate purchase requirement; *Kelly:* Deny food stamps to strikers; *Work:* Work for food stamps; *Sugar:* Raise price supports for sugar beets.

[b]*East:* Conn., Del., Me., Mass., N.H., N.J., N.Y., Pa., R.I., Vt. *South:* Ala., Ark., Fla., Ga., La., Miss., N.C., S.C., Tenn., Tex., Va. *Border:* Ky., Md., Okla., W.Va., Mo. *Midwest:* Ill., Ind., Iowa, Kan., Mich., Minn., Neb., N.D., Ohio, S.D., Wis. *Far West:* Ala., Ariz., Calif., Colo., Hawaii, Idaho, Mont., Nev., N.M., Ore., Utah, Wash., Wyo.

[c]Entries are the percentage of each category voting for the measure.

other "reform" measures: the East and Midwest, the urban and suburban districts, the 94th and 95th "reformers," and the Republican party.

But the most dramatic attempt from within the membership of the Agriculture Committee to substantially alter the committee version of the bill was that of the wheat representatives to raise the price support levels for wheat from $2.65 to $2.90 a bushel for the 1977 crop. The amendment also sought higher loan and support prices for corn for the 1977 crop to $2 each, up from $1.85 a bushel for loans and $1.75 for price supports. After being narrowly defeated in the full committee markup session by a 23-22 vote (with Chairman Foley voting 13 proxy votes against the amendment), representatives of the hard-pressed wheat states, led by Glenn English (D-Okla.) and Tom Harkin (D-Iowa) on the Democratic side and Keith Sebelius (R-Kan.) and Charles Thone (R-Neb.) on the Republican, began a campaign to win enough votes on the House floor to raise the wheat and corn price supports. The "outlaw 50," as these wheat congressmen came to be called around Capitol Hill because of their attempt to defeat the President and circumvent the position of a powerful committee chairman, employed a multifaceted strategy of information and education, persistent one-on-one persuasion, and vote trading.

In the belief that most urban and suburban representatives were ignorant of the problems faced by the grain farmer, a campaign was launched to educate them. Max Baucus (D-Mont.) brought in a movie made by college students about wheat farming and showed it to congressmen and their staffs. In order to demonstrate the financial plight of wheat farmers, Keith Sebelius (R-Kan.) wore a plastic bread wrapper on his arm, representing one cent—"about the amount a farmer gets for a loaf of bread." Dan Glickman (D-Kan.) placed a bushel of $1.50 Kansas wheat in the hall right off the House floor. Farm groups including the various wheat associations from across the country and WIFE (Women Involved in Farm Economics) were utilized by the "outlaw 50" for a coordinated lobbying effort. The thrust of these information strategies was, according to a leader of the effort, "to communicate to the urban and suburban members that wheat and corn farmers were facing a 'crisis'! That's the only thing that we in Congress respond to these days—a crisis."

Individual persuasion also was used very effectively. Keith Sebelius and Charles Thone worked the Republican side and enlisted the support of Representative Arlan Strangeland (R-Minn.). Strangeland, who took Bob Bergland's seat in Congress, though not a member of the Agriculture Committee, did an excellent job of persuading individual Republicans to vote for the higher wheat and corn supports. While many Republicans, especially from wheat and corn states, gave their support out of general concern for the wheat situation, some supported the amendment to embarrass the Carter administration. As one committee Democrat claimed, "Republicans could then take credit for the amendment if it passed, or blame Carter if it failed."

On the Democratic side, English and Harkin, along with other "reform"

Democrats on the committee, including Richard Nolan (D-Minn.), John Krebs (D-Calif.), Berkeley Bedell (D-Iowa), Leon Panetta (D-Calif.), Floyd Fithian (D-Ind.), and Dan Glickman (D-Kan.), were able to get substantial support from the "reform" members elected to the 94th and 95th Congresses. In most instances, these members supported the wheat amendment out of "solidarity with the young liberal progressives on the Ag Committee," but one member of the Agriculture committee claimed that ". . . there were many individual vote trades for minimum wage and the Consumer Protection Agency."

The Consumer Federation of America (CFA) sent a letter to all congressmen on July 20 urging them to support the English amendment. However, there was a caucus between representatives of the CFA and the leaders of the amendment where it was suggested that the CFA would oppose the wheat amendment if substantial support for the Consumer Protection Agency could not be arranged. This angered many of the supporters of the amendment, especially those in favor of the Consumer Protection Agency. One member present at this caucus stated that "The CFA was told in no uncertain terms that this would not wash. It was a thinly veiled attempt at blackmail."

The other key to the passage of the wheat amendment was the intra-commodity trading among farm representatives. According to the sponsors of the measure, the tobacco representatives were committed to the higher price supports during the time of the full committee markup session. Sugar, peanuts, and rice all "came on board" the last few days before the amendment was scheduled for debate. Finally, the day before the wheat amendment was to be introduced, the leaders reported to Chairman Foley—who had been kept abreast of developments every step along the way—that by conservative estimate they could count 240 votes for the amendment. According to Representative Glenn English,

Foley then . . . called the President and told him that they [the leaders of the wheat amendment] had the votes. Then the President called Bergland to confirm, which Bergland did. Then he [the President] told Foley and Bergland "to do what they felt they had to do" but he would not openly support the amendment.

The next day Foley himself offered the amendment, but warned that he would not support any efforts to raise this level of loans or price supports for the 1978 or 1979 crop years. Then followed an anticlimatic voice vote in favor of the amendment. Although no official roll call vote was taken to determine where support for the measure came from, one organizer of the wheat amendment claimed that of the 240 votes he counted in support ". . . probably 140 were Democrats, 100 of which were elected to the 94th and 95th Congresses, and perhaps 100 Republicans, 50 of which probably voted to embarrass Carter."

Food Stamps

We have already mentioned the importance of food stamps to the passage of agricultural legislation. The food stamp program, incorporated as it is in the farm bill, provides a ready-made issue with which rural representatives can trade votes with their urban counterparts. In 1977 Representative Frederick W. Richmond (D-N.Y.) became the key individual in putting together these trades. Richmond, a millionaire, former New York taxi commissioner, representing a Brooklyn district that contains some of the worst slums in America, is an unlikely member of the House Agriculture Committee. But as chairman of the Subcommittee on Domestic Marketing, Consumer Relations and Nutrition, he skillfully steered the food stamp bill, including the controversial elimination of the purchase requirement, through two weeks of difficult committee markup sessions.

Once the food stamp bill (H.R. 7940) was joined with the farm bill (H.R. 7171) as a separate title, Richmond had the responsibility of leading the floor action on the section. He was able to secure enough rural support to protect the food stamp program from amendments offered from the House floor which would have seriously jeopardized the significant changes made in the bill, particularly elimination of the purchase requirement. He also was able to help hold together tenuous urban support for farm legislation, in general. His urban-liberal colleagues began to look to him for guidance on farm-related issues. For instance, he persuaded several urbanites to vote for higher sugar subsidies and price supports for sugar beet growers, both positions at odds with the Carter administration. As Richmond said in a news interview, "We did build up a very good working urban-rural coalition. It was my job to convince urban members of Congress to support the family farmer and convince rural members to support cities."[11]

In Table 3-1 the vote for several of the important food stamp amendments is presented, as well as the votes on the sugar subsidy issue. The measure of Richmond's success is indicated by the fact that not one of these amendments damaged the committee version of the food stamp program. The crucial amendment offered by Representative Steven Symms (R-Idaho) to require that recipients pay for a portion of their food stamp allotment was soundly defeated by a 317-102 vote. The only support Symms was able to muster came from Republicans (54 percent) who were against the Carter administration proposal to eliminate the purchase requirement. It is interesting to note that only 28 percent of the rural members voted in favor of the Symms amendment.

An amendment offered by Representative Richard Kelly (R-Fla.) to eliminate from the food stamp program any household in which a member is on strike, unless the household was eligible before the strike, was rejected 249-170. This provision to eliminate strikers has been offered every time the House or the Senate debates the food stamp program, always drawing strong support from the South and Republicans. Table 3-1 indicates that in 1977 the same held true. The

South gave substantial backing to this amendment (69 percent), and 78 percent of the Republicans voted for it. Also more than half of the members from rural and urban/rural mixed districts voted to eliminate strikers, 54 and 57 percent respectively. Similarly, two other food stamp amendments drew support from the South and Republicans, as well as from the Midwest. Steven Symms (R-Idaho) offered an amendment, the so-called "junk food" amendment, to prohibit the use of food stamps to purchase nonnutritional foods, as determined by the Food and Nutrition Board of the National Academy of Sciences, which was rejected 227-185.

But the most interesting issue which demonstrated Richmond's ability to put an urban-rural coalition together occurred on a Paul Findley (R-Ill.) amendment to permit the Secretary of Agriculture to implement an unlimited number of pilot projects in which work would have to be performed in return for food stamps. Originally, the substance of this amendment to "work off" food stamps was to be offered by Representative Dawson Mathis (D-Ga.), a respected member of the Agriculture Committee and chairman of the Subcommittee on Oilseeds and Rice, who represents one of the largest peanut-producing districts in the House. Mathis's sponsorship of this measure would have substantially increased the probability of passage. Therefore during the floor debate over the Heckler peanut reduction Richmond threw his support, publicly, behind the higher peanut subsidies. Given the extreme closeness of that vote, Richmond's support was the difference. In exchange, Mathis dropped his plans of offering the work-for-food-stamps amendment. The Findley-sponsored version was able to draw support only from Republicans (84 percent) while only 48 percent of Southern members and 40 percent of rural districts voted for the measure.

Richmond also won urban and consumer support for an amendment offered by Kika de la Garza (D-Tex.), the third-ranking Democrat on the Agriculture Committee, to establish a price support program for sugar beet and cane producers, even though the measure was vigorously opposed by the Carter administration and would increase the cost of sugar products to the consumer. Table 3-1 indicates that 45 percent of the members representing urban districts and 46 percent of the suburban voted for the higher support levels.

Final Passage

The combination of old and new strategies adopted by Chairman Foley to secure passage of the 1977 farm food bill worked very well, and is reflected in the wide base of support H.R. 7171 and the House-Senate Conference Committee report received on final passage. In Table 3-1 the distribution of support for both versions of the bill indicates that all regions of the country supported the bill with over 80 percent of the border state members and 65 percent of the East voting for the measure. Substantial support from House Democrats (over 80 percent for both versions) was also in evidence. This was the result in no small measure of the tremendous respect House Democrats have for Chairman Foley, who is also chairman of the liberal House Democratic Caucus. Republican support for the farm food bill was also quite high (48 percent), considering that it was a Democrat-sponsored bill.

The successful development of an urban-rural coalition is evidenced by the fact that 70 percent of the totally urban congressional districts and 60 percent of the suburban supported final passage. As expected, over 90 percent of rural congressmen voted for the final bill. Those rural members voting against the bill generally did so because they felt the bill did not raise price supports for their particular commodity high enough or because they opposed the changes in the food stamp program. Finally, the "young progressives" on the Agriculture Committee were very effective in winning votes for the 1977 bill from reform-minded members elected to the 94th (1974) and 95th (1976) Congresses. Between 75 and 80 percent of these new members supported the final bill.

Conclusion

The agricultural policy-making process in the United States is in a transitional state, as is the entire agricultural enterprise. Farming has become commercialized, the sociology of rural life is changing, and new groups such as consumers and the "hunger lobby" are seeking access and influence in the formulation and implementation of our food and fiber policy. For these reasons, as well as those discussed in this chapter, agricultural politics is changing. Although it is difficult to predict the exact form of the politics of agriculture in the future, patterns which began to emerge with the passage of the Agriculture and Consumer Protection Act of 1973 and new patterns described here give us a clue.

First, the old style of intra-agricultural trading will continue, especially during Agriculture Committee consideration of new farm legislation. Weaker programs, however, such as peanuts, cotton, and rice will find it increasingly difficult to justify inclusion of high loan and price supports under the principle of "equity" for all commodities, as urban opposition to these programs mount. Perhaps at some point, wheat and feed grains representatives will determine it detrimental to their own programs to continue including these programs in one omnibus bill. The emphasis, however, will continue, as it was in 1977, to be on the wheat and feed grains programs—particularly since geographical representation on the House Agriculture Committee has shifted from the South to the Midwest, the wheat-corn belt.

A second pattern which should be very characteristic of agriculture politics is the continued development of a metropolitan-rural vote trading coalition. The primary issue involved in this coalition will be the food stamp program, unless it is eliminated by President Carter's "welfare reform proposals." Even if that should occur, rural and urban representatives will find many consumer-urban-labor-oriented issues on which to trade votes.

Finally, consideration of the 1977 farm food bill witnessed the emergence of a new and potent group of individuals led by a few younger members of the Agriculture Committee, committed to reform in general and particularly with legislation designed to save the family farm and regulate the growth of corporate agriculture in the United States. This group has been successful in gaining the support of members elected in 1974 to the 94th "reform" Congress and in 1976 to the 95th. In closing, it is interesting to point out that this group of young progressives has been the most sympathetic and responsive to the demands of the recent farm strike movement led by the American Agriculture Movement (AAM) whose basic goals call not only for "100 percent of parity" but also for family farm and rural development legislation. If this farm strike movement should solidify into a new farm interest group, the young progressives will have a ready-made grass roots constituency, and agricultural politics, particularly in the House of Representatives, could change dramatically.

Notes

1. "Quiet Persuader," *Wall Street Journal*, September 17, 1977, p. 1.

2. For a short summary and analysis of the provisions contained in the 1977 farm food bill, see "Farm Bill Cleared, Puts Government Back in Price Support Arena," *Congressional Quarterly Weekly Report*, 35, no. 39 (September 24, 1977):2029-2032.

3. For an examination of the goals of congressional committee members, see Richard Fenno, *Congressmen in Committees* (Boston: Little, Brown, 1973).

4. For an analysis of the factors leading to legislative success of the House Agriculture Committee, see Arthur G. Stevens, "Coalitions and Committee Representativeness," a paper presented at the Seminar on Mathematical Models of Congress, Chateau Roaring Fork, Aspen, Colorado, June 16-23, 1974.

5. For an analysis of the phases of agriculture policy, see Weldon V. Barton, "Food, Agriculture, and Administrative Adaptation to Political Change," *Public Administration Review*, 36, no. 2 (March/April 1976):148-154.

6. Weldon Barton, "Coalition-Building in the U.S. House of Representatives: Agricultural Legislation in 1973," in James E. Anderson (ed.) *Cases in Public Policy* (New York: Praeger, 1976), pp. 141-162.

7. For an analysis of this sort of vote trading, see Randall Ripley, "Legislative Bargaining and the Food Stamp Act, 1964," in Frederick N. Cleveland et al., *Congress and Urban Problems* (Washington: The Brookings Institution, 1969), pp. 279-310.

8. Emphasis in original interview.

9. Barton, "Coalition Building. . . ."

10. This version of H.R. 7171 contained only a skeleton food stamp section because there was no time to hold markup sessions on food stamps and complete the total farm bill before the May 15 reporting deadline for new authorizations under the new congressional budget process. In June 1977, a markup session was held on a separate food stamp bill (H.R. 7940) which contained sweeping reforms of the program. Then, during floor debate on the farm food bill (H.R. 7171), Chairman Foley proposed an amendment which substituted the text of H.R. 7940 for Title XII of H.R. 7171, the "skeleton" food stamp program. This raised the ire of many members of the House Budget Committee for they viewed it as a blatant disregard for the new congressional budget process.

11. Andy Montgomery, "Richmond Backs Rural Interests," *Lincoln Journal* (August 24, 1977):28.

4

Impacts of the Congressional Budget Process on Agricultural Legislation

Alan S. Walter

This year marks the first time that major agricultural legislation has been considered since Congress implemented a formal budgeting process in 1974. The budget process, established through the so-called Budget Act, was initiated as a means of giving Congress better fiscal control. Its objective is to provide the legislative branch with a tool to better evaluate programs that involve spending and to more fully cooperate with the executive branch in setting fiscal policy.

This chapter looks beyond 1977 to possible impacts of the process on agricultural legislation and the operation of agricultural programs in the future. Emphasis is placed on the process and its implications for agriculture; little discussion is accorded the effectiveness of the total process to date in accomplishing more general objectives. The focus is upon the formal budget process and not on simple budgetary or cost concerns which have always been expressed when agricultural programs have been considered.

Why CBO?

The budget process was implemented to give Congress a means to comprehensively and periodically evaluate all revenue and expenditure programs. Previously, Congress considered fiscal matters piecemeal. Individual committees considered authorizations for the programs under their jurisdiction without anyone formally tracking how the separate program decisions affected the aggregate budget or systematically weighing the merits of one program against another. Attempts by Congress to adjust spending or revenues during periods of recession or rapid inflation were ineffective. Fiscal leadership rested primarily with the executive branch.

It was recognized within Congress that to increase fiscal control would require new ways of operation for the Congress—more than a minor "tuneup" of current procedures. Mechanisms to fully evaluate new programs and explore their expenditure implications were considered necessary. Also, means were needed for simultaneously considering all spending and revenues to keep fiscal actions in line with macroeconomic needs and to ensure that the highest priority programs would be funded. With this information, budget adjustments can be made where required.

The budget process was therefore implemented to give Congress a greater

37

and more systematic role in setting fiscal policy. Budget committees were created in the House and Senate and vested with operating and leadership responsibilities. The Congressional Budget Office (CBO) was formed and given responsibilities which in some respects are similar to the Office of Management and Budget (OMB) in the executive branch.

Timetable for the Budget Process

Several steps are an integral part of the process. The fiscal year now begins on October 1, but the formal part of the process starts in the previous November. At that time, the President submits a current services budget which indicates spending and revenues if current programs are extended into the next fiscal year. In January, another budget with recommendations for changes from current services is submitted by the President. This year the change in administration resulted in another budget submission in February.

The first formal action by the Congress occurs after the President submits his budget. In March, all authorizing committees in the House and Senate report to their respective budget committee recommendations for spending on existing or prospective programs under their jurisdictions. The budget committees also receive testimony and recommendations on needs for the general economy. The budget committees, using the above information, then prepare budgets indicating recommended spending and revenue levels for the next fiscal year. The Senate and the House must agree to a budget by May 15, which is referred to as the First Concurrent Resolution.

The first resolution indicates a recommended spending allocation to each legislative committee for its programs. The resolution is not binding but is a preliminary recommendation of priorities. Adjustments can be made before spending allocations become binding. However, Congress has tended to stick closely to the priorities established in the First Concurrent Resolution, making it serve as a warning to the legislative committees. The resolution is not a line item in nature but gives discretion to individual committees to develop programs within their spending totals.

A second concurrent resolution which updates the first resolution must be passed before September 15. This resolution indicates to individual committees the amount by which spending programs under their jurisdiction *must* be changed to comply with the resolution. The legislative committee must then recommend specific changes, which could require legislation to implement, to accomplish changes directed by the resolution. Floor action in both Houses is completed on these recommendations by September 25, or before the October 1 beginning of the fiscal year. Therefore, by October 1, a budget has been agreed upon by Congress, and a legislative package has supposedly been passed which is consistent with the budget.

Another part of the process involves estimating costs to the government of new legislation. To facilitate an orderly consideration, all authorizing bills which involve spending in the next fiscal year must be reported before May 15, and Congress has until early September to complete action on them. The CBO makes five-year cost projections on each bill reported, and the legislative committees also may make their own cost estimates in the report for the bill.

Overall, the process tends to be heavily oriented to the next fiscal year with less emphasis on the outlying years. The budget committees and CBO make some effort to project revenues and expenditures for several years, but with mixed success. The budget resolutions are only for the next fiscal year, and it is only for this time span that the process can result in any mandates to legislative committees to recommend changes.

Budgeting Procedures for Agricultural Programs

Certain features of agricultural programs complicate using the budget process as a means to allocate spending for agriculture. Congress has periodically passed legislation which authorizes commodity programs for a specified number of years.[1] The legislation grants the executive branch authority within certain guidelines to make decisions about how the programs will be operated and provides funding to cover expenditures without further congressional action. The Commodity Credit Corporation (CCC) may borrow up to $14.5 billion from the Treasury to fund these programs. The level of federal outlays on these programs depends upon market prices, decisions of the executive branch, and program requirements as specified by Congress. Congress may have to later make an appropriation to cover the program, but this action may be years after the actual expenditure was made.

The budget process involves allocating outlays which would seem to indicate that the budget process could play a part in limiting commodity programs by controlling outlays on them. However, since the agricultural programs can operate without congressional approval except for periodic renewal or amendment, Congress cannot control spending on them in most years unless it is willing to amend the law at that time.

Congress is, in effect, estimating market conditions and decisions by the executive branch when it budgets spending for agriculture. In this light, the budgeting process seems less powerful as a tool to control programs authorized by existing legislation because spending on these programs cannot be limited by simply reducing outlays in the budget resolution. The best opportunity for Congress to allocate spending for commodity programs is through the legislation which it periodically passes to provide operating authority. This occasion may also be the time when the budget process must operate effectively if it is to allocate spending for agricultural programs.

Structure of Agricultural Programs and
the Budget Process

First, the difficulties in estimating spending for agriculture must be considered. There is general recognition in Congress that spending for agricultural programs cannot be accurately estimated months or years in advance. The discretionary authority held by the administration can affect expenditures as can market-related factors such as weather and decisions of foreign governments. There is question in the minds of some legislators about whether budget estimates should be taken seriously when there is such a large error factor. Some who favor programs may be honestly skeptical about the estimates, and others may think that discrediting the numbers may make passage easier. The availability of cost projections from the congressional estimating arm, CBO, probably served to give more credibility to U.S. Department of Agriculture (USDA) estimates since the two sets of estimates differed little. However, some members were highly skeptical about all estimates.

More credibility in the estimates of the estimators needs to be established. One indication of their reputation is given in a statement by Senator Curtis when debating over the 1977 support levels. Senator Muskie quoted some of the cost estimates, to which Senator Curtis replied, "I am sure those estimators are likable persons. I would like to see them replaced with a few farmers."[2]

A second problem contributing to ineffectiveness relates to the one-year cycle of the process (i.e., budget resolutions for only the next fiscal year) which tends to exclude consideration for most of the life of farm programs. The Senate bill has impacts through FY 1983 and the House bill through FY 1982, but the budget process does not formally extend beyond FY 1978.

Third, the small share of the budget spent on agriculture may make some members worry little about spending levels. Less than 1 percent of the federal budget has been spent on agriculture in recent years. A substantial percentage change in agricultural spending may have only a small impact on the total budget.

Fourth, the newness of the process may have restricted its introduction in the decision-making process. It takes time to gain acceptance of an important change in any system. By the time the next major farm bill is considered, the process will no longer be new and may have more of an impact because of experience with the system.

Last, political, or noneconomic, considerations cannot be ignored and may sometimes override budgetary concerns. Congress has many other considerations than the budget and will never judge programs simply on their cost aspects.

Looking Ahead

The impacts of the budget process on agricultural legislation and programs in the future will depend upon further development of the overall process and the solution of budget problems which are unique to agriculture. The process is still in its infancy and may require several years of evolution before it reaches a mature state. Changes will probably be required and will be made if the members are serious about formulating a fiscal policy in some systematic manner.

One consideration is which of the reports that must now be made as a part of the process will be taken seriously and which may be only *pro forma*. Will the March 15 report of the agriculture committees to the budget committees become a meaningful exercise in establishing a budget or only a requirement? Will the second resolution which can mandate changes in programs be taken seriously or will it be circumvented? Also, will Congress move toward longer-range targeting, or budgeting? Since most new programs can have significant long-range impacts but only small expenditures in the first year, taking a longer-run outlook offers real advantages.

Another consideration is whether better means to compare widely different programs will become a reality. Can methods be developed which allow a comparison of different programs under different committees in meeting national objectives?

In narrowing this forward look to agricultural programs, several additional problems must be considered. First, Will Congress look seriously at a part of the budget which is only 1 percent of the total? Second, Can we figure out ways to accurately estimate budget outlays on agriculture when weather and the delegation of authority to the administration have major impacts on costs, or will changes in the programs have to be made to make costs more predictable? Third, If we have a four-year bill this year, will we again be faced with the same problems in the future if we change administrations in the same year that we must consider new legislation? There would be an advantage in giving a new administration and a new Congress a year to get its people and programs in place before major issues are thrown at them.

In conclusion, the development of the process and its future impact will largely depend upon the members and their staffs because the budget process is really people more than a process. Experience with the system by those present may alone cause budgeting to be more effective and efficient. Success will also depend heavily upon new members and staff, given the rapid turnover.

It would seem that the process has not had a dramatic impact upon legislation this year. However, the same interest in fiscal soundness by Congress which caused the budget process to be implemented has made the members more carefully consider all legislation, including agriculture. The process also complemented other factors, such as the position of the administration, which has attempted to constrain outlays. The budget process, as a tool, may increase in usefulness over time as experience is gained with it and adjustments are made. Whether the process will ever be able to facilitate a rigorous comparison of widely different programs such as agriculture with the B-1 bomber, as Grommet suggested in 1975, is in doubt, but it may cause programs to compete for funding through the political process.[3]

It is possible that the process could increase spending over what would otherwise occur for certain programs, not necessarily agricultural. I could see this happening if market conditions improve, which would reduce spending on existing programs. The process may aid in efforts to transfer these savings to other programs if total spending or the deficit is a key variable in congressional decisions.

Regardless of other events, agricultural programs will face additional scrutiny as a result of the process. At the minimum, the process will serve as an informational source for decision making. At a maximum, the process will develop into a systematic means of allocating spending among programs.

Notes

1. *Agricultural Food Policy Review,* AFPR-1, Economic Research Service, U.S. Department of Agriculture, 1977.

2. Senator Tom Curtis, Remarks before the U.S. Senate, *Congressional Record,* S.8406, May 24, 1977.

3. Allen Grommet, "The New Congressional Budget Process and Implications for Agricultural Funding," paper presented to the American Agricultural Economics Association meeting, Columbus, Ohio, August 1975.

5 Subsystem Stability and Agricultural Policy Outputs

Jan E. Mabie

Introduction

The proposition that policy subsystems are important features of the broader national policy-making system may seem self-evident. From their early characterization by Griffith as "whirlpools" of activity, through Freeman's examination of executive bureau-legislative committee interactions, to numerous scholarly and journalistic case studies since, available evidence documents the existence of these "iron triangles" in many policy fields.[1] Subsystem actors—the senior agency bureaucrats, congressional committee members, and representatives of organized interest groups—are seen as decisive and fairly autonomous in structuring "mid-level" policy while at the same time imposing major constraints on "macro-level" decision making.[2]

In the area of agricultural policy, the case for the importance of subsystem activity would seem especially strong. Agricultural interests, represented by the general farm organizations and by specific commodity and production groups, are reputed to be among the most effective in Washington. The U.S. Department of Agriculture (USDA) is, itself, an old and firmly established department. Its upper level of career officials is often pointed to, fairly or not, as a classic example of entrenched bureaucracy. Finally, the agricultural committees of Congress, both appropriating and authorizing, are commonly held to include some of the cagiest and most influential legislators on the Hill.

Moreover, the notion of subsystem activity within agricultural policy, and elsewhere as well, has a great deal of intuitive appeal. At a general level, postulating some form of subsystem interaction is almost indispensable to a pluralistic interpretation of American politics and policy making. Should we suddenly be presented with hard evidence that senior bureaucrats, key congressmen, and interest group representatives did *not* communicate with one another, did *not* influence one another, and did *not* have a major impact on public policy, I suspect that the typical reaction would be outright disbelief.

More specifically, subsystems, as Redford points out, contribute important elements of stability to policy areas and serve to maintain power balances among dominant interests.[3] Agriculture would seem to have special needs for policy stability and predictability since it is an inherently risky area of production and is especially vulnerable to uncontrollable factors such as weather.

I would like to thank the U.S. Civil Service Commission's Bureau of Executive Manpower for its extensive assistance during the data collection phases of this study.

43

Do our intuitive notions and previous observations of subsystem stability in the agricultural policy field continue to stand up under systematic investigation? Since much of our knowledge of mid-level agricultural policy making comes from case studies, often journalistic in nature, we may have been perceiving greater subsystem influence than has actually been the case. Even if essential characterizations of agricultural policy making have been accurate in the past, they may not be so today. This chapter proceeds by characterizing agricultural policy subsystems in terms of the interactions of individuals in organizational settings rather than as the interactions of whole organizations conceived of as "rational actors."[4]

The Problem

Two central questions are addressed. (1) Does the degree of personnel stability in contemporary agricultural policy-making institutions warrant a "subsystem" characterization? (2) Do variations in personnel stability among policy-making institutions predict variations in the stability of budgetary outcomes for USDA agencies?

Two sides of the subsystem triangle are examined: congressional subcommittee membership and USDA bureau personnel. Interest group participation is not taken into account. Further, only some of the potential actors in Congress and USDA are considered. For Congress, only members of the Senate and House agricultural appropriations subcommittees are included. Members of authorizing committees are not. Since policy outputs are taken in budgetary terms, this is considered quite defensible. On the agency side, subsystem participants are limited to "supergrade" incumbents (G.S. 16 to G.S. 18) and equivalent Public Law incumbents.

Hence, for present purposes it is assumed that the heart of each subsystem consists of senior agency bureaucrats and congressional subcommittee members. In practical terms, if an individual leaves an agency or a subcommittee, he or she is considered to leave that subsystem. A new agency supergrade or a new subcommittee member is considered to enter the subsystem from outside.

The time periods under consideration vary. As to whether subsystem characterizations are warranted, the years 1968 through 1976 are considered. The analysis of subsystem stability and policy outputs covers 1970 through 1976.

The Agencies

The study from which these findings have been drawn utilized the following selection criteria.

1. *Organization Longevity.* An agency required an organizational history of at least twenty years prior to 1976. Agencies that had undergone name changes or which had split off from parent bureaus were included only if they retained the bulk of their programs.
2. *Size.* An average annual appropriation larger than $10 million was required.
3. *Applicability of "Normal" Appropriation Process.* Public corporations and agencies primarily engaged in the management of "public enterprise funds" were excluded.

Applying these criteria to USDA produces eight agencies: Agricultural Stabilization and Conservation Service (ASCS), Agricultural Marketing Service (AMS), Agricultural Research Service (ARS), Cooperative State Research Service (CSRS), Foreign Agricultural Service (FAS), Federal Extension Service (FES), Forest Service (FS), and Soil Conservation Service (SCS).

The Data

Data on agency personnel stability were obtained by examining lists of all incumbents to supergrade and equivalent Public Law positions. For the years 1967 onward, these listings are maintained by the U.S. Civil Service Commission. Supergrade appointments for years prior to 1967 were gathered from *The Official Register of the United States Government.* Data on congressional appropriation subcommittee membership came from *CQ Weekly Reports.*

Budgetary data are from *Budget Appendices.* Budget figures include first supplementals. Within the budgetary theory literature, questions have been raised concerning the comparability of appropriation and expenditure figures.[5] This study used a compromise measure—specifically, total obligations minus nonappropriated reimbursements. Generally, budget outcomes measured in these terms will have higher dollar values than either appropriations or expenditures. It is also felt that obligations are less subject to accounting manipulation by agencies and subcommittees.

Subsystem Stability Measures

For each agency, personnel stability is thought to involve three components: (1) supergrade longevity, (2) yearly change in composition of supergrade cadre, and (3) personnel change within the hierarchy. Initially, an individual tenure score was determined for each supergrade within an agency. New participants were assumed to produce some instability. Hence, an official's first year with an agency was scored −1, the second 0, the third +1, and so on. The official's position's grade level was taken as an indicator of position within the hierarchy.

Public Law appointees were assigned an average position grade of 17. An agency's *basic stability score* for any given year t is simply the sum of the products:

$$(\text{Individual's tenure score})_t \times (\text{individual's grade})_t$$

for each supergrade or equivalent in the agency.

To include yearly personnel change, an agency's *potential stability score* was calculated by adding 1 to the tenure score of each supergrade present in the previous year, multiplying by that individual's previous year's grade, and summing over all personnel. The ratio of an agency's basic stability score to its potential stability score serves as a summary measure of agency personnel stability on a year-to-year basis. To make scores comparable across agencies of varying sizes, average graded-tenure scores were calculated and then multiplied by the summary stability measures. The final *agency stability index* for any year t is

$$(\text{Agency stability index})_t = \frac{(\text{basic stability score})_t}{(\text{potential stability score})_t} \times \frac{(\text{basic stability score})_t}{(\text{number of supergrades})_t}$$

A similar measure was developed for the combined House-Senate membership on appropriation subcommittees. The only difference was that it did not include a special indication of hierarchy position. Subcommittee seniority, in itself, was assumed to be a sufficient indicator of relative position in the subcommittee hierarchy.

Agency-Subcommittee Stability

Two initial findings can be noted. First, the degree of overall personnel stability in most of the agency-subcommittee relationships is not as great as one might intuitively expect on the basis of a subsystem characterization. An absolute assessment is not possible since it is not known what a "normal" relationship would look like. However, the data suggest that personnel stability in agricultural policy-making institutions is not especially great. The second finding is that in the majority of agency-subcommittee relationships, relative stability has declined over the last nine years.

Considering the congressional side alone, Table 5-1 illustrates that in terms of both average subcommittee tenure and stability scores, the 1971-1976 period was substantially less stable than the preceeding six-year period.

Table 5-1
Congressional Subcommittee Membership

	Av. Member Tenure in Yrs.	Year	Stability Score	
	8.1	1965	5.55	
	8.6	1966	6.47	
1965-1970 Average = 9.1	8.8	1967	6.14	1965-1970 Average = 6.61
	9.8	1968	7.80	
	9.1	1969	5.70	
	10.0	1970	8.00	
	7.1	1971	2.77	
	8.1	1972	6.10	
1971-1976 Average = 7.9	7.3	1973	4.62	1971-1976 Average = 5.25
	8.3	1974	6.30	
	8.4	1975	5.45	
	8.7	1976	6.23	

Agency supergrade cadres present a greater source of subsystem instability. Table 5-2 illustrates average lengths of time that supergrades appointed after 1967 spent within their agency-subcommittee subsystem. Typical longevity for agency personnel in policy subsystems is not at all great. On the average, a post-1967 appointee entered a subsystem, participated, and then left, all in a space of slightly more than three years. The time periods shown for individual agencies do not seem consistent with a general subsystem characterization.

It might be supposed that when entire supergrade cadres are considered, including pre-1967 appointees, the picture would change. Table 5-3 demon-

Table 5-2
Average Time in Subsystem for Post-1967 Supergrade Appointees

Agency	Average Years	Appointees
ASCS	3.0	28
AMS	2.1	15
ARS	3.6	36
CSRS	4.0	5
FAS	3.2	25
FES	3.4	9
FS	3.6	70
SCS	2.9	29
Average =	3.3	217

Table 5-3

Distribution of Personnel by Length of Service (Percentages Are Averages of Yearly Values for 1968-1976)

Agency	Length of Service (in years) Greater than or Equal to:								
	1	*2*	*3*	*4*	*5*	*6*	*7*	*8*	*9*
ASCS	80%	60%	45%	34%	24%	18%	15%	14%	8%
AMS	85	72	65	57	51	49	45	40	40
ARS	87	76	63	51	39	29	22	20	13
CSRS	89	71	54	46	40	33	20	20	20
FAS	81	64	49	37	27	20	15	14	11
FS	82	66	51	39	24	18	15	14	8
SCS	76	55	36	25	15	10	6	6	5

strates that this is not, in general, the case. With the exception of the Agricultural Marketing Service, during the 1968-1976 period, the majority of each agency's supergrade contingency consisted of individuals having less than five years' experience with the agency as supergrades. The relative frequency of "old hands," those with nine or more years of subsystem participation, is quite low for most of the agencies.

To assess the stability of interactive relationships between agencies and subcommittees, yearly subsystem stability values were computed. Briefly,

$$(\text{Subsystem stability value})_t = (\text{agency stability index})_t \times (\text{subcommittee stability index})_t$$

For each agency-subcommittee relationship, the combined yearly value was regressed against time in years to identify trends. The results presented in Table 5-4 include simple correlation coefficients for the trends. These have no statistical significance and are simply descriptive.

Six of the agency-subcommittee relationships show overall trends in the direction of decreasing stability. Two show trends which indicate increasing stability. However, several of the relationships show ambiguous properties. For ASCS, ARS, and CSRS, U-shaped trends are apparent. Here, relative instability in agency-subcommittee relationships seems to have been greatest in the early 1970s with recovery of some stability thereafter.

Subsystem Stability and Policy Outputs

To examine the proposition that subsystem stability predicts policy stability, multiple regression models were used in which agency personnel stability and

Table 5-4
Subsystem Stability, 1968-1976

Time	*Stability Scores by Agency*							
	ASCS	AMS	ARS	CSRS	FAS	FES	FS	SCS
68	478	471	323	415	566	170	247	298
69	138	280	272	222	279	296	217	362
70	275	454	498	49	471	183	298	440
71	107	172	168	37	186	96	32	76
72	62	476	286	249	426	325	94	13
73	29	299	168	255	106	222	134	86
74	86	653	129	249	93	468	258	122
75	146	440	304	329	183	376	233	51
76	250	637	298	228	162	596	191	71
r =	−.44	+.48	−.31	−.49	−.73	+.82	−.08	−.73

subcommittee stability served as independent variables to predict *absolute percentage deviations from average percentage budget increments*. The general form of the regression model was multiplicative:

$$Y = bX_1^{m1} X_2^{m2}$$

or, in this particular application,

Current year's percentage deviation from average percent increment	= f	(agency stability index)$_t$	×	(subcommittee stability index)$_t$

rather than the more usual additive model[6]

$$Y = b + m_1 X_1 + m_2 X_2$$

There is evidence to suggest that when interactive processes are involved, multiplicative models may yield predictions superior to those obtained with additive models, and, by definition, subsystem policy making processes are interactive.[7] The sampling procedure used does not allow for statistical inferences, regardless of the type of model used. The multiple correlation coefficients reported are simply indicators of the descriptive utility of subsystem models during the specific time period considered.

Procedure

Using total obligations minus reimbursements as the basic output measure, each agency's budgets for the years FY 1971 through FY 1976 were aggregated into two output categories:

1. *General Operating Funds.* These consist largely of federal funds in expenditure categories 10 to 32, e.g., personnel compensation, equipment, transportation, and so forth.
2. *"Other" Funds.* These consist of trust funds, permanent appropriations, grants, subsidies, contributions, interest, loans, fixed charges, construction, and liquidation of contract authority.

Funds in category 2 should, in the aggregate, constitute the "noncontrollable" portion of an agency's budget, while funds in category 1 should be more discretionary in nature.[8] Hence, *the model should yield better predictions for general operating funds than for other funds.*

Since budget stability was measured in terms of each year's deviation from an average increment for preceeding years, it was necessary to choose the number of years over which obligation increments would be averaged. The limited number of data points available dictated that the three preceeding years would be the maximum practical averaging period. However, since there were no a priori grounds for assuming that a three-year period had any special properties, separate regressions were also run using a two-year period.

Similarly, it was held that subsystems probably possess certain amounts of inertia in their behavior. Consequently, the values of the independent variables were also averaged. Again, a three-year period was the maximum practical. However, a second set of regressions was run using a two-year period. With three variables and two averaging periods for each, there are a total of eight different combinations of variable averaging periods.[9] No obvious theoretical preference could be found for any particular combination. Hence, all eight combinations were used for each agency.

For each agency-subcommittee relationship and for each category of fund, there was, indeed, some variation in the quality of model fit depending upon the averaging combination used. The multiple correlation coefficient reported for each subsystem is that of the best-fitting model. The combination of averaging periods that produced it has been noted. The underlying significance of this variation has not yet been completely explored. For several of the agency-subcommittee relationships, it is possible to construct ad hoc explanations based on cyclical funding requirements for the agency's program. In one or two cases, subsystem relationships seem especially sensitive to the cycle of subcommittee turnover brought about through biyearly congressional elections. However, no single explanatory approach is satisfactory for all agencies.

As a check on the relative predictive capacity of the subsystem models, regressions were run for budget outcomes in both current dollars and constant 1972 dollars. Budget outcomes in current dollars tend to respond to inflationary pressure, a factor outside the direct control of subsystem participants. Hence, *subsystem stability should predict budget stability better for constant 1972 dollars than for current dollars.*

Finally, subsystem stability, as a predictor of budgetary stability, was compared with past budget stability as a predictor of current budget stability. In the latter case, a simple two-variable regression was used. Specifically,

$$\begin{matrix} \text{Current year's percentage} \\ \text{deviation from} \\ \text{average percent increment} \end{matrix} \quad = f \quad \begin{matrix} \text{standard deviation} \\ \text{about average} \\ \text{percent increment} \end{matrix}$$

If subsystem stability has an important influence on budget stability, then the *subsystem models should predict budget stability at least as well as, or better than, the simple budget outcome models.*

Results

Summary results are presented in Table 5-5. The numbers in parentheses indicate the combination of averaging periods that produced the best fit. In spite of the fact that the multiple R's are simply measures of goodness of fit and provide for qualitative inferences only, it is difficult not to be struck by their rather impressive values. For the years 1970 to 1976, the subsystem models generally fit well—in most cases very well and in some cases extraordinarily well.

By using the subsystem models that employed constant 1972 dollars for the dependent variable, in most cases, it is possible to explain more than half of the variation in budget stability. In the general fund category, the average percentage of variance in budgetary stability explained through the models is 61 percent. For other funds, the average is also 61 percent. This seems especially impressive when compared with the apparent descriptive capacity of the simple budget outcome models. In only one case, "other" Forest Service funds, does a budget model provide a fit superior to that obtainable with a constant-dollar subsystem model.

An overall view of the pattern of results shows a picture that is less clear. The proposition that subsystem models should fit better for "general funds" than for "other funds" is not supported. Values are in the predicted direction for two of the eight agency-subcommittee relationships, FS and ARS, while two other relationships, FES and SCS, show values that "flip-flop" depending upon whether obligations are taken in constant or current dollars. In the four remaining relationships, values are in the direction opposite from that predicted.

Table 5-5
Summary Results for Regression Models

Agency and Category of Funds	Subsystem Models		Budget Outcome Models	
	Constant Dollars	Current Dollars	Constant Dollars	Current Dollars
ASCS				
General	$R = .82$ (322)	$R = .57$ (322)	$r = -.38$	$r = -.47$
Other	$R = .86$ (323)	$R = .91$ (323)	$r = +.60$	$r = +.41$
AMS				
General	$R = .70$ (222)	$R = .69$ (222)	$r = +.01$	$r = +.03$
Other	$R = .74$ (222)	$R = .80$ (223)	$r = +.48$	$r = +.55$
ARS				
General	$R = .96$ (322)	$R = .93$ (322)	$r = +.11$	$r = .00$
Other	$R = .71$ (333)	$R = .81$ (332)	$r = +.15$	$r = +.03$
CSRS				
General	$R = .54$ (333)	$R = .50$ (333)	$r = -.38$	$r = -.46$
Other	$R = .85$ (233)	$R = .81$ (233)	$r = -.10$	$r = -.21$
FAS				
General	$R = .78$ (333)	$R = .75$ (333)	$r = +.08$	$r = +.76$
Other	$R = .96$ (333)	$R = .97$ (333)	$r = +.56$	$r = +.66$
FS				
General	$R = .86$ (232)	$R = .63$ (232)	$r = +.08$	$r = -.17$
Other	$R = .48$ (232)	$R = .44$ (233)	$r = -.76$	$r = -.60$
FES				
General	$R = .75$ (322)	$R = .60$ (322)	$r = +.30$	$r = -.51$
Other	$R = .67$ (333)	$R = .86$ (323)	$r = +.67$	$r = +.74$
SCS				
General	$R = .75$ (333)	$R = .96$ (333)	$r = +.40$	$r = +.35$
Other	$R = .87$ (322)	$R = .87$ (322)	$r = +.15$	$r = +.24$

An analysis of the standard deviations of yearly obligation increments for the eight agencies showed that, in general, "other funds" were actually *more* variable than "general funds." It is possible that in aggregating agency budgets, mistakes in judgment were made as to which obligation items should be assigned to the noncontrollable category and which to the discretionary category. However, the classification procedure used seems quite consistent with others employed in the budget theory literature.[10]

A final observation is necessary concerning the proposition that subsystem models should fit better when obligations are taken in constant dollars rather than in current dollars. As Table 5-5 indicates, this does seem to be the case for "general funds." In seven of the eight relationships, the constant-dollar fit is at least as good or is marginally better. However, just the opposite pattern is found for "other funds." The fit for current dollars is as good or better in seven of the eight cases.

Discussion

Any discussion of these results must stand in light of several important qualifications. First, only two sides of the subsystem "triangle" have been considered. It is probable that at least some supergrades, and perhaps congressmen, departed to take positions with interest groups in their subsystems. If this "absorption" were total, or nearly so, the stability measures used here would overstate personnel change, and the results would be rendered spurious. It is considered highly unlikely that this is the case in general. A casual inspection of the data showed that many departing supergrades were clearly of retirement age, while others departed to take positions with different agencies of USDA or with agencies of other departments. Still, systematic investigation of interest group recruitment sources would seem necessary for a complete assessment of subsystem personnel stability.

Second, the possibility must be considered that agency personnel are oriented toward the prevailing norms, goals, and budgetary behavior of their policy subsystem, through socialization processes within their agency, prior to assuming supergrade positions. A similar argument can be made for junior members of the congressional subcommittees. Both arguments would certainly find at least some support in the literature.[11] Since the study did not consider agency positions graded G.S. 15 and below, a more inclusive characterization of subsystem participation may well be indicated for future research. Nonetheless, the findings cast some doubt on the assertion of well-developed socialization processes, at least within the agencies examined here. Given the high turnover rates observed among supergrades, the question must be asked, Who transmits prevailing values and norms to lower-level officials?

Finally, the period covered by the study may have been somewhat anomalous. During this period, an unusually high proportion of career officials, the late New Deal and World War II "age lump," became eligible for retirement. Additionally, it is probable that this period saw unusually hostile relationships between the political heads of the Nixon administration and career bureaucrats in many governmental agencies. These factors, combined with a generally unsettled political environment, may have produced enough distortion in subsystem activity so as to reduce the appropriateness of inferences about "normal" policy-making processes.

In spite of these qualifications, it is obvious that the subsystem models used here provide a reasonably good description of policy outcomes during the period considered. The results tend to encourage the contention that subsystem activity is an important factor in agricultural policy making. However, a paradox is also apparent. The results do *not* imply, either statistically or descriptively, that individuals in agricultural policy-making institutions actually operated as healthy subsystems during the period under consideration. The qualitative inferences that one can draw from the overall data presentation suggest rather the opposite conclusion. For the period, personnel stability in agencies and Congress seems fairly low in absolute terms and is clearly lower than for the period of the middle to late 1960s. Significantly, the period also saw a considerable degree of instability in budgetary outcomes for the agencies in question. Hence, it is the correspondence of personnel and budgetary *instability* which has, on the whole, tended to produce the good descriptive fit obtained with the subsystem models. What the models may very well be describing is the breakup, or perhaps more accurately, the "transformation" of most of these policy subsystems.

Notes

1. See, respectively, Ernest S. Griffith, *The Impasse of Democracy* (New York: Harrison-Hilton Books, Inc., 1939), and J. Leiper Freeman, *The Political Process: Executive Bureau-Legislative Committee Relations* (Garden City, N.Y.: Doubleday and Company, Inc., 1955).

2. For a useful discussion of various levels of policy making and an overall characterization of subsystem politics, see Emmette S. Redford, *Democracy in the Administrative State* (New York: Oxford University Press, 1969), especially chap. 4.

3. Ibid., pp. 96-106.

4. See Graham T. Allison, *Essence of Decision* (Boston: Little, Brown and Company, 1971) for a lucid discussion of the implications of alternative conceptual models. The approach taken in this study would probably fall most nearly under Allison's "organizational process" paradigm.

5. See, for example, John Gist, "Mandatory Expenditures: The Defense Sector and the Theory of Budgetary Incrementalism," Sage Professional Papers in American Politics (Beverly Hills, Calif.: Sage Publications, 1974) vol. no. 04-020.

6. When variable values are logarithmically transformed, the multiplicative model is equivalent to an additive model having the form

$$\text{Log } Y = \text{Log } b + m_1 \text{ Log } X_1 + m_2 \text{ Log } X_2$$

7. For an excellent discussion of the potential usefulness of multiplicative models in political research, see Walter Dean Burnham and John Sprague,

"Additive and Multiplicative Models of the Voting Universe: The Case of Pennsylvania: 1960-1968," *APSR,* June 1970, pp. 471-490.

8. For a discussion of noncontrollability in the federal budget, see Murray Weidenbaum, "Institutional Obstacles to Reallocating Government Expenditures," in R. Haveman and J. Margolis (eds.), *Public Expenditures and Policy Analysis* (Chicago: Markham Publishing Co., 1970), pp. 232-245.

9. Taking the variables in the order agency stability, committee stability, and budget stability, the combinations of averaging periods, in years, would be

$$2, 2, 2 \quad 2, 3, 3 \quad 2, 3, 2 \quad 2, 2, 3$$
$$3, 3, 3 \quad 3, 2, 2 \quad 3, 2, 3 \quad 3, 3, 2$$

10. See Wiedenbaum, "Institutional Obstacles."

11. See, for example, Herbert Kaufman, *The Forest Ranger: A Study of Administrative Behavior* (Baltimore, Md.: Johns Hopkins Press, 1960), and Richard F. Fenno, Jr., "The Appropriations Committee as a Political System," in Robert L. Peabody and Nelson N. Polsby (eds.), *New Perspectives on the House of Representatives* (Chicago: Rand McNally, 1977), pp. 139-166.

6 Building Bureaucratic Coalitions: Client Representation in USDA Bureaus

Kenneth John Meier

The conventional wisdom concerning agricultural policy is that it is formed in policy subsystems where interest groups, U.S. Department of Agriculture (USDA) bureaus, and congressional committees operate autonomously without the intervention of major political forces such as Congress or the President. According to Theodore Lowi, "That agricultural affairs should be handled strictly within the agriculture community is a basic political principle established before the turn of the century and maintained since then without serious reexamination."[1] Tripartite policy subsystems such as those in agricultural policy can operate in isolation from major political forces because each element of the subsystem provides all the essential needs of the other participants. Bureaus receive the appropriations and legislative authority they need from the congressional committees and in return deliver services to the interest groups. Interest groups receive the services offered by the bureaus and in return give political support to members of Congress in their legislative and political battles. Members of the congressional committees receive political support from the interest groups which permits them to maintain themselves in positions of power and grant appropriations to the bureaus.

A policy subsystem can operate essentially as a closed system with regard to the remainder of the political system if (1) the scope of issues that the subsystem considers is narrow, so that others are not concerned with the issues, and (2) the program costs are relatively small. With narrow issues and small costs, other political actors do not have the incentive to intervene in the subsystem because the rewards of successful intervention will be small relative to the costs. As a result, the members of the policy subsystem can focus and resolve all conflict in the subsystem and present the major system with a fait accompli on most policy issues.[2]

Subsystem politics is an important political phenomenon because it affects the outputs of the political process. Numerous students of agricultural policy[3] have argued that agricultural policy reflects the policy preferences of the organized agricultural interests and excludes broader farm and consumer interests. The stability of agricultural subsystems,[4] however, has been affected by recent events that created incentives for other political actors to intervene in agricultural policy.

The events creating incentives to intervene in the agricultural policy subsystem were the emergence of food as a systemic issue and the continued demographic changes in the nation. First, international population growth plus declining harvests changed the market for farm products from one of surpluses to one of shortages. Changes in international supply and demand caused large increases in domestic food prices (20 percent in 1973, 12 percent in 1974, 7 percent in 1975), mobilizing many nonfarm policy makers. Second, the flow of people from farms to the cities further weakened rural strength in the U.S. Congress, the major forum for agricultural policy.[5] With fewer rural members of Congress and greater urban interest in food policy, major farm legislation in the mid-1970s could be passed only with the aid of urban votes.[6] As a result, the power of the agricultural policy subsystems declined.

Given these recent changes in the agricultural policy environment, this chapter will examine the ability of Department of Agriculture bureaus to build interest group coalitions and the change in this ability over the past fifteen years. First, a measure of clientele support based on appropriations hearings will be presented. Second, all operating bureaus in the Department of Agriculture will be ranked according to their clientele support. Third, clientele support for the USDA bureaus in the mid-1970s will be compared with the clientele support for the same bureaus in the mid-1960s, to determine the impact of the recent environmental changes on the bureau coalitions. Fourth, the reasons why certain bureaus in the Department of Agriculture were able to build large interest group coalitions will be examined. Finally, the benefits and costs of interest group support will be assessed on variables crucial to the survival of the bureaus.

Measuring Clientele Support

Any attempt to measure the clientele support of USDA bureaus must meet two criteria. First, the measurement of clientele support must focus on a process where the bureaus are the entities being considered. Interest group support on major farm legislation, therefore, while adequate to assess interest preferences on general agricultural policy, will reveal little about agency clientele coalitions. Major farm issues that occupy the policy-making system for extended periods of time center on USDA-wide issues such as target prices, nutrition, or exports.[7] Second, the measurement of clientele support must focus on a process where the interest group activity is visible. Day-to-day policy-making actions of the USDA bureaus implementing general legislation obviously involves contact with interest groups, given the decentralized nature of agricultural programs, but such interaction is usually informal and rarely visible to the policy analyst.

The only portion of the policy-making process where bureaus are the units being considered and the interest group activity is open is the appropriations process. Agricultural appropriations are organized along bureau lines, and the appropriations subcommittees permit interest groups to appear before them on behalf of a bureau. The interest group data used in this analysis were gathered from a content analysis of testimony before Senate and House Subcommittees on Agriculture Appropriations for fiscal years 1975 through 1976.

The testimony of each interest group was content-analyzed and coded for a variety of information. First, the characteristics of the interest group were identified—whether the group testified in person or via written communications, whether the group was a mass association, a peak association, or a single petitioner (one person seeking benefits for himself, his company, or locality). Second, the intensity of the group's testimony was coded from the content analysis. Testimony before the appropriations subcommittees falls into two categories—testimony concerning the agency in general and testimony on specific programs that the agency administers. "Agency testimony" means that the interest group supports the agency in general rather than a single specific program that the agency administers. Because agency-based support is more beneficial to the bureau since it indicates a more permanent type of support, agency testimony was coded as being more intense than programmatic testimony. Testimony regarding the bureau, therefore, was coded as a +3 while that on a program was coded +2. Based on these initial codes, all group testimony was given an intensity score from Table 6-1.

The testimony of some 800 groups for 21 bureaus was reduced to just four variables for analysis in this research: the number of interest groups testifying, the number of members of Congress testifying on each bureau, the mean intensity of group testimony for each bureau, and the mean intensity of congressional testimony for each bureau. Interest groups and congressional testimony were kept separate for theoretical reasons. Francis Rourke, interpreting a study of Richard Fenno, contends that support in Congress allows agencies to avoid budget cuts while support among outside interest groups permits an agency to grow and aggrandize power.[8] This distinction is also supported by the perception of many policy analysts[9] that the best lobbyist an organization can have is a member of Congress.[10]

Much of the information gathered in the content analysis was deleted from the remaining analysis because the information duplicated the above four variables. The number of interest groups present and the number of positively testifying interest groups were almost perfectly correlated with the number of groups ($r = .99$ in both cases). Almost all groups appearing before the appropriations committees came to praise an agency, not to condemn it. Despite the

Table 6-1
Testimony on the Program

		Pro	Neutral	Con
	Pro	+5	+3	+1
Testimony on the agency	Neutral	+2	0	−2
	Con	−1	−3	−5

theoretical reasons for retaining the total membership of all interest groups (since large membership in theory can be translated into electoral consequences), the size variables were dropped because they could not be measured unambiguously. Many of the organizations were peak associations, and adding a membership of 140 organizations to a membership of 450 farmers results in a figure difficult to interpret. Even if the researcher could accept the problems of peak and mass associations, the size of each agency's interest group following would vary little from bureau to bureau because a few large organizations such as the American Farm Bureau testify for all agencies.

Variations in Clientele Support

Tables 6-2 and 6-3, respectively, present the House and Senate clientele scores for the USDA bureaus.[11] Even a cursory examination of the tables reveals that

Table 6-2
Clientele Support before the House Appropriations Committee. 1974-1976

Agency	Number of Groups	Intensity	Members of Congress	Intensity
ARS	72	2.53	18	2.67
APHIS	26	2.65	2	4.00
CSRS	41	3.12	10	2.40
NAL	0	0	0	0
Extension	14	3.14	3	2.33
SRS	16	1.75	1	−1.00
ERS	3	2.67	2	2.00
CEA/CFTC	0	0	0	0
PSA	7	1.29	0	0
FCS	1	3.00	0	0
FAS	16	3.13	0	0
Export	0	0	0	0
ASCS	27	2.11	4	2.25
FCIC	1	3.00	0	0
CCC	2	4.00	1	2.00
RDS	3	3.00	2	3.50
REA	10	3.60	3	4.00
FmHA	25	2.72	12	2.08
SCS	42	2.40	43	3.58
AMS	12	1.42	0	0
FNS	15	0.60	7	0.64

Table 6-3

Clientele Support before the Senate Appropriations Subcommittee on Agriculture, 1974-1976

Agency	Number of Groups	Intensity	Members of Congress	Intensity
ARS	45	2.29	32	2.22
APHIS	26	2.04	9	2.33
CSRS	32	2.06	17	2.24
NAL	0	0	0	0
Extension	18	2.06	5	2.20
SRS	10	2.10	5	2.00
ERS	3	2.33	3	2.67
CEA/CFTA	0	0	0	0
PSA	6	2.00	0	0
FCS	0	0	0	0
FAS	13	2.00	1	2.00
Export	0	0	0	0
ASCS	24	1.75	9	2.00
FCIC	2	2.00	0	0
CCC	3	2.00	0	0
RDS	11	2.00	10	2.30
REA	7	2.57	4	2.00
FmHA	14	1.43	18	2.94
SCS	20	2.10	9	2.11
AMS	4	2.00	11	2.00
FNS	5	1.16	9	2.00

the values for clientele support roughly correspond to perceptions of clientele strength. The agencies with large clientele support include ARS, SCS, CSRS, FmHA, ASCS, and APHIS. With the exception of APHIS, all these agencies are major distributive agencies in research, conservation, or subsidies—ideal programs for building a strong clientele base. The exception, APHIS, appears on this list because the mid-1970s appropriations hearings received a fair amount of testimony on the APHIS quarantine programs.

The mid-level clientele agenices (Extension, FNS, SRS, AMS, REA, and RDS) are a mixture; none are known for strong clientele support except for the Extension Service and the Rural Electrification Administration. The Extension Service heads the list of the middle six agencies and therefore may not belong in the middle group. The REA, on the other hand, has seen the importance of its function decline as it successfully achieved rural electrification. As the need for additional rural electrification declines, so should support for REA.

The remaining nine organizations with little clientele support are staff agencies, regulatory agencies, or foreign affairs-related agencies. None of these agencies has significant positive distributive impact on the traditional clientele of the Department of Agriculture.[12]

The intensity of support scores in Tables 6-2 and 6-3 is self-explanatory, though some figures reflect positively on the validity of the measures. The agency with the least positive support (in terms of intensity) is the Food and Nutrition Service, the agency administering the food stamp program. During this period the food stamp program was controversial especially on the issue of food stamps for striking laborers. As a result, the FNS has been unable to build a strong clientele among the agricultural community.[13] The high scores achieved by the Rural Electrification Administration reflect the Nixon threat to eliminate the agency. As the number of REA supporters dwindled, the agency had sufficient symbolic value to its remaining clientele to elicit strong support from a few groups.[14]

Comparing clientele support in both the House and the Senate reveals striking similarities. The rank-order of interest group support for the bureaus is almost identical for both houses ($r = .86$). Although fewer members of Congress testify, thus making the scores less reliable, House and Senate support scores are still positively correlated ($r = .5$). The intensity scores form the same pattern with the correlation .67 for interest groups and .57 for members of Congress. The high intercorrelations are reassuring since they reflect on the reliability of the selected measures and indicate that little information will be lost by combining the scores for the House and the Senate. The remainder of this research, therefore, will use one set of clientele support scores based on both houses of Congress.

The similarities in clientele support should not blind the reader to differences in clientele style and procedure in the two houses of Congress. Although both committees attract generally the same number of clientele, more emphasis is placed on appearing in person rather than sending a statement in the House subcommittee (76 versus 46 percent). Clientele testifying before the Senate subcommittee are slightly more positive about the agency (97 versus 93 percent); in fact, Senate testimony tends to be predominantly programmatic support rather than agency support (90 percent in the Senate, 43 percent in the House). The reasons for these differences in clientele testimony can be found in the role that each appropriations subcommittee established for itself. The House Committee on Appropriations sees itself as the guardian of the public purse and cuts budgets that agencies present to it.[15] The Senate Appropriations Committee acts as an appeals board in regard to House action and hears requests from the bureaus, restoring those requests that it feels have merit.

Because House hearings develop most of the factual testimony,[16] the Senate concentration on appeals naturally generates more programmatic testimony. General declarations of agency support are not needed in the Senate. Since the Senate restricts itself to appeals, the preponderance of testimony is positive because the Senate serves as an appeals board only for negative House decisions. Groups who receive most of their request from the House, therefore, can risk sending written testimony rather than appearing in person.

Clientele Support in the 1960s

Because the environment of agricultural policy has changed so dramatically in the past decade, an interesting issue involves the relationship of the policy environment to the bureau's ability to maintain clientele support. This section examines the testimony before the House Appropriations Subcommittee on Agriculture during the mid-1960s with this objective in mind.[17] The time period 1963 through 1965 was selected with great care because it represents a time when subsystems clearly dominated agricultural policy.[18] In 1963 President Lyndon Johnson gathered together all the major farm interests and asked them to write the new farm bill. The Wheat-Cotton Bill of 1964 was a classic example of subsystem politics at work in agricultural policy.[19] Since farm prices were low, commodities were in great supply, and food prices were low, the major actors in the system were relatively unconcerned with agriculture, unlike the present situation. The change in policy environments, therefore, predicts a decline in bureau coalitions.

The clientele support rankings for the 16 bureaus that spanned the fifteen years are shown in Table 6-4. The stability of the bureaus' relative positions vis-à-vis one another is remarkable ($r = .68$), but the size of the coalitions has suffered an absolute decline. In 1965 the 16 USDA bureaus averaged 36 clientele while eleven years later 21 bureaus averaged only 20 clientele. Of the major clientele bureaus, the ARS clientele support dropped 48 percent, the ASCS lost 47 percent, the REA 31 percent, the SCS 39 percent, and the AMS 90 percent. The dissipation in USDA bureaus' clientele is not just a statistical artifact, because the incentives for attracting more clientele support are greater now than they were in the 1960s. In the 1970s many members of Congress questioned the need for many USDA functions. Under such conditions, the bureaus would rationally expend greater effort to secure clientele testimony to provide a record of service and thus demonstrate their worth. The decrease in clientele support, therefore, likely reflects an absolute decline in the constituencies of the USDA bureaus.

Although the relative clientele support rankings for the bureaus remain similar and the entire agricultural policy system has suffered a decline in clientele support, some agency coalitions have changed relative to others. The relative strength of each bureau's coalition in both time periods is shown in Table 6-5. The rise of the Cooperative State Research Service (CSRS) is easily explained.[20] Until 1962 CSRS was part of the ARS and as a new agency was not able to build sufficient clientele by 1965; by 1975, operating in an area similar

Table 6-4

Clientele Support before the House Appropriations Subcommittee on Agriculture 1963-1965

Agency	Number of Groups	Intensity	Members of Congress	Intensity
ARS	129	1.92	50	1.88
CSRS	15	2.00	6	2.16
NAL	0	0	0	0
Extension	9	3.29	8	3.29
SRS	9	2.00	1	2.00
ERS	5	3.00	0	0
FCS	3	4.33	0	0
FAS	36	3.00	0	0
Export	0	0	0	0
ASCS	26	1.77	27	2.00
FCIC	3	2.00	0	0
CCC	1	2.00	0	0
REA	41	−0.72	2	3.00
FmHA	7	1.43	5	4.20
SCS	56	2.23	82	2.65
AMS	67	2.36	16	2.00

to that of the ARS and the Extension Service, the CSRS was able to develop a large following. The two major agencies with strong clientele in the 1960s but much weaker clientele in the 1970s, the REA and the AMS, declined as their functions declined in importance. The Rural Electrification Administration saw the bulk of its major task completed. The Agricultural Marketing Service lost several programs to other agencies.[21] With the decline in the relative importance of bureau functions, interest groups switched their attention to other policy makers.

Coalition Size: An Explanation

USDA bureaus vary greatly in the amount of clientele support they can rely on in policy-making operations. The Agricultural Research Service and the Soil Conservation Service are blessed with numerous groups willing to support them in the appropriations battles, while the Farmer's Cooperative Service and the Federal Crop Insurance Corporation must interact almost alone. This section will examine the reasons why some agencies are so fortunate and others lack clientele support. According to students of bureaucratic coalitions,[22] two variables affect

Table 6-5
Clientele Support, 1963-1965 and 1974-1976

1963-1965 Clientele Support	1974-1976 Clientele Support		
	Weak	Moderate	Strong
Weak	NAL ERS FCS FCIC CCC		
Moderate	FAS Export	Extension SRS	CSRS FmHA
Strong		REA AMS	ARS ASCS SCS

the ability of a bureau to build strong clientele support. First, the bureau must be able to offer the interest group something in exchange for its support,[23] some service the interest group needs. Positive benefits also tie members of Congress to the bureau by benefiting the constituents of a member. Second, the bureau should have a reputation for expertise—the ability to perform a task and perform it better than other bureaus. Expertise is especially important in conjunction with the ability to deliver services to clientele because Congress usually lacks the expertise to provide these services directly.[24]

The two theoretical factors—benefits and expertise—affecting the strength of clientele support can be operationalized through five indicators. First, the number of personnel each agency has is an indicator of both ability to deliver services and expertise. Since USDA bureaus tend to be decentralized—the entire Department has less than 15 percent of its employees in Washington—the more employees an agency has, the more clientele can be contacted and can receive services. Larger personnel numbers also mean that an agency can specialize its personnel so that it can apply more expertise to the problems facing its clientele. Second, the agency's ability to contract out for services affects the size of clientele because agencies with contract authority gain additional clientele among those organizations receiving contracts.[25] The Department of Defense, for example, is widely known for its ability to create clientele through the use of government contracts. Third, according to Francis Rourke, the ability to produce tangible achievements augments the bureau's political support.[26] Agencies that produce conservation projects, new plant hybrids, or rural electrification have a more direct appeal to clientele than those that produce reports or maintain liberties.[27] The former provide some direct benefits to the clientele while the latter's benefits are indirect and often not recognizable by the clientele. Fourth, access to technical information that lay people cannot easily understand is a major element of expertise.[28] This expertise is translated into clientele support because technical specialists such as agronomists, agricultural economists, and geneticists can provide benefits to the producers that they cannot provide for themselves.[29] Fifth, the number of computers to which the bureau has access via either ownership or rental agreement is a good indicator of the bureau's expertise because little research on major agricultural problems is possible without access to computer technology.

The five variables listed above were combined in a linear model to predict the level of clientele support for each of the bureaus in the Department of Agriculture. Each of the variables was used as an independent variable in a regression equation in an attempt to explain the variation in the four clientele measures.[30] The results are presented in Table 6-6. The first aspect of Table 6-6 worthy of note is the multiple correlations at the bottom of the table. The model predicts extremely well for the number of interest groups and the number of members of Congress supporting the bureau. The five variables account for 90 percent of the variance in clientele support. For intensity of support the model works less well (.68 for congressional intensity and .46 for interest group intensity), but it is still respectable.

The regression coefficients of the independent variables indicate that the process works much as the theory predicted. In terms of attracting large numbers of clientele, access to computer expertise has the largest impact followed by specialization potential (size of personnel).[31] Ability to deliver services in terms of both contractual authority and ability to produce tangible benefits also has a major impact.[32]

Intensity of clientele support relationships is not as interpretable as the size of support relationships. Congressional intensity is related strongly to whether the bureau can deliver tangible benefits and the size of the bureau. This relationship indicates that USDA bureaus large enough to deliver substantial

Table 6-6
Standardized Regression Coefficients for Clientele Support

Independent Variables	Number of Interest Groups	Members of Congress	Group Intensity	Congressional Intensity
Number of personnel	.34	.40	.13	.40
Contract authority	.28	.27	.07	.11
Tangible achievements	.30	.39	.09	.35
Technical knowledge	.11	.02	.36	.11
Computers	.49	.40	−.15	−.09
r =	.95	.94	.46	.68

services in a number of congressional districts can attract strong congressional support. Interest group intensity, on the other hand, is fairly unrelated to either expertise or ability to deliver services, with the single exception of access to technical information that the lay person does not have.[33]

The implications of the model predicting clientele support and intensity are important for any student of agricultural policy. Clientele support is strongly related to expertise and ability to deliver services to potential clientele groups. For most agencies these variables are fairly constant, being defined by the legislative function of the organization. If the function of a bureau is to deliver services to a target population and if substantial expertise is needed to do so, the agency should fare well. If a bureau function is lacking both these characteristics, it must suffer the liabilities of a weak clientele.

These findings indicate that agency leadership has very little room to operate in building additional clientele. If the size of clientele is dictated by expertise and function, leadership actions to attract more clientele can offer only a marginal improvement. Given the past history of the Department of Agriculture, especially the close relationships between the Extension Service and the American Farm Bureau, this finding may well be relevant to the 1970s only. A bureau leadership positively attuned to the needs of a clientele cannot help but make at least marginal improvements in clientele support, especially when contrasted with a leadership hostile to the clientele.[34] These generalizations apply only to absolute size of a clientele. An agency that attempts to alter the composition of its clientele faces different constraints, and this chapter does not empirically address that problem.

The Impact of Clientele Support

Case study evidence has demonstrated repeatedly that clientele relationships do have an impact on public policy.[35] These studies consistently argue that the nation's agricultural policy has demonstrated a bias toward large, progressive farmers.[36] Case studies demonstrating the impact that clientele relationships have on public policy in other areas are too numerous to cite.

A more interesting question concerning the impact of clientele support is whether the bureaus benefit from strong clientele support. Freeman, Fenno, Wildavsky, and other students of subsystem politics believe that bureaus with strong clientele support receive additional fiscal resources and autonomy in the use of those resources.[37] Congress, in short, responds to the expressed needs of interest groups by favorable treatment of the groups' bureau.

Not all scholars of public policy agree, however, that interest group support is an unmitigated blessing for an agency. Students of regulatory policy in particular feel that interest group support may well be harmful to an agency. Huntington found that the ICC's response to its clientele led to the ICC's decline as an effective organization.[38] Marver Bernstein developed Huntington's case study and others into his life cycle theory of regulatory agency decline.[39] When diffuse political support for a regulatory agency wanes, agencies attempt to woo the regulated as their clientele. Since strong clientele relationships with the regulated are perceived as illegitimate by the major policy actors, Congress and the President respond to the captive agency by ignoring its needs, cutting its budget, and constantly meddling in its administrative activities. Regulatory agencies are actually harmed by strong clientele support.[40]

This section empirically examines the question of the impact that clientele support has on the bureau's ability to receive greater resources and autonomy in their use. If clientele support is positively related to an agency's ability to extract additional resources from its environment, then this ability should be reflected in the following four measures of budget success. *Budget growth* is the annual percentage growth in congressional appropriations.[41] *Budget success* is the ability of the bureau to avoid budget cuts at the hands of Congress; operationally, success is the ratio of congressional appropriations to the bureau's initial request of Congress. *Presidential budget support* is the analogue of the congressional growth rate; it is the annual percentage growth rate in the President's grants to the bureau compared with the previous years' congressional appropriations.[42] *Supplemental appropriations* are requests by the agency for additional funds after the budget is passed; these funds cover new programs, unexpected expenses, or deficiencies.[43]

Table 6-7 shows that agency budgets are unaffected by the clientele support for the bureau; none of the 16 possible relationships are statistically significant. Bureaus with strong clientele support are no more likely to avoid budget cuts, to

Table 6-7

Simple Correlations between Clientele Support and Measures of Resources and Autonomy

Budget Measures	Number of Interest Groups	Group Intensity	Members of Congress	Congress Intensity
Growth	−.01	.03	−.05	.10
Success	.06	−.02	.02	.21
Presidential support	.15	.08	.26	.18
Supplemental appropriations	−.03	.03	−.14	.15
Autonomy Measures				
Trust funds	−.07	−.01	−.04	.06
Permanent authorizations	−.00	.08	−.24	−.02
Budget detail	.03	.10	−.28	.01
Rules-to-laws ratio	−.01	.07	−.06	.11

grow, or to get supplementals; neither are they more likely to be punished. A bureau's clientele support and its budget record are essentially unrelated.[44]

The skeptic might argue that the lack of results is related to the special circumstances surrounding American agriculture in the 1970s. With the decline in importance of agriculture and the increasing cost of food, agricultural policy became an issue on the systemic agenda; therefore, national political forces may have countered the impact of clientele support. If the skeptic were correct, then a positive relationship between clientele support and budget growth and success should be found during the mid-1950s when agricultural policy subsystems were still strong. This is not the case. Clientele support is not significantly related to either budget growth ($r = .21$) or budget success ($r = -.11$) during the 1963-1965 period.

If clientele support does not lead to greater resources, perhaps it yields greater autonomy in the use of these resources. Four measures of autonomy were used to test this hypothesis. *Trust funds* are funds established by legislation with their own sources of generation. Possession of trust funds exempts a portion of the agency from the appropriations process. One measure of autonomy, then, is the percentage of bureau funds that are received from trust funds. *Permanent authorizations* are legislative authorizations for expenditures that do not have an expiration date; with permanent authorizations an agency can avoid the annual authorization struggle. Another measure of autonomy is the percentage of agency resources covered by permanent authorizations. *Budget detail* is the ratio of the dollars in the bureau's budget to the number of lines the agency's budget takes in the congressional budget; if this ratio is large, then Congress can examine the budget in great detail.[45] The *rules-to-laws ratio* is a measure of legislative autonomy; it is the ratio of the number of pages of administrative rules promulgated by the bureau to the number of pages of legislation that concerns the agency. Autonomous agencies will tend to have brief laws but issue a great many rules to clarify the legislation.

Table 6-7 shows that bureau autonomy is unrelated to strong clientele support; none of the 16 possible relationships are statistically significant. Bureaus with strong clientele support are no more or less likely to enjoy the benefits of budget or legislative autonomy.

The findings concerning the relationship of budgets and autonomy to clientele support must be qualified. Table 6-7 does not prove that clientele support is not helpful in aggrandizing additional resources for a bureau, only that the two variables are uncorrelated. This conclusion is counterintuitive and as unsatisfying as the finding that campaign contributions do not affect election outcomes. The rival hypothesis that bureaus with clientele support would likely suffer great losses of resources if their clientele support dissipated cannot be ruled out. Neither can the hypothesis that clientele support helps isolate the bureau from environmental influences; clientele support may well lead to small but secure increases in resources. If the bureau were at the whim of environmental influences such as public opinion, we would expect that the agency would make large gains when it was favored but sustain large losses when it was in disfavor. In that circumstance, clientele support may be beneficial. The findings of this section, however, cast doubt on the hypothesis that clientele support is directly translated in larger resource allocations for the bureau.

Conclusions

This research attempted to create measures of interest group support for 21 bureaus in the Department of Agriculture. By using data from agricultural appropriations, measures were created that generally reflected the perceived strength of bureau's clientele support. From this data base several generalizations about clientele support in agriculture were possible. First, as the importance of agriculture declined from the mid-1960s to the present, the size of agricultural bureau coalitions also declined. Second, individual bureau coalitions were related to both the expertise of the bureau and the ability of the bureau to provide tangible benefits. The size of the bureau's coalition was positively related to both these variables, as was the intensity of congressional support; the intensity of interest group support was not related to either. These relationships suggest that bureaus are restrained somewhat in their clientele-building activities by the defined mission of the agency. Finally, clientele support does not appear to be helpful in gaining and maintaining resources and autonomy; agencies with strong clientele fare no better and no worse than agencies with weak clientele.

Notes

1. Theodore Lowi, *The End of Liberalism* (New York: W.W. Norton, 1969), p. 103.

2. E.E. Schattschneider, *The Semi-Sovereign People* (Chicago: Holt, Rinehart and Winston, 1960).

3. Charles L. Schultze, *The Distribution of Farm Subsidies* (Washington: The Brookings Institution, 1971); Don F. Hadwiger and Rickard Fraenkel, "The Agricultural Policy Process," in James E. Anderson, *Economic Regulatory Policies* (Lexington, Mass.: D.C. Heath, 1976), pp. 39-50; Reo C. Christenson, *The Brannan Plan* (Ann Arbor: University of Michigan Press, 1959); Sidney Baldwin, *Politics and Poverty* (Chapel Hill: University of North Carolina Press, 1968); Jim Hightower, *Hard Tomatoes, Hard Times* (Washington: Agribusiness Accountability Project, 1972).

4. Grant McConnell, *The Decline of Agrarian Democracy* (Berkeley: University of California Press, 1953); Ross Talbot and Don F. Hadwiger, *The Policy Process in American Agriculture* (San Francisco: Chandler, 1968).

5. Garth Youngberg, "U.S. Agriculture in the 1970s: Policy and Politics," in James E. Anderson, *Economic Regulatory Policies* (Lexington: D.C. Heath, 1976), pp. 51-68.

6. Weldon Barton, "Coalition Building in the United States House of Representatives," in James E. Anderson, *Cases in Public Policy-Making* (New York: Praeger, 1976), pp. 141-161.

7. Recent agricultural issues that have been of concern to Congress have been the Agriculture and Consumer Protection Act of 1973, efforts at reforming the food stamp program, protection of market stability and other issues surrounding the Soviet grain purchases, the question of sugar profits and subsidies, and the inclusion of rice under a similar system as wheat, feed grains, and corn. Many of these issues either concern the entire Department of Agriculture or omit a great many bureaus with other functions so that interest group activity cannot be translated into bureau coalitions.

8. Francis Rourke, *Bureaucracy, Politics and Public Policy* (Boston: Little, Brown, 1976); Richard F. Fenno, *The Power of the Purse* (Boston: Little, Brown, 1966).

9. Aaron Wildavsky, *The Politics of the Budgetary Process* (Boston: Little, Brown, 1964).

10. Although the distinction between interest groups and members of Congress is theoretically useful, it is difficult to maintain empirically. Bureaus that are successful in recruiting one type of clientele are generally successful in recruiting the other. The correlation between number of interest groups supporting the bureau and the number of members of Congress is .92; the intensity scores are also correlated ($r = .62$).

11. The figures presented in Tables 6-2 and 6-3 differ somewhat from similar tables presented in Kenneth John Meier, "The Agricultural Research Service and Its Clientele: The Politics of Food Research" paper presented at the 1977 annual meeting of the Southwestern Political Science Association, April 1977. Adding the number of groups and the members of Congress in the present tables yields a figure equal to, or slightly larger than, those found in table 2 of that paper. The remaining differences result because that paper dealt only with supportive clientele; all negative testifiers were deleted. Since intensity is used here specifically, both negative and positive testimony were included.

12. The weak clientele group contains two interesting agencies: the FCIC and the Farmer's Cooperative Service. Since each of these agencies provides some positive benefits through either crop insurance programs or cooperative assistance, they are likely candidates for support. Since the farmer pays for most of, though not all, FCIC benefits and since the FCS benefits to the farmer are indirect, their visibility may be too low to generate support.

13. Former Secretary of Agriculture Earl Butz often publicly stated his preference that the food stamp program and the school lunch programs be transferred to the Department of Health, Education, and Welfare. The FNS

programs are perceived more as welfare programs than food disposal programs by the producers; therefore, interest group support for food stamps is weak. The food stamps program has suffered little, however, since it has sufficient visibility to attain the systemic agenda.

14. The number-of-groups variable is probably a more valid indicator of interest group support than the intensity score. The positions of fewer of the agencies on the number of clientele variables are out of line with expectations. Explaining why the Foreign Agricultural Service has very intense supporters or why the intensity of group support for the Farmer's Home Administration varies between the House and the Senate is difficult.

15. The behavior that Fenno described in the 1950s and 1960s is no longer true. During the Nixon-Ford administration, the pressures of inflation caused the President to cut agency budget requests more severely than normal. As a result, agencies appealed to the House Appropriations Committee to restore the cuts. With both committees performing the role of appeals board, the guardian of the purse role, while still enunciated, no longer is an accurate description. In fact, the agriculture bureaus for the period from 1971 to 1976 actually received 5.5 percent more from Congress than they were authorized to request by the Office of Management and Budget.

16. See John Wanat, "Bureaucratic Politics in the Budget Formulation Arena," *Administration and Society* 7 (August 1975): 191-213.

17. The House Agriculture Appropriations Subcommittee was selected rather than both subcommittees because the previous evidence indicated that similar information could be gained by examining either committee. Since little information is lost by examining only one committee, the House committee was selected because of its preeminent role in the budget process.

18. Lowi, *End of Liberalism.*

19. Ibid., pp. 100ff.

20. The Farmer's Home Administration's increase in clientele support occurs for no ostensible reason.

21. Portions of two contemporary agencies, APHIS and PSA, were at one time programs in the Agricultural Marketing Service. These agencies have since developed clientele relationships of their own.

22. Rourke, *Bureaucracy, Politics, and Public Policy,* pp. 85-90.

23. Peter Blau, *Exchange and Power in Social Life* (New York: Wiley, 1965).

24. In theoretical terms, the ability to deliver services may well be more important than expertise. NASA with its expertise is in a far worse position than the Law Enforcement Assistance Administration that lacks expertise but provides tangible benefits. Together these two factors augment each other; separately they may not have the intended impact.

25. The variable "contracting" is a dummy variable coded 1 if the agency had legislative authority to contract out for services and 0 if it did not.

26. Rourke, *Bureaucracy, Politics, and Public Policy,* p. 84. This statement actually extends Rourke more than he originally intended. Rourke contended that the production of tangible achievements was an element of expertise that led to additional power for a bureau. To Rourke, clientele support was a different factor. The logic of producing tangible achievements, however, applies equally well to bureau power or to gathering clientele support.

27. The variable "tangible achievements" was coded as a dummy variable: coded 1 if the agency produced some tangible good such as conservative projects or new hybrids and 0 if the agency's product was less tangible.

28. Rourke, *Bureaucracy, Politics, and Public Policy,* p. 84.

29. Technical information is included as a dummy variable with the agency coded as 1 if it had access to technical information and 0 if the information that it possessed was comprehensible by the lay clientele.

30. The text of this chapter is deliberately brief on the methods used in the section because they are common to much behavioral research and would needlessly lengthen the argument. In simple terms, the size of an agency's clientele support is a function of the number of personnel, the ability to contract out services, the ability to produce tangible achievements, the access to technical information, and the number of computers. Mathematically the model is as follows:

$$IG = a + b_1 P + b_2 C + b_3 T + b_4 I + b_5 Cm$$

where IC = the number of interest groups supporting the bureau
P = the number of personnel at the bureau
C = whether the bureau can contract
T = the bureau's ability to produce tangible achievements
I = the bureau's access to technical information
C_m = the number of computers the agency has
a = a constant

The parameters of this equation were estimated using standard multiple regression techniques. Similar equations were estimated for the number of members of Congress supporting the bureau, the intensity of interest group support, and the intensity of congressional support.

31. The interpretation of the regression model makes more sense if one treats the variables used as indicators of a more theoretical concept. The actual number of computers that an agency has probably does not have anything to do with its ability to attract clientele, but the access to expertise which can be partially measured by number of computers does have an impact on clientele support.

32. All coefficients for the size of clientele support are positive, which is another indicator of the appropriateness of the model. All the relationships

discussed earlier predicted positive associations between the independent variables and the clientele scores.

33. One methodological reason why the model works better for extent of support than it does for intensity is that the variable "intensity" contains more measurement error than the size of clientele. The results of the measures in Tables 6-2 and 6-3 were much as anticipated for the size of clientele, indicating little measurement error. The intensity scores were not as easily explainable perhaps because the measurement used was more crude.

34. The reason that so little is left as residual variance and, therefore, explainable by omitted variables such as leadership is that leadership may be constant in its attempt to attract clientele. A bureau chief actively hostile to the major clientele of a bureau would likely not remain as a bureau chief for a long time.

35. See Lowi, *The End of Liberalism*; Hightower, *Hard Tomatoes Hard Times*; Schultze, *Distribution of Farm Subsidies*; Baldwin, *Politics and Poverty*; and Christenson, *The Brannan Plan.*

36. The bias of agricultural policy does not mean that the USDA and its bureaus are conservative or ineffective within their expressed goals. Many of the bureaus have an excellent reputation for effectively meeting stated goals. The USDA as a whole was also known for innovative management in the past. The USDA, for example, implemented a zero-base budgeting system ten years before the state of Georgia did.

37. J. Leiper Freeman, *The Political Process* (New York: Random House, 1956); Fenno, *The Power of the Purse*; Wildavsky, *Politics of the Budgetary Process.*

38. Samuel P. Huntington, "The Marasmus of the I.C.C." *Yale Law Journal* 61 (1952):467-509.

39. Marver H. Bernstein, *Regulating Business by Independent Commission* (Princeton, N.J.: Princeton University Press, 1955).

40. The differences noted here actually may not be contradictory. Agencies engaged in distributive policy are often encouraged to serve clientele while regulatory agencies are not. Distributive policy bureaus, therefore, should be rewarded for their success in serving their clientele while regulatory agencies must be punished for failing to serve their clientele. The results of this study appear to detract from this theoretical dichotomy since neither type of agency fares well as a result of clientele support.

41. This analysis uses the fiscal years 1971 through 1976. The actual years used are unimportant because clientele support is very stable over a short period. Similar analysis with the budget years 1974 through 1976 which match the clientele support years found identical results.

42. Ideally a Presidential success measure that compared the amount bureaus received from the President with the amount they asked for from the President would be used. Unfortunately bureau requests to the President are not part of the public record.

43. The variable is operationally defined as the number of supplemental appropriations that the bureau was granted in fiscal years 1974 through 1976.

44. Additional analysis by the author shows that this pattern holds for all agencies of the federal government. Budgets appear to be influenced by outside events such as national priorities, public opinion, crises, etc., but not clientele support.

45. The budget document used in this analysis is actually the *Budget Appendix* published annually along with the much shorter budget. The budget document itself contains very little detail; the *Budget Appendix* treats each of the agencies in greater depth.

7

Politics of the Agricultural Research Establishment

Alex F. McCalla

Introduction

This chapter discusses the set of organizations, public and private, which fund and/or do agricultural research in the United States. Its purpose is to attempt to unravel the "politics" of that establishment. The term *research establishment* might imply a unitized, cohesive organization dedicated to a collectively agreed-upon common purpose. It is the thesis of this chapter that such a characterization is not accurate. Rather the "agricultural research establishment" is a morass of loosely related, sometimes complementary, sometimes competitive, organizations, so intertwined with the "publics" they serve that it defies simple definition. Its magnitude in recent years is approaching a $2 billion a year enterprise about 50 percent public and 50 percent private. There are substantial interconnections between elements in the system, complete with an elaborate maze of formal and informal overlapping organizations and directorates.

This chapter presents a view of how this system operates as seen by a former participant in the process.[1] However, participation does not guarantee a full understanding of the formal and, more importantly, the informal operations of the system. A full understanding would require longer involvement, and even then it might be elusive.

The Origins of the "Establishment" and Its Current Form and Magnitude

Most discussions of the current agricultural research arrangement in the United States begin with the year 1862. In that year the Morrill Act established federal land grants to the states for the establishment of Land-Grant Colleges. In the same year the U.S. Department of Agriculture (USDA) was created. Early emphasis of both organizations was on education. Formal recognition of the need for direct support of research came 25 years later in the Hatch Act of 1887, which established federal matching support to state experiment stations to be established in conjunction with the land grants. That act with subsequent amendments also authorized direct federal support for in-house research in an organization that later became the Agricultural Research Service (ARS).[2] Thus the two major public components of the agricultural research establishment have been in place since before the turn of the century. The original justifications of public support for agricultural research were that farms were too small to support their own research and that productivity increases in agriculture benefited both farmers and consumers and therefore society.

From the beginnings outlined above, the public portion of the establishment has grown and become more diversified. The strong push for general federal support of research resulting from Sputnik also channeled increased resources, particularly for basic research, into agriculture. Thus the National Science Foundation (NSF) and the National Institutes of Health (NIH) among many other federal agencies increased funding of research. More recent entries are, for example, the Environmental Protection Agency (EPA) and Energy Research and Development Agency (ERDA). The number of funders of agricultural research as well as the number of doers has increased greatly.

The origins and magnitude of private agricultural research are much harder to trace. It is likely that proprietary firms such as machinery companies pursued developmental research from their beginnings. It has increased in magnitude with the industrialization of United States agriculture. The most recent published estimate of industry support of agricultural research was made in 1966 when it was estimated that industry spent $473 million for research, which represented 54 percent of total funds available for agricultural research.[3]

The current form and magnitude of the agricultural research enterprise, as seen by a National Academy of Science study team,[4] are presented in two categories: sources of funds and research performers. The four major sources of funds are the federal government, state governments, private industry, and foundations. It is estimated that in 1976 these sources provided $1.9 billion for food research. About half of this came from federal and state sources. The federal government provided $645 million, state governments $425 million, industry $800 million, and foundations $100 million. In terms of appropriations, 85 percent of federal support went to the USDA. The remainder was appropriated through agencies such as NSF and NIH, which in turn contracted for research primarily in universities. Of the money appropriated to the USDA, $370 million was spent in-house, with the largest single agency being the Agricultural Research Service, which received $285 million. Most of the remainder was passed through to universities, the majority through formula funding under the Hatch Act and administered by the Cooperative State Research Service (CSRS).

Categorized in terms of expenditures by research performers, the breakdown is as follows:

1. $370 million is spent in-house in federal research agencies.
2. $737 million is spent by universities, public and private. Of this, $425 million comes from state sources, $272 million from federal sources, $40 million from industry, and $9 million from foundations.
3. In-house industry research spent an estimated $720 million, virtually all of which comes from industry sources.

4. Private research firms spent between $50 and $100 million, most of which also comes from industry sources.

Thus the current magnitude of the research enterprise is large, and the number of participants is large and growing.

The Formal Structure and Principal Actors

Before we turn to a description of how the system works in theory and in fact, it is useful to know the names and numbers of the principal actors in the process. These are presented in three categories: those who authorize and appropriate funds for agricultural research, those who broker and/or spend research funds, and those who attempt to influence the direction and magnitude of research activities.

Funders of Research

Authorization and appropriations for agricultural research at the federal level comes through Congress, which acts on legislative and budget proposals from the executive branch. In the 85 percent of federal expenditures that go to the USDA, the principal actors are as follows:

1. The House Agriculture Committee involved with defining the scope and character of research—a large committee with substantial urban representation
2. The House Subcommittee on Agricultural Appropriations, which deals with annual budget requests
3. The Senate Committee on Agriculture and Forestry, which performs similar functions to the House committee, though it is much more dominated by senior Southern Democrats and Midwestern Republicans
4. The Senate Appropriations Subcommittee on Agriculture and Forestry

In terms of general directions of what is included within the rubric of agricultural research, the Senate and House Agriculture Committees are important. However, in terms of year-to-year research content, the appropriations subcommittees and particularly their chairmen are very powerful. For example, during his long tenure as chairman of the House subcommittee, Whitten probably has been the single most influential person on agricultural research directions. This influence may have been diluted slightly with recent revisions in the congressional budget process. Other congressional committees are involved in non-USDA research, but these are relatively less important in determining overall directions. In state legislatures, the particular committees involved in appropriating money for agricultural research are diverse. However, most Agricultural Experiment Station budgets are submitted as elements, usually line items, in Land-Grant College budgets. As such, they go to education committees and budget subcommittees in both houses of the state bodies. Again, as with federal funding, committee chairmen are of particular importance. However, at the state level the access of interest groups to particular legislators may be greater, which could increase the influence of full legislative decisions on the research outcome. For example, in California, a subcommittee of the Assembly Education Committee included specific control language with respect to social impact statements on agricultural research. Both agricultural industry groups and the university lobbied on the floors of both houses to have it eliminated.

Agricultural industry support of agricultural research falls into three predominant types. The first and largest is in-house proprietary research conducted to improve the firm's profitability. Historically, this has been predominantly applied and developmental technological research on inputs. Recently, however, increased expenditures on basic research have occurred in some very large firms. The second form of industry research support is direct contracts, grants, or gifts from proprietary firms to public and private research organizations. These are generally for very specific short-term projects. The third mechanism of industry support is producer check-offs through either market orders or voluntary associations. This is a particularly important vehicle for industry funding in many states, particularly those with large specialty-crop industries. Historically, these funds have gone to Agricultural Experiment Stations, although recently the ARS has been a more important recipient.

Foundation support of agricultural research has never been large in absolute terms and has shifted in recent years predominantly in the direction of international agricultural research. In general, as with industry research, the funding has been quite specific and generally shorter term.

The Brokers and Spenders of Research Funds

Appropriated funds for research may go directly to a research organization or be brokered by an intermediate agency.

Federal Level. At the federal level, prominent research brokers for agricultural as well as other kinds of research are NSF, NIH, EPA, ERDA, and CSRS. These agencies presumably allocate research funds on a grant or contract basis with relatively clear priority guidelines on a project or program basis. Thus an additional set of political inputs is possible in determining research priorities. The possible exception is CSRS, which essentially passes through formula Hatch and other federal grant funds to State Experiment Stations without specific programmatic thrusts being identified. Their primary role, despite rhetoric to the contrary, is to ensure that legislatively mandated minimums are met by the individual stations. Only in the case of competitive grants does CSRS have a direct input into research programs.

Of the other agencies, NIH, EPA, and ERDA also conduct their own in-house research. Thus these agencies, along with ARS, the Economic Research Service (ERS), the Forest Service (FS), and the Farmer's Cooperative Service (FCS), have internal mechanisms for identifying priorities and allocating funds. We shall return later in the chapter to discuss at least some of these mechanisms.

State Level. At the state level, the dominant spenders of research dollars are the State Experiment Stations. Here the situation varies from state to state with respect to organizational structure and the form of state appropriations. These appropriations could come either as a lump-sum budget as part of a university's organized research budget or as rather specific line items from the legislature. The means by which other federal, industry, and foundation funds enter the university system also vary. In some cases, this money will come to the university via general research administrations as opposed to Agricultural Experiment Station administration. This further complicates an already complex arrangement in the land grants where teaching, extension, and state public service functions compete for faculty time and institutional rewards. Of particular importance in the large university is the relative importance of state-appropriated funds, federal formula funds, and extramural public or private funds. Those who provide the most funding are likely to have the most influence.

Also at the state level other public and private universities can and do conduct agricultural and food-related research using federal grants, industry, and foundation funds.

Industry and Private Research Firms. Little is known in the public sector about the character of much of the research done in industry or by private firms such as the Stanford Research Institute and Batelle. In the case of the former, it is proprietary research, presumably profit-motivated, which finds its expression in new technology or techniques merchandised by the firm. In the case of private research firms, virtually all the research is done on a client basis, and thus the character of the research and its results do not generally enter the public domain.

Thus, in summary, the major doers of agricultural research are USDA in-house agencies ($370 million), Land-Grant Colleges ($600+ million), and private industry ($700+ million). These spenders of research dollars operate under a diverse set of goals and economic and political pressures. The dominant characteristic worthy of note at this point is that the establishment is diverse and highly decentralized, with no one agency at any level having the prerogative or power to oversee and direct anything more than small pieces of the action.

Organizations, Committees, and Lobby Groups Involved

The already complicated maze of agencies that fund, broker, and do research is overlaid with a further network of public, quasi-public, and private organizations, committees, and interest groups, all of whom in one way or another have interests in agricultural research. What follows is a partial road map to that network.

Let's begin with the public sector first. In the federal government, obviously the departments and agencies directly concerned—the USDA, Department of Interior, EPA, ERDA, NSF, etc.—all attempt to influence Congress to increase support for research of their liking. In addition, federal agencies, such as the Office of Management and Budget (OMB), the Council of Economic Advisers (CEA), the General Accounting Office (GAO), and the Office of Science and Technology Policy (OSTP) evaluate and make recommendations on federal research funding as part of their general involvement in the federal policy process. Obviously the directors of ARS, CSRS, FS, etc., are advocates for their programs as they seek additional funds, often at the expense of other federal agencies. At the state level, state departments of agriculture, county agricultural commissioners' associations, and other agencies also are involved.

In the quasi-public domain, the National Academy of Sciences is involved through its Board on Agriculture and Renewable Resources.[5] Until 1973 an organization called the Agricultural Research Institute (ARI) was an adjunct of the academy. In that year it became a separate entity which, however, maintains close ties with the National Academy of Sciences. The ARI was originally established by industry scientists but now contains in its membership land grants and USDA agencies as well as industry groups.

Also in the quasi-public domain is the National Association of State Universities and Land-Grant Colleges (NASULGC). This organization has its origins in the Association of American Agricultural Colleges and Experiment Stations formed in 1887, the year of the passage of the Hatch Act. As such, it became the first educational lobby in the United States and one of the earliest lobbies of any sort.[6] NASULGC has within it a Division of Agriculture (no other element of the modern state university is accorded this status), which in turn is subdivided into three sections for extension, resident instruction, and experiment stations. Within the experiment station section, the Experiment Station Committee on Policy is charged with organizing and developing policy positions on legislation and appropriations relevant to the experiment stations.

In an effort to promote coordination and joint action, a joint committee of NASULGC and the USDA, cochaired by an experiment station director and the Assistant Secretary for Conservation, Research and Education, exists. This committee, the Agricultural Research Policy Advisory Committee (ARPAC), also has a member representing the Agricultural Research Institute, an industry association.[7] Its stated purpose is to "... make recommendations on broad aspects of research objectives, budget and program coordination."[8] A newer joint arrangement is the International Science and Educational Council (ISEC) which advises on teaching, research, and extension.

A myriad of private interest groups are interested in agricultural research at both the federal and state levels. These include the general farm organizations such as the American Farm Bureau Federation, the National Farmers Union, the Grange, and the National Farmers Organization, which operate at both federal and state levels. There are a great many commodities groups which support elements of the research program that are in their particular interest. These groups are probably more effective at the state level. In fact, in some states the enlargement of state appropriations for the experiment station came about by commodity groups lobbying state legislatures to augment support for research on their particular commodity. In addition, a large number of groups represent input industries, such as the National Agricultural Chemical Association, which attempt to influence research policy and appropriations. In recent years a newer diverse set of groups representing consumers, environmentalists, small farmers, and the rural poor have increased their efforts to make their voices heard regarding directions and priorities of the agricultural research establishment.[9]

How the System Is Supposed to Work

In any research system, there are four major factors which influence the character of the operations. These are mechanisms for *priority setting, planning, budgeting,* and *evaluation* or at least reporting of results. The fractionated budgetary sources have already been discussed under the section on the funders of research. It is to the formal organization for priority setting, planning, and evaluation that we now turn. In the early years of the system, there was little attempt at joint planning of the federal and state public components of the system. Each experiment station had its own mechanism of planning and priority setting influenced both by internal institutional needs and by state agricultural industry interests. At the federal level, various mechanisms were attempted to set priorities, but here congressional interests had strong influence. In the pre-World War II period, the only potential source of coordination between the two systems was the USDA Office of Experiment Stations which was charged with ensuring that (1) states match federal dollars and (2) various legislative mandates regarding special categories be met. The mechanism was through federally approved experiment station projects which required annual reports and were subject to periodic reviews. But these were largely ex post and delved only occasionally into the substance of research. Given that most state experiment stations mixed federal and state funds on most projects, it did give the potential for at least ex post collating of the joint state-federal effort.

The successor agency to the Office of Experiment Stations, the Cooperative

State Research Service (CSRS), continued the same function with the added responsibilities of monitoring marketing requirements and approving regional research projects through a statutory committee called the Committee of Nine. This committee is made up of two representatives from each of the four regional experimental station associations and chaired by a representative of CSRS. Each of the regional associations has committees on regional research which approve projects, but in recent years they have had no budget allocation authority as individual station directors allocated formula Hatch funds to regional contributing projects.

The first major national effort at long-range planning for agricultural research was a study jointly sponsored by NASULGC and the USDA conducted in 1965 and 1966. The study committee, made up of a large array of people from the experiment station and the USDA, produced a document *A National Program of Research for Agriculture,* which identified 10 major goals for agricultural research. The goals were further subdivided into 98 research problem areas (RPAs). The committee also proposed priorities for the allocation of new resources, if forthcoming, to the system. It did not, however, seriously come to grips with priorities for reallocation of existing resources. Given the resource constraints of the period following the report, it had little to offer in terms of readjustment of research priorities. Thus these remained dominantly oriented toward the production efficiency of commercial agriculture.

The RPAs also formed a basis for a cross-classification system of research reporting which was incorporated into the Current Research Information System which is a computerized reporting system of experiment stations and now USDA research.

In the next attempt at comprehensive planning and priority setting, initiated in the early 1970s, the totality of USDA in-house research as well as that of the experiment stations was involved. This attempt followed closely the reorganization of the Agricultural Research Service. Prior to 1972 ARS was centrally organized on a commodity or subject matter basis with field staff reporting to national headquarters at Beltsville. The reorganization created regions (four) and areas which in many instances were coterminous with states. Under the reorganization, total research programs in an area reported to an area director, who in turn reported to the regional director. Thus, the structure of ARS became more closely parallel to that of the state experiment stations. The rationale for the reorganization was to bring the ARS program closer to users and to enable closer cooperation and coordination with the state stations. The result will probably be a shift in ARS research toward a more localized and developmental research program. As I shall argue later, it also enhanced the likelihood of competition and the possibility of individual congressmen influencing microresearch priorities.

Following the reorganization, ARPAC established a subcommittee called the National Planning Committee. In turn, four regional planning committees were established. These regional planning committees were to establish up to 50 task forces in each region to develop specific plans for agricultural research. The National Planning Committee, the regional planning committees, and the task forces were to contain representatives of the state experiment stations, ARS, ERS, FS, and the Agricultural Research Institute. In total, if all task forces were activated, this system would involve 205 committees with a minimum of eight people on each. I have computed that if each committee met twice a year for two days, the cost of the system in terms of time and travel costs would exceed $2 million. Since the process is not yet complete, it is not possible to judge the final outcome. It is an attempt to involve the research scientist at the working level in planning and as such has merit. However, the complete separation of the planning process from the budget process makes the probability of the exercise having much impact very low indeed.

Two other planning and priority-setting activities need to be mentioned. The first was a working conference held in 1975 and sponsored by ARPAC. The conference was unique in the sense that for the first time the majority of voting participants represented users of research rather than researchers and research administrators. The users also contained representatives of nontraditional groups such as consumers and environmentalists. The results of the conference were published in two volumes[10] and contain recommended priorities in terms of future directions.

The second is the major National Academy of Science (NAS) study on future food and agricultural research needs.[11] This study involved scientists both from within and beyond the Land Grant-USDA complex whose task was to identify long-range research priorities. This study, using expert panels and the Delphi technique, attempted to identify important research needs, their probability of solution, the cost of solution, and the potential impact of solution. The report also comments on research organization.

Thus, as it stands today, the public component of the agricultural research establishment is made up of a myriad of research organizations, funded from diverse sources, which through an elaborate maze of planning committees, advised by periodic conferences and studies, gives the impression of being a coordinated, planned research effort dedicated to the public good. At the same time, each research component (and the researchers in it) seeks to maintain independence to pursue its own interests. This, then, is the agricultural research establishment and how it is supposed to work. The national planning effort augmented by expert and user inputs is to establish long-range *macro* goals for the system with ARPAC and the Agricultural Research Institute providing mechanisms for national cooperation and coordination. Micro priorities at project and program levels are to be determined within that framework by the local administrators and scientists, giving due consideration to local conditions and needs.

How the System Appears to Really Work

The remainder of the chapter is devoted to a personal analysis of how the system appears to actually work. The analysis begins with the premise that the single most important factor influencing the character and outcome of a research enterprise is financial or budget support. Funding has two facets—the macro level of financial support and the micro budget decision-making process which allocates that level of expenditure. Other factors such as quality of personnel, rewards systems, organizational structure, and peer pressure are important but of lesser influence. Formal planning mechanisms, administrators, and the public at large have the least influence. This is a sweeping proposition which hopefully will be supported by the following analysis. First we discuss *macro* issues.

Money is, after all, the lifeblood of a research organization. It influences the number and quality of people that can be employed. It provides the wherewithal to buy equipment, conduct field trials, and disseminate results. Given the decentralized fragmented system we are discussing, competition for monetary support becomes a continuing concern of all involved in the system. It follows, then, that actors in a position to directly influence the level of monetary support are vitally important. In this category fall the appropriations subcommittees in both federal houses, state legislatures, granting agencies, Office of Management and Budget (OMB), Congressional Budget Office (CBO), GAO, commodity groups and industrial firms which provide direct support, and foundations. All these actors can and do have powerful influences on the overall magnitude of research budgets. Therefore it follows that individuals who hold positions of power in these groups can by the amount of funding and the conditions attached thereto influence annual and longer-term directions of research. These, then, are the most important political forces influencing macro research priorities and in many instances micro priorities.

These funding entities are obviously influenced in their judgments by other actors in the system, and it is worth noting briefly the potential influence of some of these. Agricultural organizations and lobby groups have potential but likely declining influence on research outcomes.[12] Research funding, particularly at the federal level, tends to be general rather than commodity-specific. Thus general farm organizations like the Bureau and the Farmers' Union could influence general funding levels. However, as the overall political process relating to agricultural policy has become more commodity-fractionated and at the same time more macro (i.e., involving many other groups besides agriculture), the analyses in this regard have been conducted by Bonnen,[13] Youngberg,[14] Hadwiger and Fraenkel,[15] and Barton,[16] all of whom argue that the control of the agricultural political agenda is rapidly shifting. Given that research tends to be general and not immediately obvious in terms of its specific or commodity outcome, it tends to attract less attention from groups with specific objectives. At the state level, however, commodity groups continue to have potential influence. But in general it is my judgment that the influence of farm organizations on macro priorities and general funding levels is not strong.

Other diverse actors such as NASULGC, NAS-BARR, ARPAC, and the administrators of research-doing agencies and universities probably have a good deal less influence on macro research priorities than they think they do. This is true for several reasons. First, in an era of public skepticism about research and technology, these agencies are viewed as more self-serving than in the public interest. Second, the diversity of their organizational makeup is so immense that, by the time all competing internal influences are taken care of, their action is either too watered down or too late to have much influence on budgetary issues. Two examples support the point. One case in point was the protracted battle of NASULGC with AID over Title XII of the International Development and Food Assistance Act of 1975, which in the end led to an outcome not generally to the liking of either. A second case is the protracted battle between large and small experiment stations over the issue of competitive grants versus formula funding under Hatch provisions. This has prevented the Division of Agriculture of NASULGC from taking a strong position in favor of competitive grants, a position recommended by the NAS study. Third, these organizations are so overstructured in terms of committees and overlapping memberships that their ability to influence even their own components is severely limited by their greater attention to process and internal politicking than to substantive issues. Finally, most of these organizations adhere to the view that the best researchers and the best research organizations are those that have maximum freedom. Thus, coordination and group positions are fundamentally contrary to their basic inclinations.

The other element in the budget process is the spending decisions at the micro level of projects, programs, and departments. It is here that the actual character of the research enterprise is determined in terms of topics studied, including relative emphasis among commodities, applied versus basic etc. At this level there are three powerful factors at work. The first is the individual scientist and his or her immediate superior, the department chairperson, who by the choice of project and methodology determine the character of the basic building blocks of a research enterprise. Their choice is influenced by several factors—peer recognition, rewards, their own perception of research needs (often heavily influenced by clientele groups), and availability of resources. This suggests not that scientists are perverse and antagonistic to broader concerns, but rather that the good scientist is a person whose personal curiosity is his or her greatest asset and therefore must first and foremost be interested in what he is doing.

The second major factor influencing micro research outcomes is the "untied" research dollar. Most continuing appropriations to agricultural research establishments are inevitably invested in the necessary conditions for research productivity, namely personnel, equipment, and continuing operating expenses. In some cases this could be $50,000 to $100,000 per scientist-year. However, to do a specific research project, additional "flexible" resources are required. The agency or group that provides the marginal addition of "spendable cash" can influence entire research activity including substantial magnitudes of permanent state and federal funds. Thus federal agencies such as NSF and EPA may, via large research grants, co-opt major additional resources by providing flexible resources to research programs. Similarly commodity groups, foundations, and proprietary firms can significantly influence micro research directions by relatively small investments and without having to participate in complicated and time-consuming planning bureaucracies.

The third major influence on micro research priorities is much more subtle. This is the influence of perceived peer groups on the selection of research topics by individual researchers. This peer influence is of two (sometimes opposing) sorts. The first is that of disciplinary peer recognition which tends to move scientists in the direction of more basic research that is acceptable and recognized in the basic disciplines. The second is that of clientele groups. Historically, substantial portions of applied agricultural research have been organized on a commodity basis and with strong relationships to commodity user groups. Many people in the agricultural research establishment have grown up with this association, so that to a considerable extent those inside the system share the same values as clientele groups. Therefore, they implicitly identify with their objectives. It is by this access more than any other that commercial agriculture has had, and continues to have, pervasive influence on the scope of agricultural research. This access point is facilitated by the Cooperative Extension Service.

The role of higher-level administrators—directors of experiment stations, deans of agriculture, university presidents, assistants, deputy and regional directors of USDA research units—in micro priority setting is limited in the short run. This is so because they control few discretionary funds which allow them to compete with outside funding agencies. In the longer run, they can influence directions somewhat by their role in the rewards system and the allocation of vacant positions. Even more unlikely to have much impact is the recently established National Planning Network. This is so for two fundamental reasons. First, it is made up of people in the system who probably prefer it as it is. And second, even if it recommended significant changes, they likely would not happen because the planning mechanism is uncoupled from the budget process.

Thus the actors that influence the direction and character of the agricultural research establishment have greatest influence through general funding levels at the top of the complex and at the bottom with the micro spending level. At the macro level, the actors providing funds to agricultural research also provide funds to many other activities. Thus their continued interest in agricultural research is limited at best. Occasionally the system is shocked by major shifts in funding interest, such as a world food problem, but these interests tend to be crisis-oriented and transitory. Further, the absence of full annual budget reviews means that even the major permanent funders of research have little possibility of forcing major shifts in direction by normal incremental budgetary methods. At the project level, the system is constantly undergoing marginal changes, but these seldom cause deviation from established patterns because the people and the flexible funding sources remain largely unchanged. Thus the research establishment has a tremendous tendency to maintain the status quo and to continue its lumbering, disjointed movement along well-trodden paths.

In concluding this analysis, two additional influences need to be noted. The first is the changing nature of the Land-Grant institutions themselves. As they have grown larger and more complex, the dominant role that agriculture had played has diminished. Within the institutions, pressures for more teaching and general university and community service add competitive options for research workers' time. This long-term trend, in conjunction with recent rapid enrollment increases in colleges of agriculture, has tended to increase general institutional influence on agricultural researchers.

The second factor is the potential impact of the regionalization of the Agricultural Research Service. This action, taken to foster cooperation and coordination with the Land-Grant system, also greatly enhances the possibility of external political influence on both systems. First the reorientation of ARS programs to an area and regional basis increases the visibility of their program to individual congressmen and to state and local agricultural interest groups. Thus an individual congressman or interest group with a special interest has direct access to ARS research activities via the funding process at both the federal and the local level. Second, the regionalization of ARS has placed their programs in direct competition at the state level with experiment station programs. This now gives commodity groups the opportunity of playing one agency against the other, using the carrot of flexible funding. In California, for example, Market Order Boards now have the opportunity of funding either University of California researchers or area ARS programs. Given perceived resource shortages in both organizations, this gives industry groups as well as private business firms greater influence at the project level.

The Establishment in Summary

When viewed as a paper organization, the agricultural research establishment is a large set of independent research organizations sharing common purposes and voluntarily cooperating in planning and coordination to ensure the most efficient and effective product in the public interest. Elaborate reporting systems ensure continuing feedback of results to funding sources and at the same time prevent duplication of efforts.

However, I have argued that the reality of the establishment is quite different. It is an amorphous hulk of disjointed and often competitive components, each of which is being tugged and pulled by myriads of special interests. It does not have a unified program but rather is influenced by annual budget decisions at the macro level and the project level while the whole complicated bureaucratic superstructure that separates the two levels moves along unchanged. As such, the establishment *in its totality* is largely impervious to political manipulation in the short run. The converse is also probably true, namely, that establishment as a whole wields little direct political power. Only major unhappiness of the funders which resulted in major budget reductions would significantly alter its character. Reorganizations, new administrators, and different names are cosmetic rather than real. At the same time as the totality of the establishment is politically protected, specific interests, particularly if they have money in hand, can materially influence micro priorities which over time would slowly alter the total.

Much of the above may sound negative and cynical. To some it may seem that I have described a monster moving along with no one in charge, and in part that is correct. But the fact that the system is disjointed, unplanned, uncoordinated, competitive, and slow to change may in fact be its greatest strength. No one can argue that the United States agricultural research "establishment" has not yielded results. It has produced research that has created the most technologically efficient agriculture in the world. It has participated in many fundamental research developments which have had wider application than just agriculture. And it has provided an environment for training superb scientists who work all over the world. It has accomplished this, in my judgment, for three principal reasons. First, it has been sufficiently well supported that overlap, competition, and, yes, nonproductive research could be afforded. In other words, it has not prevented a good deal of exploration and chancy research as a "well-planned" bureaucratic system might. Second, it has preserved to a considerable extent, given all the potential pressures, sufficient intellectual freedom to allow first-rate scientists to be productive. And third, it has been very adept at fitting itself into the political and social fabric of the United States. Its survival and growth over the last century, while still maintaining control of its own destiny, attest to this. In sum, it has been a remarkable political system which has enmeshed itself into the broader system in such a way that it has prospered and produced effective research results.

Notes

1. The author served as dean of the College of Agricultural and Environmental Sciences and associate director of the California Agricultural Experiment Station, University of California, Davis, 1970 to 1975.

2. 91st Cong., 2d Sess., *A Brief History of the Committee on Agriculture and Forestry United States Senate and Landmark Agricultural Legislation*

1825-1970. Senate Document 91-107, Government Printing Office, Washington, 1970, p. 16.

3. *Research to Meet U.S. and World Food Needs,* vol. 2, Report of a conference sponsored by the Agricultural Research Policy Advisory Committee (ARPAC), Kansas City, Missouri, July 9-11, 1975, pp. 53-54.

4. National Academy of Science, "Research Organization in the United States: Conclusions and Recommendations," draft report of Study Team 14A, September 25, 1976.

5. Formerly the Agricultural Board, which was established in 1944 on the joint recommendation of the National Research Council (an element of the National Academy) and the then Association of Land-Grant Colleges and Universities.

6. See Charles M. Hardin, *The Politics of Agriculture* (Glencoe, Ill.: The Free Press, 1952), p. 23.

7. For an official description of the federal-state system and its many actions, see *Research to Meet U.S. and World Food Needs,* vol. 2, chapter 6, pp. 42-60.

8. Ibid., p. 44.

9. See Don Paarlberg, "A New Agenda for Agriculture," paper presented to the 1977 Agricultural Policy Symposium, Washington, July 26, 1977.

10. *Research to Meet U.S. and World Food Needs,* vols. 1 and 2, Report of a Working Conference sponsored by the Agricultural Research Policy Advisory Committee (ARPAC), Kansas City, Missouri, July 9-11, 1975.

11. National Research Council, *World Food and Nutrition Study: The Potential Contributions of Research* (Washington: National Academy of Sciences, 1977).

12. See, for example, Paarlberg, "A New Agenda for Agriculture."

13. James T. Bonnen, "Observations on the Changing Nature of National Agricultural Policy Decisions Process: 1946-1976," presented to Conference on "Farmers, Bureaucrats and Middlemen: Historical Perspectives on American Agriculture," sponsored by the National Archives and the Agricultural History Society, April 27-29, 1977.

14. Garth Youngberg, "U.S. Agriculture in the 1970's: Policy and Politics," in James E. Anderson (ed.), *Economic Regulatory Policies* (Lexington, Mass.: D.C. Heath, 1976), pp. 51-68.

15. Don F. Hadwiger and Richard Fraenkel, "The Agricultural Policy Process," in ibid., pp. 39-49.

16. Weldon V. Barton, "Coalition-Building in the U.S. House of Representatives Agricultural Legislation in 1973," paper presented at 1974 annual meeting of the American Political Science Association, Chicago, August 29-September 2, 1974.

8 Agricultural Scientists and Agricultural Research: The Case of Southern Corn Leaf Blight

Johnston Nicholson

The emergence of a world food crisis has focused attention on food and agricultural policies of the United States. In discussions of the food crisis, agricultural research is frequently held to be one of the keys to eventual solution. Policies for agricultural research, once considered the province of agriculturalists and their clients, have become an issue of national concern. Whether the budget for agricultural research ought to be greatly expanded in response to a food crisis depends in part upon the likely quality of the research and upon who will benefit from the results of research. The "agricultural research establishment" has come under administrative, congressional, and public scrutiny several times in the last decade.[1] The scientific quality of research and the distributive impact of federal investment in agricultural research have been questioned. One of the recurring criticisms of present policy for agricultural research is that basic research receives too little support in relation to applied research and development. The mechanisms by which federal funds for agricultural research are distributed put excellent scientists, both within and outside the agricultural research establishment, at a disadvantage. More money should be awarded through competitive grants, and improved arrangements should be made for peer review by practicing scientists in the awarding of these grants. Only then will scientific excellence compete successfully with relevance to practical tasks as a criterion for awarding funds for agricultural research.[2]

Grants to Study Southern Corn Leaf Blight

The epidemic of southern corn leaf blight in 1970 reduced the total harvest of corn by 20 percent. A disease of such agronomic importance drew the attention of the agricultural community, from farmers to congressmen. One response was for the United States Department of Agriculture (USDA) to request, and Congress to appropriate, $1.5 million in funds for "special grants" to study the disease, its causes, and effects. The immediate issue was economic loss. A longer-term issue was that most major crops are genetically similar and therefore "genetically vulnerable" to epidemics of diseases and insect damage.

The epidemic of Southern corn leaf blight in 1970 was caused by a new race

93

of a known pathogen, the fungus *Helminthosporium maydis.* The new race attacked plants with the genetic characteristic Texas male sterile cytoplasm—a characteristic of 80 to 90 percent of the corn grown in the United States in that year. The disease began in the South and spread rapidly northward because of the nearly universal susceptibility of corn to the disease. It was quickly apparent that one major solution to the problem for future crop years was to replace the susceptible T cytoplasm with varieties of the normal cytoplasm type.

By early 1970 some scientists at state agricultural experiment stations were studying Southern corn leaf blight. Later that year, additional commitments were made on the part of experiment stations. In January 1971, an interregional meeting of administrators of experiment stations was held with administrators of the Cooperative State Research Service (CSRS). In a subsequent meeting, the groups drafted a request for special grant funds which was submitted to CSRS for action by Congress. The process of appropriation was rapid, and funds for grants were available by late 1971.

In order to distribute the funds, administrators of CSRS called together the directors of several state experiment stations in a third meeting to identify expertise important to the problems of leaf blight and to recommend where the funds could be allocated most effectively. The scientists at experiment stations thus identified were asked to submit proposals, and authorization from CSRS was rapidly granted. In 1973, when the original projects were underway, additional grants were made to study the mechanisms of disease resistance.

Interview Schedule and Respondents

Thirty-two Ph.D.-level scientists and three science administrators who were involved with the special grants from CSRS to study Southern corn leaf blight were interviewed either personally or by mail. The interview schedule consisted of a number of open-ended questions and a series of agree-disagree statements. Among the scientists, all but three were principal or coprincipal investigators receiving support from the special grants from the Cooperative State Research Service, all but two of whom held regular appointments in departments in colleges of agriculture or at state agricultural experiment stations.

Scientists were asked to characterize their work as basic, applied, or both. More than half the scientists characterized their work as exclusively or primarily basic research. The basic scientists tended to be from the disciplines of plant pathology, plant physiology, biochemistry, and microbiology. They were generally younger, having earned their doctoral degrees since 1960. There is a slight relationship between basic science and lower academic rank. State and geographic regions fail to distinguish basic scientists from others.

Most of the scientists interviewed said they were at least partly engaged in basic research. Only two said that they were engaged exclusively in applied research. The systematic differences between the first group (basic scientists) and the group of scientists who also engage in applied research might be much greater if more scientists had been interviewed whose exclusive area of research had been applied. Scientists in the more applied group preponderantly received their Ph.D. degrees before 1960, and more than half were full professors. They were primarily plant breeders, geneticists, and plant pathologists.

Status of Agricultural Scientists

In the scientific community at large, prestige attaches to those who seek knowledge for the sake of knowledge. A theoretical rather than a practical orientation is expected of the "true" basic scientist. The traditional seat of basic science in this sense is the university.[3] The agricultural research establishment, however, has been closely identified with the practical missions of USDA. According to some spokesmen, agricultural scientists have low status in the scientific community because of this practical orientation.[4]

Respondents were asked a series of questions to determine their perceptions of the status of agricultural scientists and whether a low status was "deserved." Table 8-1 presents the responses to the agree-disagree questions.

An overwhelming majority (92 percent) of the scientists agreed that "agricultural scientists have for some time been considered 'second class citizens' of the scientific community." Among the more applied group, all agreed with the statement. A somewhat smaller proportion (76 percent) agreed that "life scientists in colleges of agriculture are well-trained, creative and competent as are life scientists in other fields." The applied scientists were more likely to agree than the basic scientists. By inference, the basic scientists were more critical of the standards within the agricultural research establishment. The basic scientists also were disinclined to say that the status of agricultural scientists has improved with the "emergence of the world food crisis." Although the evidence is very sketchy, it may be that the basic scientists identified more with the scientific community and were unwilling to see their star rising unless their nonagricultural colleagues in science awarded them prestige. The more applied group may value approbation by society at large more highly. In general, these scientists were conscious of and concerned about the low status of agricultural scientists.

Structure of Support for Agricultural Research

The appropriate mechanisms by which governments ought to support scientific research have long been a matter of controversy. From the perspective of basic science, government ought to support the best scientists, as determined by their peers. Individual investigators submit proposals which are reviewed competi-

Table 8-1

Scientists' Attitudes toward the Status of Agricultural Scientists by Type of Scientist's Research (*Percent*)[a]

	Agree Strongly	*Agree*	*Disagree*	*Disagree Strongly*	*N*
Agricultural scientists have for some time been considered "second-class citizens" of the scientific community.					
All scientists	42	50	4	4	26
Basic scientists	33	44	11	11	9
Basic-Applied scientists	47	53	0	0	17
Life scientists in agriculture are as well trained, creative, and competent as are life scientists in other fields.					
All scientists	40	36	16	8	25
Basic scientists	22	22	33	22	9
Basic-Applied scientists	50	44	6	0	16
With the emergence of the world food crisis, scientists in agricultural fields are now getting the respect they are due.					
All scientists	4	46	42	8	24
Basic scientists	0	14	71	14	7
Basic-Applied scientists	6	59	29	6	17

[a]Some row totals do not equal 100 percent because of rounding.

tively by practicing scientists in the same discipline and are awarded to scientists primarily in universities.[5] This structure of peer review has generally characterized the awarding of funds for basic research in the National Institutes of Health (NIH) and the National Science Foundation (NSF).[6] The proponents of the system argue that it results in federal support for scientific excellence. Critics charge that pure peer review substitutes the politics of science in awarding funds for the politics of the larger society. The Agricultural Research Service (ARS) represents the converse model: research is closely tied to practical tasks by employing scientists directly. Relevance to missions may take precedence over scientific excellence when the two conflict. The direction of research programs is overseen by administrators who may or may not share the scientific discipline of the researcher.[7] Proponents of mission orientation argue that this ensures that taxpayers, or agricultural clients, support research which is of direct benefit. Critics charge that the quality of science gets lost in the struggle between corn and soybeans, cotton, and milk.

The Cooperative State Research Service is between NIH and ARS as a model of government support for research. CSRS supports scientists in universities, where the tradition of basic research is strongest. But CSRS does not adhere to the peer review system of NIH. Awards are made by formula, or awarded to scientists at the experiment stations identified as experts by science-administrators. Respondents were asked to comment on a number of aspects of federal support for agricultural research.

Basic Scientists

When asked the purposes of the grants for Southern corn leaf blight, the basic scientists said that the grants either were or should have been devoted to understanding the basic mechanisms of this and other plant diseases. Many distinguished between the political goals—to "demonstrate that the agricultural research establishment could respond quickly and decisively to an 'emergency' "—and the scientific goals—"a pool of basic knowledge necessary to predict and stop impending epidemics on major crops." The basic scientists were unanimous that basic science in agriculture is inadequately supported. Most argued that the U.S. Department of Agriculture has the responsibility to support basic agricultural research and that present arrangements for doing so are inadequate:

Funding of agricultural research is a highly political process and it is very difficult to set up and carry out a long-range program of really basic research. This program got me started on a problem and then the money was cut off at about the time I was geared up to do something worthwhile. I finally got a small amount of money from NSF to continue but I feel USDA or some other agency should be offering continuing support rather than feast-and-famine support to basic research.

Scientists gave several reasons for the inadequacy of present arrangements, in addition to their opinion that the total amount of support for basic research is insufficient. Another criticism was the brief duration of support for projects. Many saw the grants to study leaf blight as a step in the right direction but said that support should have been for five or ten years rather than for three or four. Others said that USDA maintains a proprietary interest in research by agricultural scientists, so that scientists in colleges of agriculture have difficulty in competing for funds from the National Science Foundation and the National Institutes of Health. Still others thought that the reputation of agricultural scientists as second-class citizens of the scientific community prevented them from competing successfully for funds from other sources.

The frustration with the policies of USDA was that the "bureaucracy" emphasizes solution to immediate problems, whereas the scientists would like an opportunity to build up a body of basic knowledge whose usefulness is not so readily demonstrated.

The basic scientists seemed to agree that the Cooperative State Research Service was the appropriate agency within USDA to sponsor basic research. Most expressed satisfaction with the tasks performed by CSRS in administering the grants on Southern Corn Leaf Blight and agreed that once the initial commitment of support had been made, they were given considerable latitude to pursue promising leads in their research. Most said that administrative tasks associated with the grants were kept to a minimum and that administrators at CSRS were responsive and helpful when contacted but that contact was infrequent.

When asked whether they would have funded the SCLB projects, the basic scientists were more critical than others. Many said they would have eliminated some projects which had not produced much. Others said that the grants should have been made on the basis of competition and peer review:

It was given to the wrong people; some would certainly have been scrapped. I think CSRS is okay—but it should be done on a competitive basis with peer evaluation.

Some projects are led by incompetent, scientifically nonaggressive people. Would have changed the project monitoring—made people cooperative—gotten rid of dead wood. CSRS is good but is hampered by some backwards thinkers (not many but just enough).

Among the basic scientists the message was clear that the Cooperative State Research Service is the most appropriate institution within the Department of Agriculture to support basic research but that CSRS, too, is hampered by political constraints and relies insufficiently on practicing scientists to make awards.

Basic Applied Scientists

The more applied scientists were more satisfied than the basic scientists with the present institutions for supporting agricultural research. None of the scientists in this group considered basic research unimportant. They emphasized the need for a balance between basic and applied research:

I would get a better balance. In these grants 80 percent of the research was biochemical basic research. I would give more money to mission-oriented research.

In general we need to expand production [applied] research but not at the expense of basic research. Until recently, there was disproportionate emphasis on basic research. This has changed somewhat in the last few years. The pendulum swings too much—we need more of both basic and applied and a better balance.

Most of the scientists in this group saw basic and applied research as complementary and saw no conflict between basic research and "mission orientation." They were less concerned than the basic scientists that there be funds set aside for basic research; nor were they disturbed that administrators rather than practicing scientists made the selections of whom to support. None recommended a new institutional mechanism for peer evaluation. Most saw the Cooperative State Research Service as the appropriate institution within the USDA to sponsor such programs as the grants for Southern corn leaf blight. CSRS was appropriate, partly because "CSRS personnel are familiar with workers and research under way across the country to a greater extent than any other agency." The basic-applied scientists generally found the intermediate model of federal support for research, represented by CSRS, to be a congenial one.

Administrators

The administrators shared the view that basic research is both important and difficult to defend to political officials. The variations on this theme seem to follow from the position of the administrator.

One administrator from the Cooperative State Research Service was especially sympathetic to the strains of basic agricultural scientists. He was eager that the scientists help him make a case for the success of the special grants for Southern corn leaf blight, in order to argue for further projects with such relatively unfettered conditions. He stressed that scientists can be asked to have eventual beneficiaries in mind in posing questions for research but that basic biological research is not amenable to stringent cost-benefit analysis. He suggested that one likely consequence of binding basic scientists to specifying quantitative benefits is the encouragement of "entrepreneurs who put out numbers that don't mean a thing."

Though enthusiastic about the promising directions of basic research supported by the special grants, the administrator was concerned for an eventual policy that would "not earmark vital research money but would support continuity." In short, the attitudes of the CSRS administrators toward agricultural research policy were closely akin to the attitudes of the basic scientists.

A second administrator had been assigned to evaluate the projects on Southern corn leaf blight, as a regular part of USDA evaluation of all programs. He found "mission-oriented" research less problematic than his colleague at CSRS. He was especially sensitive to the difficulty of defending "knowledge for the sake of knowledge" to political decision makers.

The third administrator, an associate director of a state agricultural experiment station, emphasized the constraints under which science administrators at the state level operate. He suggested that basic research is especially difficult for a science administrator to defend in a state in which agriculture is a major sector of the economy:

The end product of a zoology department is not the same and it need not be, it shouldn't be the same as the end product of the agronomy department of the college of agriculture. The zoology department is interested for knowledge's sake and they can and will pursue this kind of thing without any social reward or payoff at the present time. But the agriculture experiment station can't afford that kind of luxury or they can't afford too many people doing those things that have no payoff at the end.... Some states, like New Jersey, have had a tremendous number of SMY [statistical man-years] on their faculties for long years and have virtually solved every problem a farmer can think of. They don't reduce their faculties, they turn their faculties to things that are not highly applied. . . . It's a relative thing—where you find yourself.

As a group, the administrators expressed much the same range of attitudes toward policies of agricultural research as the scientists. Not surprisingly, the administrators devoted much attention to political and economic constraints in allocating resources for agricultural research. To some extent the administrators took those constraints as given and learned to operate within them. Whether the constraints toward mission-oriented research are desirable was in dispute among both scientists and administrators.

Agricultural Scientists and Agricultural Research

There clearly emerged a sense of pride in the ability of agricultural scientists to respond to practical problems and crises. As they saw it, the community of agricultural scientists is much better organized than the medical science community—the most frequently drawn comparison—to anticipate and alleviate major disasters. Though many would emphasize basic research, few would isolate the basic scientists from concern with agriculture's problems. At the same time, few saw themselves as engaged exclusively, or even primarily, in the service of a narrowly defined agricultural clientele.

The world food crisis has put agricultural research policy in the national policy arena. The very success of agricultural research directed toward increasing productivity and decreasing labor has reduced the size of the agricultural clientele. When most Americans were farmers, agricultural research was clearly in the "public interest." The decline of the proportion of the population engaged in agriculture made agricultural interests less "public" and more "special." The response of the Department of Agriculture has been to isolate itself from politics in general, depending upon a political subsystem supported by their shrinking but vocal clientele in agriculture.

For their part, the agricultural scientists find themselves in a box. They have allowed the Department of Agriculture to speak for them for so long that they are identified by lay outsiders as servants of large farmers and agribusiness, in part because the research organizations within USDA institutionalize that bias. They lose prestige among their scientific colleagues outside schools of agriculture by being identified with applied rather than basic research.

Many of the scientists in this study were committed both to scientific excellence in basic research and to food problems rather than agricultural clients. Their situation, however, is unlikely to change markedly, even if the nation became committed to attacking world food problems through research. If the proponents of scientific excellence won, the scientists in colleges of agriculture might well be passed over in favor of the more scientifically prestigious "centers of excellence" in biomedical research. If the Department of Agriculture won, the basic scientists would continue to compete with applied scientists on the basis of relevance to the Department's missions. The scientists are caught between the politics of science and the politics of agriculture.

Notes

1. U.S. Congress, House, Committee on Science, Research and Technology, *Special Oversight Review of Agricultural Research and Development,* Report of subcommittees of the Committee on Science and Technology, House of Representatives, 94th Cong., 2d Sess., 1976; National Research Council-National Academy of Sciences, *Report of the Committee on Research Advisory to the U.S. Department of Agriculture* (Washington: National Academy of Sciences, 1972), known and hereafter referred to as the *Pound Report*; National Research Council-National Academy of Sciences, *World Food and Nutrition Study, Enhancement of Food Production for the United States,* Report of the Board on Agriculture and Renewable Resources (Washington: National Academy of Sciences, 1975); Jim Hightower, *Hard Tomatoes, Hard Times: The Failure of the Land Grant College Complex* (Washington: Agribusiness Accountability Project, 1972); National Academy of Sciences, *The Life Sciences,* Report of the Committee on Research in the Life Sciences (Washington: National Academy of Sciences, 1970); U.S. Congress, House, *Agriculture, Environment and Consumer Protection Appropriations for 1975,* Hearings before a subcommittee of the Committee on Appropriations, House of Representatives, 93d Cong., 2d Sess., 1974; Philip M. Boffey, *The Brain Bank of America* (New York: McGraw-Hill Book Company, 1975).

2. Pound Report, pp. 1-43; National Research Council, *World Food,* pp. 29-33; Subcommittee on Science, Research and Technology, *Special Oversight Review,* pp. 1-14.

3. Michael Polanyi, *The Republic of Science* (Chicago: Roosevelt University, 1962); Robert Gilpin and Christopher Wright (eds.), *Science and National Policy Making* (New York: Columbia University Press, 1964).

4. Subcommittee on Science, Research and Technology, *Special Oversight Review,* pp. 71-75; National Research Council, *World Food,* p. 10.

5. Norman W. Storer, *The Social System of Science* (New York: Holt, Rinehart & Winston, 1966); Daniel S. Greenberg, *The Politics of Pure Science* (New York: New American Library, 1967), pp. 16-17; Marlan Blissett, *Politics in Science* (Boston: Little, Brown, and Company, 1972), pp. 50-65.

6. Greenberg, *Politics of Pure Science,* p. 21; Stephen P. Strickland, *Politics, Science and Dread Disease* (Cambridge, Mass.: Harvard University Press, 1972), pp. 234-239; Heather Johnston Nicholson, "Autonomy and Accountability of Basic Research," *Minerva* 15 (Spring 1977):32-61.

7. Letter from Richard H. Alsmeyer, United States Department of Agriculture, November 4, 1975.

9

The Commodities Exchanges and Federal Regulation, 1922-1974: The Decline of Self-Government?

Jonathan Lurie

The development of private commodities exchanges, and other kindred institutions, into quasi-public regulatory agencies is one of the more important but little studied aspects of American administrative law.[1] By 1920 the major exchanges had become well-established organizations, providing commodities marketing facilities for producer, processor, distributor, and consumer. For reasons detailed elsewhere, they had largely avoided federal regulation. In part, this "accomplishment" resulted from increasingly effective internal policing ultimately endorsed by the United States Supreme Court in 1905.[2] Further, the deeply rooted American ambivalence toward speculation, risk, and commercial gain had effectively discouraged national regulation.[3] Yet, proponents of such a measure persisted, making numerous efforts between 1890 and 1920 to enact a regulatory statute, but with no success. Finally in 1921, with an effective political agrarian "farm bloc" in Congress, with a frequently articulated if not deeply held desire to return to certain prewar societal values typified in the phrase "return to normalcy," and with an extremely bad and protracted decline in agricultural prices, federal regulation of the commodities exchanges became a fact.[4]

The sponsors of the Grain Futures Act argued that the new law introduced federal *supervision* rather than federal *regulation,* emphasizing that its provisions enhanced existing internal regulatory authority. Compelling an exchange to enforce its own rules was, after all, very different from imposing rules upon the exchange itself. Yet the distinction between regulation and supervision has been tenuous at best. While the Grain Futures Act of 1922 remains the basis for all subsequent commodities exchange federal regulation, Congress enacted major revisions of the statute in 1936, 1968, and 1974. How have these changes affected the exchanges' long-established powers of self-government? What insights do they offer into the interplay among private enterprise, a free and open market, and external regulation?

In the report for 1930, the Secretary admitted that the exchange facilities "should be improved and in some respects fortified with additional safeguards to prevent abuses."[5] He further urged that the internal rules adopted by these organizations should be subject to review by an agency "in the interests of the producers or the consumers" and called for tighter rules against bucket shopping and misuse of customer orders by traders who were themselves involved in market transactions.[6] By 1933, Secretary Henry J. Wallace warned that "uncontrolled speculation . . . always obnoxious, becomes particularly obnoxious when the country is engaged in efforts to regulate farm production. Uncontrolled speculation does not go well with controlled production."[7] In 1934 Wallace wrote that the need to amend and strengthen the Grain Futures Act "has been apparent for many years." In 1935 the House passed by voice vote major amendments to the law, providing for, among other things, the prohibition under heavy penalties of "the bucketing of customers' orders, the making of wash sales and fictitious trades, and cheating and fraud in connection with the handling of customers' orders."[8] By 1936 the Senate had passed a very similar measure. The House, again by voice vote, concurred in the Senate amendments, and the changes became law.[9]

The 1936 amendments altered the scope of federal commodities exchange regulation, giving it a different direction from the original act that persists to the present. The federal regulators now could place limits on the amount of futures traded each day. Ironically, this action, taken in the hope of maintaining a free and open market responsive to the laws of supply and demand, has succeeded over the years in making the market relatively stable even as it permanently foreclosed the open market prevalent during the nineteenth century. Even more important, the 1936 amendments confirmed the fact that self-regulation by the exchanges had apparently become less than effective. The new changes gave the Secretary of Agriculture broad powers to impose such rules as "are reasonably necessary to effectuate any of the provisions or to accomplish any of the purposes" of the statute. In the event of violation, either past or occurring, the Commodity Exchange Commission (CEC) (consisting of the secretaries of Commerce and Agriculture and the Attorney General) could issue cease-and-desist orders, subject to court appeal. If the board of trade involved, or a director, officer, agent, or employee thereof, refused to obey or comply, the new amendment levied a fine of not less than $500 nor more than $10,000 and/or imprisonment for not more than a year. "Each day during which such failure or refusal to obey such order continues shall be deemed a separate offense."[10] In the 1936 amendments, the organized boards of trade were treated much more stringently than the individual traders.

For the next thirty years, Congress enacted no fundamental changes in the Commodity Exchange Act. During this period, which included World War II as well as the Korean conflict, the futures markets expanded dramatically. Although commodity trading in both amounts and monetary value increased between 1964 and 1975, its growth between 1969 and 1974 is noteworthy. Trading in 1969 was 20 percent higher than in 1968; in 1970, the increase was 22 percent; in 1972, 26 percent. During 1973, the volume of commodity trading increased by over 40 percent. In 1969 the total number of contracts traded reached more than 11 million. By mid-1973, the number had more than doubled.[11] It is not surprising, then, that by the mid-1960s federal interest in expanding national commodity exchange regulation was evident. While the proposed changes in the law remained somewhat within the original framework of internal self-regulation, it is clear that, congressional and exchange rhetoric not withstanding, this concept seemed to diminish even as the commodities markets expanded.

During 1966 and 1967, Congress considered changes in the law that were sought by the Commodity Exchange Authority (CEA). In hearings before the committee, the spokesman for the U.S. Department of Agriculture dismissed the pleas that "the exchanges can and have regulated themselves" as unfounded. He emphasized that the proposed injunctive provision, one that would permit the CEA to halt suspected violations in progress, was "the most vital element . . . the major amendment we offer."[12] Of course, representatives of the exchanges were uniform in their opposition to the change, calling it dangerous and unnecessary. Further, extensive questioning by skeptical members of the committee brought out the facts that during the last 45 years, the number of criminal actions brought by the CEA averaged about one a year.[13] Of the six cases taken to the courts on appeal, the CEA was reversed on three of them. Noting that "use of the injunctive power . . . would be almost like making a surgical incision with a meat axe," the representative of the Chicago Board of Trade added that "being right just half the time doesn't demonstrate the kind of certainty required for proper use of injunctions."[14]

By a 28-1 vote, the committee endorsed, and Congress duly enacted, major amendments to the Commodity Exchange Act. Not only could the Secretary of Agriculture disallow any rule or regulation adopted by an exchange that appeared to contravene federal law, but also the new amendments compelled the exchanges to enforce all their rules and regulations that had not been disapproved by the Secretary. In addition, the exchanges had to preserve all books, records, minutes, and journals of its governing committees "in a manner that will clearly describe all matters discussed" by them. The implications of these changes for self-regulation were not lost on witnesses for the various boards of trade. The president of the New York Cotton Exchange insisted that the Secretary would have the power to keep disapproving an internal regulation "until you write it the way the Department wanted you to write it in the first place. . . . The result will be that the CEA instead of the exchanges will be writing . . . the trading rules, and the governing boards might as well retire."[15] Robert Martin, chairman of the board of the Chicago Board of Trade, argued that this provision "is inconsistent with the principle of responsible self-regulation." It injected the Secretary's authority "at least indirectly—into the very heart of the board's most responsible exercise of self-regulation."[16] On the other hand, the president of the Board of Trade of Kansas City objected both to the Secretary's power of disapproval and to the requirement that the boards of trade enforce their rules and regulations. These changes, he claimed, meant that "full responsibility is thrust upon the market and its employees for enforcing the Commodity Exchange Act and rules approved by the Secretary, or they shall suffer the penalties. . . . We maintain that this is an unwarranted shift of responsibility from the Commodity Exchange Authority to the commodity exchanges."[17] Apparently self-regulation did not extend to enforcing federal authorities!

The 1968 amendments to the Commodity Exchange Act represent the last congressional effort to maintain a trichotomous system of regulation—one that had been in effect since 1922. The exchanges, the Secretary of Agriculture, and the commission (consisting of the Secretary of Agriculture, the Secretary of Commerce, and the Attorney General or their designated representatives) all had important regulatory input into the commodities markets. Originally the balance had been in favor of exchange internal policy power. By 1936, the shift had begun toward increased federal authority over the exchanges. By 1968, the thrust of federal supervision had expanded into areas that traditionally had been within the purview of the exchanges, and, as has been noted, the new amendments required these institutions to enforce their rules and regulations. In back of this requirement lay the threat that federal enforcement would follow in the absence of local action.

Between 1969 and 1973 the amount of traded futures contracts more than doubled. Yet the CEA failed to grow with it. Lacking an independent legal staff, subject to the various budgetary vicissitudes that affected the Department of Agriculture during the early 1970s, exercising very limited powers of enforcement—these conditions made it virtually impossible to carry out the mandate of the 1968 amendments. Further, according to the House Committee on Agriculture, the requirement that the exchanges must enforce their rules "coupled with only limited federal authority to require the exchanges to make and issue rules appropriate to enforcement of the Act" may have actually worked to weaken internal regulation.[18] The committee noted that some boards of trade on advice of counsel had reduced, not expanded, internal regulations, "since there is a growing body of opinion that failure to enforce the exchange rules is a violation of the Act which will support suits by private litigants."[19] Moreover, there was clear evidence of illegal practices committed on various exchanges, not the least of which was the alleged manipulation of the Kansas City Board of Trade September 1972 wheat future as it related to the Russian grain sales. Although the congressional reports continually praised the concept of self-regulation, legislative action ultimately taken indicated that the rhetoric did not correspond to the reality. Self-regulation, according to the House Committee, "is a commendable and noble concept." However, it "cannot be viewed in this and later decades as an argument against greater Federal regulation. . . . It cannot continue to function without a strong Federal regulatory umbrella over self-regulatory activities of the industry."[20]

The end result of congressional deliberation on this topic was the abolition of the Commodity Exchange Authority and the creation of a new, independent regulatory agency, the Commodity Futures Trading Commission (CFTC) in 1975. All futures trading was placed under its jurisdiction. Although a representative of the Department of Agriculture could attend and observe all proceedings and deliberations of the commission, he or she could not vote. In effect, the Department was removed from any active role in commodity regulation. Further, the commission could either by itself or through the Attorney General go to court to seek injunctive remedies against any contract market or person engaged in any violation of the law. A new system of administrative disciplinary procedures was established, and the penalties for violation of the statute went from $10,000 to $100,000.[21]

It is, of course, too soon to gauge the effectiveness of this latest regulatory commission. There are about as many differing views among scholars on the effectiveness of federal regulatory commissions as there are commissions themselves. Yet, as this chapter has sought to imply, the growth of federal regulation in commodity exchanges and trading raises troublesome questions: (1) To what extent is the commodity trading system, as it has evolved since the 1920s, representing a *free, open* market? (2) How is federal regulation compatible with private exchange self-regulatory responsibilities? One of the fears often voiced by observers of the American judicial system is that reliance on federal judicial review lessens the obligation and responsibility of legislatures to exercise proper and reasoned judgment in the passing of statutes. Is the situation of the commodity exchanges somewhat similar? Are they less inclined now to exercise primary responsibility, knowing that a full-time independent regulatory commission is overseeing their activities? To what extent should federal regulation go in order to protect the "public interest" in maintaining privately administered commodity markets? (3) To what extent does our current commodity regulatory framework involve movement toward a "planned economy," in that the prices of commodity futures can only rise or fall to a level established by law, within which level the forces of supply and demand presumably are free to operate? (4) Is it wise to continue emphasizing self-regulation powers held by the exchanges in the light of federal developments noted during this chapter?

Notes

1. Jonathan Lurie, "Commodities Exchanges as Self-Regulating Organizations in the late 19th entury: Some Perimeters in the History of American Administrative Law," *Rutgers Law Review* 28 (1975):1107-1140.

2. *Board of Trade v. Christie,* 198 U.S. 236 (1905).

3. J. Lurie, "Speculation, Risk and Profits: The Ambivalent Agrarian in the Late 19th Century," *Agricultural History* 46 (1972):269-278; J. Lurie, "Commodities Exchanges, Agrarian 'Political Power' and the Anti-Option Battle, 1890-1894," *Agricultural History* 48 (1974):115-125.

4. 42 Stat. 998 (1922). See also J. Lurie, "Regulation of the Commodities Exchanges in the 1920's: The Legacy of Self-Government," paper to be published in the proceedings of the 1977 National Archives Conference on Farmers, Bureaucrats, and Middlemen.

5. *Report of the Secretary of Agriculture,* 1924, p. 59.

6. Ibid., p. 55. See also p. 92 of the 1931 report.

7. Ibid., 1933, p. 55.

8. Ibid., 1934, p. 82; ibid., 1935, p. 116.

9. 49 Stat. 1491 (1936).

10. Ibid., p. 1500.

11. 93d Cong., 2d Sess., *House,* Report #93-975, p. 42, (1974).

12. 90th Cong., 1st Sess., House Committee on Agriculture, Hearings, "Amend the Commodity Exchange Act," Serial T, p. 71, (1967).

13. Ibid., pp. 61-83.

14. Ibid., p. 110.

15. Ibid., p. 89.

16. Ibid., p. 111.

17. Ibid., p. 37.

18. 93d Cong., 2d Sess., *House,* Report #93-975, p. 46, (1974).

19. Ibid.

20. Ibid., p. 48.

21. 88 Stat. 1389 (1974), p. 1404.

10 Interest Group Strength and Organizational Characteristics: The General Farm Organizations and the 1977 Farm Bill

William P. Browne and
Charles W. Wiggins

"The general farm groups? The traditional farm interests don't seem to have their former importance. They lack visibility. They just don't seem to be around." That was the comment of one veteran Capital Hill agriculturalist, a congressional staff member. But a contrary opinion was expressed by an equally experienced agricultural policy maker from the U.S. Department of Agriculture (USDA). "Where are the general farm organizations? Just where they've always been—wherever the decisions affecting farmers are being made. Let me tell you something. No interest group in town will get its way more in 1977 than the Farm Bureau, and it won't be by accident."

Such were the assessments being made around Washington as the 1977 farm bill was nearing its final legislative stages. And both viewpoints were equally represented. In listening to agricultural observers, the only clear thing about the general farm organizations was the lack of consensus concerning their present influence.[1]

Organizational Background

The political influence of the general farm groups has been derived from several factors relative to their own political structure.

(1) Each is a national association of local affiliate units, all supported by dues-paying local members who select their own grass-roots leaders.[2]

(2) The American Farm Bureau Federation (NFBF), National Farmers Union (NFU), and Grange each have intermediary autonomous and politically active state-level organizations between the national and local units.

(3) Organized lobbying is officially carried on at the state and national levels as a result of resolutions passed at annual legislative conferences.

(4) Each organization maintains a small Washington staff for the expressed purpose of implementing the group's annual policies statement from the legislative conference. AFBF employs nine lobbyists for that purpose, NFU

designates three lobbyists, the Grange has two, and National Farmers Organization (NFO) one; the organizations also employ a small number of research
personnel who supplement the lobbyists' work.

(5) All four organizations are much more than political voices for agricultural interests. In fact, the lobby staffs are only one minor component in the
overall organizations. Other services include social activities, marketing information, marketing assistance, credit exchanges, insurance, and cooperative purchasing agreements. The organizations employ far larger numbers of staff
members with backgrounds and skills related to these services than they do for
their lobby operations. Since these staff members are skilled in subject areas
frequently related to legislative matters, they can and do serve as a valuable
information source for the lobbyists. The same type of use is made of those staff
members who are employed in communicating with the members through
newsletters, magazines, and specially prepared literature. These employees are
often called on to draft statements, releases, and reports distributed to or
prepared for government policy makers.

(6) Formal policy making for all national organizations rests with officers
and committees elected by and from the general membership. Although
day-to-day operations are in the hands of the full-time staff, ideas and even
actual organizational control are, contingent upon heavy demand, free to
emanate from the ranks of practicing farmers and ranchers. This situation
produces two results. First, the general farm organizations have legitimacy in the
eyes of government officials who want to gain a practitioner's viewpoint.
Second, these elected officers, since they are respected for the insights they
possess, can be used to testify before committees and make direct contact with
legislators and Department of Agriculture officials. In other words, they also
expand the lobbying potential of each group.

(7) All four organizations see their role as spokesmen for the whole of
American agriculture. As such, resolutions appear and some lobbying goes on in
support of almost every conceivable issue affecting the business and social life of
farm families.

(8) With the on-and-off exception of both the NFU and the Farm Bureau,
these groups do not purport to stand alone as the champions of agricultural
interests. The general farm organizations along with the commodity groups have
consulted regularly since 1921 to coordinate lobbying efforts and present a
united front.[3] Even in 1977 with the wide discrepancies in farm price demands,
35 farm organizations, this time excluding NFU, were able to formally and
informally present a well-coordinated compromise on price levels under the
auspices of the National Farm Coalition. As the director of one Washington
office stated, "There is always disagreement on issues, but more often than not
most of the organizations are lined up together. You might be temporarily
opposed to one group on a specific matter, but you know you'll be working
together on something else before long. There is a tremendous amount of mutual
assistance and cooperation in this town."

The combined impact of these eight factors has created a comfortable climate of opinion in national politics for the general farm organizations. And, since they have traditionally operated within the "subgovernment" of agricultural policy, their reception has been even more hospitable than it might have been were these interests airing their differences with one another in a more open setting.[4] However, the times are and have been changing to at least some degree. As Don Paarlberg claims, a "new agenda" confronts agricultural policy makers, and the farm groups are affected by it.[5] Today a united front spearheaded by the legitimate representatives of a broad interest group of agriculturalists no longer automatically carries the day merely because its components have attained internal consensus. Yet the general farm groups have, over time, created a set of organizational conditions from which they cannot escape, and they must react to changes in terms of their capabilities. The remainder of this chapter will address the constraints these conditions impose on the operation of these interest groups and also what latitude the groups have for flexible operation.

Membership Constraints

For too long, political scientists viewed interest groups as single-dimension institutions. Group theorists like Arthur Bentley argued that the group could be defined only in terms of its interest.[6] If you knew what the composite membership of the group needed, you knew what the group was about politically. Although Bentley was not necessarily referring to the organized interest group, generations of political scientists applied his logic to them anyway.

More recently political analysts have begun to hack away at the notion of the interest group as a cohesive force. Mancur Olson and then Robert Salisbury contended rather persuasively that members join and pay dues for reasons other than the political issues addressed by the organization.[7] In doing so, they demonstrated that the interest group was far more complex in its organizational structure than others have assumed. The interest group, as Salisbury made it real, could not be considered to be just the interactive elements with varying commitments seen by David Truman.[8] Members do belong who have differing and even conflicting political goals.

The diversity of interests within the group and the need to serve a variety of reasons for affiliation place a tremendous burden on the staff personnel who must maintain the organization.[9] In the final analysis, keeping the organization together is the ultimate goal. Political victories, profitable commodity agreements, and successful insurance operations have very little value to the great bulk of the membership if they cannot be expanded on later or fully utilized over an extended period.

The general farm organizations, perhaps even more than most interest groups (because of the dramatic yearly decrease in farm residents), continuously see maintenance as foremost a problem of numbers of members—and not without good reason. The NFU and the Grange have stabilized their membership in recent years but only after precipitous fall-offs beginning in the 1950s. The NFO recently reorganized its field staff because of a large backlog of nonpayment of dues among members that was troublesome to the Securities and Exchange Commission as well as to the group itself. Only the Farm Bureau with its new inroads into the South has increased to record membership.

The membership problem that faces the staff is not, however, just one of recruitment and retention logistics. As Browne has shown elsewhere, the staffs of urban interest groups recognize that their members drop out because they fail to see the rewards of membership.[10] The behavior of the general farm staffs indicates that they believe the same thing. Periodicals are continuously sent to members advertising organizational accomplishments and citing threats to agriculture; direct staff-member contacts are encouraged; nonpolitical services and information about them are widely distributed; and marketing assistance is frequently given priority status as the most significant function of more than just the NFO. In short, the membership problem cannot be handled by designating just one office to work with local units. It confronts and involves everyone on the staffs because they must contribute to a common effort; and this produces considerable stress within each of the organizations.

Staff Tensions

The physical distance that separates the lobbying staff from headquarters presents some difficulty for three of the organizations. Simple communication is one problem since officials in the home office must be kept abreast of legislative changes, bureaucratic rulings, new proposals, appointments in government, serious rumors about farm policy, and any changes in the group's lobbying strategy. But tensions result less from the bulk of communications than they do from the shared nature of decisionmaking within each organization.

Although the Washington representatives are the policy experts, the lobbyists are not entirely autonomous. Instead their role is more one of political advisor; and their opinions, while always respected, are often weighed quite carefully by other ranking staff personnel as well as the elected national officers. Decisions are made when all three sides of this organizational triangle either agree with one another or agree to defer to the lobbyist's judgment. This situation makes coordination as much of a problem as communication.

At first glance, the communication-coordination problem might not seem membership-related; but some probing into the perceptions of the lobbyists reveals it to be. Lobbying, as the Washington staff sees it, requires more than just promoting the goals of the organization. The job demands careful attention to the changing problems of a wide variety of political participants, flexibility in bringing the needs of these people together, and a willingness to compromise, sometimes quickly. However, the lobbyists are not entirely convinced that the rest of the organization understands this. These staffers see other employees as interested primarily in the details of their own jobs, especially member services, and they feel elected officers are often too wedded to their own carefully cultivated visions of what they as farmers themselves consider to be "down on the farm needs." "As I see it," one lobbyist emphatically stated, "the question should be 'Will the committee staff [in the House of Representatives] buy it?' But, oh no, somebody [in the home office] will want to know how we could ever let anyone propose to regulate one of our operations any further and what our members will think about this when they walk in and see more government involvement."

To some extent, these staff tensions would exist even if the headquarters were in Washington because personal responsibilities still would vary. Many of the same concerns over being understood were cited by Grange officials as well as those of the other three groups. But proximity allows them to talk over their problems more directly. And constant exposure to the political realities of the nation's capital gives Grange officials, like those of the urban interest groups studied earlier, more insight into and understanding of the problems of lobbying.[11] AFBF, NFU, and NFO do not appear to be as cohesive organizations as might be expected, and the repeated comment that "things would be different if they were in town" seems a revealing one.

A Forum for Issues

The presence of too many points of view as a problem for lobbyists does not end when staff differences are resolved. The many concerns of the members as they are directly expressed to the organization also affect lobbying.

As a big smile swept over his face, the lobbyist in charge of one Washington office proclaimed that "we go by the book in lobbying. The book tells us what to do." Officials from all four farm organizations have multipage statements to dispense to those who inquire about their organization's public policy positions. These range from the 77-page indexed booklet of the AFBF to the four-page stapled Xerox copy of NFO's resolutions. In Washington lexicon, these are "the book," the complete listing of those political issues that move and inspire those members who offer ideas and vote at the annual conference.

The policy statement of conference delegates represents many things to each of the farm groups, and it colors their lobbying in several ways; but it is not a mandate for their lobbying. "This statement goes in the drawer and if anyone asks whether we have a position on this or that issue, I tell them," offered another head lobbyist when asked about "the book." But the collective sentiment of the staff members was best expressed by the blunt statement of one young lobbyist: "These things make us look more than a little goofy to congressmen and other people who don't know what kinds of things actually interest us. They think we're really pushing all this trash."

Because voting delegates are able to argue for the insertion of whatever issues they want, the resolution statements are cluttered with things of personal interest that have limited impact on current agricultural problems. These fall in three broad categories: (1) current major issues including regulatory reforms, abortion, and social security; (2) current minor issues such as elimination of six-day mail delivery and legalizing marijuana; (3) traditional, repeating resolutions of the organizations including sentiments in support of progressive human welfare programs and in opposition to land-use planning beyond the county level. To a great extent, these resolutions exist to satisfy the expressive needs of the membership.[12] Everyone with a burning issue to champion or a pet peeve to complain about can take it through the resolutions process and, especially if a responsive cord is struck, satisfy himself as to the openness of the American democratic system. Even the NFO, which consciously tried to discourage the inclusion of such items, finds them impossible to resist entirely.

The resolutions statement is also an historical commentary on the traditions of the organization. Over time each organization has worked in coalition with both farm and nonfarm groups. The Farm Bureau, for instance, has long maintained a working relationship with the National Association of Manufacturers. These and shorter-term partnerships as well as the rationale for such cooperation have been regularly sold to the members. Because many members have long memories and since several staff personnel find it desirable to rhetorically keep their bridges to old friends in good shape, a great many resolutions included each year refer to past challenges that remain unresolved or call for continued extension of old legislative pushes that have long since waned.

Unfortunately, from the lobbyists' standpoint, all this produces several negative effects. First, the organizations appear to lack a specific and clearly defined agenda of goals. Some of the major issues, such as reserve policies, get lost. Second, the organizations appear, as they have historically, overly ideological or partisan.[13] As one House committee staffer remarked, "The Farm Bureau reads Conservative Republican. I don't know specifically what they want, but I bet I know where their head's at." Third, they threaten many potential political allies. A call for reorganization of USDA antagonizes people with whom the staff must work. Likewise, a resolution opposing revenue sharing rankles staff members at the National Association of Counties who serve a similar constituency to the farm groups.

Issue Emphasis

Fortunately for the staff lobbyists, they do not feel too constrained by such resolutions. First, the resolutions are stated quite generally in most instances, leaving them flexibility in their work. For example, the Farm Bureau mentions the need for minimal price supports while still condemning their necessity in the 1977 group resolutions. And the Grange, which tends to be the most specific in its resolutions, calls for fair target prices in 1977 rather than demanding specific figures. Thus all four staffs are given quite some latitude in implementing what the members have proposed. As an AFBF staff member noted, "The policy of the organization is not to hamstring our legislative efforts."

Second, the staffs do not see the members getting aroused if work is not done on most of the resolutions. Instead, they feel that accomplishing some objectives, and making the members aware of those accomplishments, is quite important. And they feel that the items on which they succeed should produce real benefits that are easily seen by farmers as affecting their business environments. As an example, the Farm Bureau cited 1976 estate tax reform as an issue of great significance to their members and one that reflected very positively on the organization. On the other hand, the members "won't blame us if pornography continues or if the army is unionized, but they've expressed themselves on those too."

Apparently, only a relatively few issues would produce a great reaction from the membership if the staffs were to drop their lobbying efforts. And, not unexpectedly, they are all "bread and butter" issues. Farmers Union members "insist on high price supports and we have to deliver." Grange members are adamant about target prices and only somewhat less insistent on better loan rate provisions. NFO members see price supports and the reserve issue as most crucial. Only the Farm Bureau seems to face a dilemma. Its members, especially wheat farmers and other Midwesterners, demand price support levels even though the organization has committed itself to a free market position. So AFBF lobbyists feel they must push for supports while they must also satisfy their member demands for freedom from government interference in international trade and with reserves. Other issues, it seems, while crucial to the health and well-being of agriculture, are entrusted to the judgment and safe keeping of the Washington representatives.

On balance, the need to satisfy membership expectations complicates the task of lobbying. The staff and national officers of the farm organizations worry about keeping members happy for fear, they feel, that unhappy members are short-term members. From the lobbyists' perceptions, this fear is largely unfounded, but it puts them in potential conflict with many organizational colleagues nonetheless. The fact that the members have so much to say, rather than that they insist on so many prescribed public policy results, is the one direct membership problem faced by the lobbyists. If the lobbyists can convince the members that they're doing as much as possible on the basic farm incomes issues, they don't expect to be too troubled by those who pay dues.

Demands of the Political Environment

Were the general farm lobbyists to be hampered by too forceful an involvement by group members, they would find it nearly impossible to lobby effectively. Their efforts would be spread too thin in attempting to satisfy "the book," and no time would be left to deal with emerging issues of new importance. There are too many offices to cover and too many "assistant lobbyists" from the membership ranks to coordinate with too few Washington representatives for the group to even demonstrate their presence under those conditions.

Staff personnel agree that a "new agenda" has opened up the politics of agriculture. Even without worrying about revenue sharing, social issues, and transportation, an astonishing number of legislative committees and bureaus control programs that have a direct farm impact. "Our staff has grown and our contacts are increasing even faster," said one senior lobbyist. "If we're not so visible to some people anymore it's only because we can't restrict ourselves to the same old places any longer. It's a new ball game." The House Committee on Banking and Currency, with its emphasis on international trade, demands attention as do separate committees dealing with public lands, agricultural labor, water resources, taxation, consumer affairs, and innumerable other items. As a result, the farm groups have had to work with several relative strangers to sponsor bills of particular interest.

Most of the lobbying workload now falls in the administrative arena. And the White House constitutes only a small portion of that. Representatives from each of the groups agree that there are several reasons for the vast amount of time spent in the bureaucracy. First, most farm bills have substantial bureaucratic input prior to introduction. Second, several agencies such as the Federal Energy Administration are newly involved in writing bills related to farm activities. Third, there is a need to work with bureaucratic agencies in implementing each piece of legislation that passes since "only the skeleton comes from the Congress. Flat out, you succeed or fail during implementation." Fourth, regulations are constantly being rewritten both within the Department of Agriculture and by such new agencies as the Occupational Safety and Health Administration (OSHA). Fifth, there is an increasing need to work with bureaucrats to establish the economic and environmental feasibility of programs. That entails more information gathering from various sources. The importance of contacts on these matters is underscored by the recent modest growth of some staffs, each instance of which was attributed to a need for increased bureaucratic ties.

Lobbying, as the farm lobbyists see it, goes considerably beyond the need to contact federal officials and their staffs. Within Washington, it also means considerable involvement with other interest groups. Although the National Farm Coalition serves as an ideal forum for such interaction and allows the interacting groups to "unofficially" announce their own compromise positions without backtracking on promises made to the membership, it is not the only vehicle for cooperation. Some is on the spur of the moment: "It's hard to imagine a week going by, for any (group) representative, without the need to call someone in," opined one lobbyist. At other times it is on relatively minor issues such as securing help for the OSHA difficulties or a member having problems in the field. "Even the Farmers nion needs help sometimes," maintained another staffer, "they can't be informed about everything so they come over. Nobody is self-sufficient. We all have to work together."

This cooperation should not be surprising even though the groups are noted for their diversity of opinions. Actually it is a logical extension of the very traditional manner in which each organization's staff views their lobbying role. To the farm groups, lobbying is making yourself known to those who will listen, carefully explaining your position, and producing information to sustain your case. These organizations attempt to persuade by demonstrating the legitimacy of their claims, not by castigating enemies. They prove that they have the facts, member support, allies, or votes to demand attention. With such an orientation, lobbying other farm organizations or seeking support from them only makes sense. Perhaps, in certain instances, the farm lobbies even go somewhat further. "We have to cooperate with the consumer groups," was the advice of a long-time Washington lobbyist. "Other people listen to them and so should we. And they should listen to us; farmers are consumers too, and they should understand that fact."

Finally, lobbying goes on outside Washington as well. In fact, while bureaucrats may command more personal attention, there seems to be no more of a concerted effort anywhere than the one to convince the rest of the organization of the lobbyists' sagacity and worth. And this process brings an element of unreality to the grass-roots structure and the notion of open organizations. Part of the effort is to ensure internal support in order for the groups to appear credible before government. Most of the farm lobbyists agree that it does little good to articulate a position that isn't backed up by the sentiments of the membership. And several of them noted that government officials have considerable insights into grass-roots opinions. "The worst thing you can do to ensure defeat is to claim widespread member support when there is none," offered one lobbyist. "There are too many clues available elsewhere."

However, "farming the membership" is done to reduce internal pressures on the staff as much as it is to build credibility. Representatives from each organization noted a greater need to increase "educational efforts" among the members. "For our purposes," said one senior lobbyist, "there can never be enough effort to educate our members about basic farm issues as they are affected by national politics. This office, and a few others like it in town, are the one real source of information farmers have about government's very real impact on their lives." The expressed reason for this was clearly stated and universally shared: "We still haven't convinced them [the members] of what's right."

To accomplish these ends, the general farm groups all emphasize communication and interaction. Newsletters, pamphlets, special publications, the media, and the resolutions statements are employed to the extent that funds are available to prepare and distribute them. In addition, the Farm Bureau has recently added telecommunications equipment to ensure nearly instantaneous output to the various national and state components of the organization. Almost all the deployed material is either prepared or coordinated from the Washington offices. For example, AFBF houses its editor in its small Washington suite even though all other nonlobbying activities are centered in the spacious Illinois headquarters.

The lobbying staffs also work with the members to ensure thorough issue coverage in the annual resolutions statements. Although they seldom succeed, or even try very hard, at fending off the inclusion of items, the staff of each organization is involved enough in these deliberations to suggest where the document is weak or what impending public policies are neglected. This process not only gives the staffs a chance to predefine their lobbying agenda, but also gives them an excellent opportunity to appear before the delegates and explain what issues are of special urgency. An active state president of one group commented on the effect produced by this opportunity: "I've never been to a conference on politics where (the staff) didn't scare the beJesus out of me with their tales. So I come home and can really scare hell out of my neighbors. You and me out here, we don't know enough about what's going on [in Washington]."

The Potential of the Farm Organization

Two opinions about the general farm organizations were cited at the beginning of this chapter. To some extent, we can explain both remarks. Obviously the farm groups have been spreading their staff operations over a far broader range of activities than ever before. Therefore, it's unlikely that individual political participants will perceive them as having the same visibility as they were noted for in years past. With regard to the 1977 success of the Farm Bureau, it must be noted that the comment was made in reference to only two issues—the farm bill and international trade. And the trade prediction was based on the judgment that the climate of public opinion would disallow government interference at this time. However, our analysis of internal group operations goes quite far in explaining why AFBF could have gained a reputation for considerable influence on the basis of the 1977 farm bill.

(1) To begin with, the farm bill was handled in the traditional centers of agricultural power. Although Senator Herman Talmadge was often referred to as "no friend" by farm group lobbyists, there were obviously a few around who were willing to listen to the need for a high support since the Talmadge proposal was continuously hiked. The same was true of USDA input. And, significantly, there were few consumer interests seeking entry into this policy arena to support Talmadge.

(2) AFBF, contrary to the expectations of many who hold an ideological view of the organization, had to be price support-oriented and, therefore, was able to gain strength by drawing on a coalition of other farm groups, both general and commodity. Member sentiments and the need to avoid intergroup warfare left AFBF with no other alternative position. This seemed to minimize intrastaff tensions as well.

(3) AFBF was able to concentrate on the farm bill since membership interests were strongly committed to its contents. There was no need to worry about other issues. They could be postponed or given back-burner attention without member reprisal.

(4) The political environment was not jammed with too many other agricultural issues. Only energy proposals seemed to be demanding much attention and concern. The second major renewal bill being debated, food stamps, was being wished away to the Department of Health, Education and Welfare by AFBF and much of the rest of the agricultural establishment.

Interest group strength, it appears, is a matter of who controls the issue and what problems the organization faces in mobilizing to handle it. The Farm Bureau would probably not draw plaudits for its effectiveness were several issues to appear at once, widely dispersed through the committees of Congress and bureaus of the administration. Nor could it stand alone on an issue, be adamantly ideological, or try to meet every member's expectations. However, in a period of economic hardship for farmers, integrated grass-roots demands confronted, as they also had in 1933, a political system organized to be predisposed to be of assistance and, as a result, produced strong economic relief.[14] When ideas and principles must be given a back seat to the economic concerns of agriculture, the 1977 farm bill shows that AFBF can emerge as an influential, strategically sound lobby.[15]

What of the other three farm organizations? They could indeed be influential. In fact, they have been. NFO, in popularizing "producer power" for example, helped spearhead many of the institutional reforms needed to assist the collective commodity bargaining efforts of farmers. And, in their hearts, perhaps many of that organization's staff were even more pleased with the 1977 farm bill than AFBF personnel. However, each of the three other organizations has problems that AFBF need not face in being an effective lobby. Their lobby staffs are far smaller than the Farm Bureau's and as a result more restricted in what they can attempt. NFU is placed in the member-related bind of having to insist on high parity-based price support levels. And the Grange lacks an activist style of lobbying, relying too heavily on sending out statements by mail. In the final analysis, these and other limitations of the general farm organizationss give new life to David Truman's compendium of those variables that affect the lobbying strength of the group: internal organization, number and distribution of the members, authority, financing, time, quality of the leaders, skills within the organization, strategy, and nature of the membership.[16] Certainly no one group has the best of all these. So interest group politics becomes an exercise in making do with what you have.

Notes

1. The major findings of this study result from a series of detailed personal interviews by Browne with one dozen Washington staff personnel from the farm groups. A series of open-ended questions were used to elicit systematic responses about legislative priorities, member involvement in goal setting, member expectations about goal setting, and lobbying success.

Prior to these interviews, another series of interviews was conducted focusing on the attitudes of congressional staff, USDA officials, and group members. This information was used as background for the development of the lobbyist questionnaire. Similarly, farm group publications were examined as a guide to the interviews. This published material was also useful in writing the chapter.

2. We recognize, of course, the regional strengths and weaknesses of each organization.

3. Harmon Zeigler, *Interest Groups in American Society* (Englewood Cliffs, N.J.: Prentice-Hall, Inc., 1964), pp. 176-179.

4. Theodore J. Lowi, *The End of Liberalism* (Univ. of Chicago Press, 1969), pp. 102-115.

5. Don Paarlberg, "The Farm Policy Agenda," *Increasing Understanding of Public Problems and Policies—1975* (Chicago: Farm Foundation, 1975).

6. Arthur Bentley, *The Process of Government* (Chicago: University of Chicago Press, 1908).

7. Mancur Olson, Jr., *The Logic of Collective Action* (Cambridge, Mass.: Harvard University Press, 1965); Robert H. Salisbury, "An Exchange Theory of Interest Groups," *Midwest Journal of Political Science* (February 1969):1-32.

8. David B. Truman, *The Governmental Process* (New York: Alfred A. Knopf, 1951), p. 24.

9. William P. Browne, "Organizational Maintenance: The Internal Operation of Interest Groups," *Public Administration Review (PAR)* (January-February 1977):48-57.

10. William P. Browne, "Benefits and Membership: A Reappraisal of Interest Group Activity," *Western Political Quarterly* (June 1976):258-273.

11. Browne, *PAR,* p. 56.

12. Salisbury, "Exchange Theory of Interest Groups," pp. 15-19; Peter Clark and James W. Wilson, "Incentive Systems: A Theory of Organization," *Administrative Science Quarterly* (September 1961):129-66.

13. Ross B. Talbot, "Farm Organizations and the National Interest," *The Annals of the American Academy of Political and Social Science* (September 1960):112-114.

14. Robert H. Salisbury and John P. Heinz, "A Theory of Policy Analysis and Some Preliminary Application," in Ira Sharkansky (ed.), *Policy Analysis in Political Science* (Chicago: Markham, 1970), pp. 48-49, 55.

15. This analysis is of special interest, given Graham K. Wilson's study of agricultural groups through the early 1970s, especially his final conclusion. "Special Interests, Interest Groups and Misguided Interventionism: Explaining Agricultural Subsidies in the U.S.," *Politics* (November 1976):139.

16. Truman, *Governmental Process,* chap. 5.

11 Consumer Organizations and Federal Dairy Policy

L. Guth

Since 1933 milk prices in the United States have been heavily influenced by two interrelated federal programs: price supports for manufactured products and federal marketing orders for fluid milk. Policy has usually been determined within a classic "subgovernment," consisting of the National Milk Producers Federation (NMPF), other dairy industry and farmer organizations, the House and Senate Agriculture Committees, and the U.S. Department of Agriculture (USDA) marketing authorities.[1]

From the 1930s through the late 1960s, decisions were usually arrived at by negotiation among subgovernment actors, with relatively little input from "consumer" or "public" representatives. Although local consumer groups were active in the early stages of federal order development, they lacked the finances, expertise, and political sanctions necessary for continued influence. Protection of consumer interests was left therefore to various public officials, who were only sporadically able to counter subgovernment policies. Urban congressmen generally left milk questions to rural colleagues, depriving in-house consumer advocates such as the USDA Consumers Counsel of vital political support. The Office of Price Administration (OPA) was more effective in overriding subgovernment policy during World War II, but generally public officials were effective consumer spokesmen only when rapidly rising prices aroused widespread concern.

Despite the frequent absence of external controls, various forces within the subgovernment provided some protection for consumer interests. Many industry groups shared pricing objectives heavily conditioned by anticipated consumer responses. Milk dealers, processors, and manufacturers always preferred low farm prices to maintain sales volume, minimize unit costs, and fatten profit margins. And although NMPF cooperatives were understandably more sensitive to farmer price demands, a similar "managerial" outlook influenced many of them, especially the manufacturing and fluid milk "operating" cooperatives. These groups, which actually handled members' milk, were always more skeptical of administered price hiking than colleagues in purely "bargaining" cooperatives. In addition, manufacturing and fluid milk cooperatives usually preferred only modest federal price assistance in the other's sector so as to avoid overproduction which might threaten their own markets.

After 1953, as a chronic price slump gradually drove the NMPF toward a more aggressive policy, other factors limited subgovernment price boosting. Growing fragmentation of producer interests along regional, product, and organizational lines reduced the NMPF's cohesion and political influence. At the same time, general farm organizations such as the Farm Bureau, National Farmers Union (NFU), Grange, and National Farmers Organization (NFO) introduced their own demands, greatly complicating the bargaining process. Especially crucial was the powerful Farm Bureau demand for reduced federal price assistance, improved productivity, and greater milk sales—a policy prescription suited for a hypothetical milk consumers' lobby. This subgovernment "pluralism" did not destroy existing programs, but stymied proposals for higher price supports, production restrictions, greater industry self-regulation, and augmented cooperative bargaining authority, all potentially adverse to consumer interests.

The rising milk prices and the Milk Fund scandal of the early 1970s revealed that these traditional checks on the subgovernment were no longer even partially effective. Although rising prices resulted in part from broader economic forces, the cooperative merger wave of the late 1960s had indeed altered the traditional economic and political balance. New interregional "supercooperatives" such as Associated Milk Producers, Inc. (AMPI), Mid-America Dairymen, and Dairymen, Inc. not only controlled a considerable portion of the nation's milk, but used this economic power to manipulate many federal orders and even the price support program. In addition, their innovative use, for farm groups, of massive campaign contributions and ability to reconcile previously competing producer factions enhanced the industry's political power.[2]

By 1973 these developments drew a number of consumer groups into dairy policy debates, including the Consumer Federation of America (CFA), the National Consumers Congress (NCC), the Congress Watch, and several research and educational groups. This rising wave of consumer interest also prompted creation of the National Association for Milk Marketing Reform (NAMMR) by milk dealers hoping to counter increasing cooperative power. Despite a common concern for dairy policy, these groups often focused individually on specific issues or used different forums. Most exhibited the consumer movement's reliance on exposure and through litigation (such as Nader's suit against the 1971 price support increase), conferences, economic studies, and press releases managed to generate an impressive amount of publicity. Popular exposes of the supercooperatives and scholarly critiques of the milk marketing system combined to put dairy issues on the political agenda.

In converting public awareness into public policy, results were more mixed. NAMMAR and the NCC enjoyed only modest success in evoking House and Senate Judiciary committee investigations of the industry, but consumers enjoyed some victories on more conventional farm legislation. In 1973, when the supercooperatives sought to solidify their organizational position in federal orders, the NCC and Congress Watch raised the alarm in the press and relevant provisions were quickly deleted from the farm bill by overwhelming Senate majorities. Still, consumer action was probably less instrumental in this result than the work of Senator Philip Hart and lobbying by the NFU and NFO, bitter commercial rivals of the supercooperatives.[3]

That the consumer camp was not monolithic is revealed by the 1975 farm bill debates. CFA's Carol Foreman forged a compromise dairy provision acceptable to the labor unions, liberal farm groups, and the swollen contingent of consumer-minded legislators. This compromise helped rescue the bill on the House floor, but did not prevent a veto by President Ford, whose charge that higher price supports would harm consumers was applauded by the NCC, which opposed the Foreman compromise as mere tinkering with an archaic system. This episode also disclosed the differing pricing standards used by consumer groups: the CFA, allied with the liberal NFU and NFO, argued for a "fair return" on farmer investment as the proper basis while the NCC preferred free market economics as a better guide.[4]

Despite these qualified legislative successes, consumer groups made few inroads into the administrative process, failing to gain USDA positions of authority over milk issues. In the Nixon-Ford administration, consumer adviser Nancy Steorts' efficacy was limited by a lack of marketing expertise, exclusion from policy deliberations, and isolation from her own consumer constituency. Carter's choice of Carol Foreman as Assistant Secretary for Marketing and Consumer Services met with concerted farm opposition, relegating her to a new post without marketing order duties. Although Foreman pledged to "jaw-bone" against high food prices, one of her first official statements found "defensible" a March 1977 price support increase even the NMPF opposed as excessive. For the most part, Foreman has been too preoccupied with her own extensive domain of food programs to intervene in dairy politics.[5]

Nor has consumer experience in formal USDA proceedings been very encouraging. An NCC petition for a USDA finding of "undue price enhancement" by cooperatives operating in several federal orders was dismissed in December 1976, and a rehearing was denied. Consumer groups have seldom intervened in federal order hearings; although the NCC testified at one or two national price hearings, effective participation was first precluded by a dearth of expert witnesses and later, when the NCC developed a pool of consultants, by the cost of frequent appearances at widely separated hearing sites.[6]!

The limited consumer penetration of the USDA was offset somewhat by the activism of other executive agencies, taking their cue more from a general proconsumer atmosphere than from organized consumer groups. During the Nixon-Ford years, the Cost of Living Council under John Dunlop, the Antitrust Division of the Justice Department, the Federal Trade Commission, the Council of Economic Advisers, and other traditional consumer-oriented agencies moved to the forefront, fighting USDA efforts to increase prices, bringing major antitrust suits against the supercooperatives, and criticizing both the cooperatives and the federal regulatory system. These activities were applauded by consumer groups who in turn drew ammunition for their own warfare from the results.[7]

In the final analysis, consumer activism of the early 1970s helped sustain widespread public concern over milk questions, translated into some legislative influence, and supplied a favorable milieu for administrators in consumer-oriented agencies. Generally, however, consumer groups' ability to capitalize on public concern was circumscribed by limited finances, expertise, and lobbying manpower. More fundamentally, their efforts were reactive and episodic, suffering from particularism and poor coordination, as involved organizations responded in ad hoc fashion to single aspects of a larger and extremely complicated policy question.[8]

Whatever its limitations, for a time it seemed that consumer involvement might be permanent; indeed, by 1975 industry leaders warned that farmers were losing their grip on policy. More recent events, however, indicate considerable subgovernment resilience. The USDA has issued spirited public justifications of cooperatives and federal orders, launched internal investigations to eliminate any cooperative manipulation of price programs, and even chastised publicly "one ruthless dairy cooperative" (Secretary Butz's description of AMPI) for actions threatening to discredit the entire movement.[9]

Dairy cooperatives also geared up extensive consumer education programs and, more importantly, initiated direct contacts with some consumer groups. Although the NMPF's traditional hostility toward consumer groups persisted, several regional cooperatives including the supercooperatives invited consumers to attend board meetings, inspect members' farms and cooperative offices, and explore mutual policy concerns. These exchanges did moderate some criticism; as one consumerist observed, "it's a little harder to talk about 'milk monopolies' after walking around all day with manure on your boots." In late 1975 some cooperatives even proposed a national commission of producer, dealer, and consumer representatives to develop a consensus price policy. Although this idea died from cooperative apathy, by 1976 even the NMPF was cautiously sponsoring a public conference with the Community Nutrition Institute and cooperating with other groups on FDA ice cream standards.[10]

Whether these contacts represent a modest recognition of consumer organizations as permanent subgovernment fixtures is still in doubt. As the rapid price increases and Milk Fund of the early 1970s recede in public memory, consumer groups may find it difficult to remain active. Although several organizations still profess interest in dairy policy and a substantial reservoir of expertise on milk issues is gradually building up outside the subgovernment, obstacles to enhanced consumer influence remain. These are well illustrated by the experience of the NCC, in the forefront of consumer activities until a 1977 merger with the National Consumers League (NCL) and suspension of its "milk project." Aileen Gorman, who headed the work, cited difficulties in maintaining press, staff, and membership interest in an extremely technical issue, lack of vital foundation support, and competing priorities pressing upon limited resources as reasons for the suspension. That similar factors influence other consumer groups is suggested by their quiescence on dairy provisions of the 1977 farm bill.[11]

Ironically, there is evidence that consumerism may actually have revitalized the subgovernment. The cooperatives and their allies were jarred out of some well-worn but increasingly archaic strategies into recognition of political realities confronting farmers in an urban society. Consumer attacks also encouraged dairy and farm groups to close ranks, putting aside some long-standing fraternal feuds. Finally, by creating a real "market" for information and analysis of dairy issues among urban congressmen but not servicing it, consumer groups allowed the dairymen to fill the void, often developing access to previously hostile or indifferent legislators. Reinforced by campaign contributions, these new alliances have greatly improved the atmosphere for the cooperatives on Capital Hill and, indirectly, in executive councils. Although the dairymen will still confront obstacles in the Justice Department, the OMB, and in the congressional budgeting process, the old subgovernment is clearly far from dead.[12]

Notes

1. Randall B. Ripley and Grace A. Franklin, *Congress, Bureaucracy, and Public Policy* (Homewood, Ill.: Dorsey, 1976), pp. 76-79. The following discussion of the dairy subgovernment is based on the author's "Interorganizational Relations in Agricultural Policymaking: The Case of the National Milk Producers Federation," unpublished Ph.D. dissertation, Harvard University, 1973, chaps. 7 to 11.

2. For a critical review of these developments, see Tanya Roberts, "Review of Economic Literature on Milk Regulation," paper prepared for the Council on Wage and Price Stability by the Public Interest Economics Center, December 1975.

3. *Hoard's Dairyman* 118 (July 10, 1973):803.

4. *Wall Street Journal,* April 9, 1975, pp. 1, 27; author's interview with Aileen Gorman, former executive director of the NCC, July 19, 1977, Washington, D.C.

5. *Dairy Record* 78 (February 1977):18; *The New York Times,* April 2, 1977, p. 8.

6. *News for Dairy Co-ops,* 34 (December 30, 1976); Gorman interview.

7. See, for example, *The New York Times,* October 5, 1975, p. 7, and March 15, 1977, p. 51.

8. For similar problems affecting other consumer groups, see Jeffrey M. Berry, *Lobbying for the People* (Princeton, N.J.: Princeton University Press, 1977).

9. *American Dairy Review* 38 (April 1976):25-25.

10. *Hoard's Dairyman* 120 (January 25, 1975):82; *American Dairy Review* 37 (February 1975):26; *Dairy Record* 78 (January 1977):22.

11. Gorman interview; *Wall Street Journal,* April 8, 1977, p. 6.

12. Author's interviews with NMPF staff members, July 12, 1977, Washington, D.C. Also, Richard T. Kaplar, "The Dairy Co-ops: A Leader of the PACS," *National Journal* 8 (October 23, 1976):1516.

Part II
New Agenda Issues

Introduction to Part II

Don F. Hadwiger

Don Paarlberg (Chapter 12) saw them coming, from his subcabinet offices in the Benson, Hardin, and Butz administrations. The agricultural "establishment"—an amalgam of former, successful challengers—was challenged by advocates of a new agenda, and Paarlberg says flatly that the establishment did everything possible to resist this new agenda.

The new agenda included food stamps, environmental protection, and a number of other neglected food and agricultural issues. The new agenda advocates successfully expanded the conflict and thus increased the number of elites interested in food issues.

Paarlberg assumes that the new challengers will ultimately become part of an expanded "establishment"; indeed, this has already happened, through the selection of new agenda advocates as principal officials in the Carter administration's USDA. Several new agenda congressmen (who may also be "farm" congressmen) sit on the congressional agriculture committees; and major provisions of the many-faceted 1977 agricultural act were products of this new food politics coalition—for example, a new legislative research charter which authorizes funding increases for black colleges, research on small farms, solar energy, and energy conservation.

Joseph Hajda (Chapter 13) maintains, however, that regular farmers, farmworkers, and consumers still do not have access to the "strategically located intersections of the decision system." Hajda is referring to interdepartmental coordinating committees which have become heavily involved in food policy because of its impact in other major policy areas. Hajda cites a General Accounting Office study which found that 30 congressional committees and 26 executive departments and agencies play a part in food and agriculture decision making. And state and local governments also have stakes in agricultural policy, as emphasized by several studies presented in this book.

The nonpolitical environment adds other major variables determining agricultural policy. High world demand for American grain temporarily ended farm subsidies, conveniently releasing funds for expansion of the food stamp program. As farm subsidies now resume, and so long as food stamps endure, there is pressure upon the USDA to meet these costs by robbing funds and personnel from other missions on the new or old agendas. Market development, for example, has been somewhat neglected despite its potential contribution to farm income and the United States trade balance. And agricultural research, lacking new resources, faces the double challenge of a faltering technology within commercial agriculture and several new agenda legislative mandates.

While articles in Part II make use of the concept of old and new agendas,

they introduce a more complex reality. On some issues the old and new agendas
are reconciled. The agricultural subsystem has formed a coalition with new
agenda advocates—a new food politics coalition—to champion food issues as
against other national priorities. In Jeffrey Berry's study of food stamp policy
(Chapter 14), the respective proponents of farm programs and food programs
have realized that farmers no longer have many votes, but consumers, who do
have votes, nevertheless desire to preserve the system which has given them a
variety of low-cost and attractive foods. Indeed, the food stamp program, which
expanded agricultural markets as well as providing urban congressional support
for farm programs, could have been resisted by farm leaders only on the basis of
racism and kindred antipathies. The agricultural establishment has now accepted
a serious commitment to nutrition research and education, although the
resulting efforts to change diets may provoke sharp conflict from some
producers.

While there is also general agreement on the need for use of inorganic
chemicals in food production and processing, as well as on the need to restrain
chemical use and abuse, differing interests and technical complexities remain for
scientists, producers, and consumers to argue. Maney's chapter on the fire ant
campaign reveals a divided scientific community, yielding first to its ambition to
"eradicate" insects (an ambition nourished by leading farm politicians) and then
to the consciousness-raising tactics of environmentalists.

Mercifully, there is no chapter in this book on the issue of food additives,
with arguments—buoyed by an absence of facts—which have involved a large
public, for example, on the question whether one is more likely to get cancer by
eating bacon preservatives or by eating the mold which occurs in their absence.
There are, however, chapters on issues supposedly on the new agenda which are
not being given much public attention and are not being resolved. Bill Payne,
previously with the U.S. Civil Rights Commission, helped establish one of the
first new agenda items, and he now concludes that the USDA's responsibility for
providing jobs and services to rural blacks, Mexican-Americans, Indians, and
other minorities has been half-heartedly pursued (and was pointedly neglected
by Secretary of Agriculture Earl Butz), with the result that the USDA, by strong
implication, continues largely to ignore the rural poor (the food stamp program
being the one major exception).

Isidro Ortiz' study of California's farm worker bargaining law (Chapter 17)
reports the difficulty faced by California's government, even under a sympathetic administration, in providing for farm workers what is now a "right" under
federal law for most other workers.

Scarcity of water, land, and energy has introduced myriad pathologies into
American agriculture. A few states or local governments have tried to deal with
several of these problems that have not yet attained priority on either the new or
old federal agendas. On one issue, Esseks reports (Chapter 18) that state or local
governments have found only one promising mechanism for preserving farmland

against urban and industrial encroachment, and this has been usable only in one or two high-income megalopolitan enclaves. John Richard found (Chapter 19) that the fight for water being waged in Wyoming features a "multiplicity of agencies and groups," which results in "fragmented and complex administrative approaches to policy making often frustrating rational reallocation of water resources." The municipalities and industries are winning water from agriculture, retiring prime farmland almost as surely as if it were overlaid by concrete.

Thus the challenge to the old establishment, although broad-ranging and invigorating, has as yet failed to address several major problems which have slow fuses. One of these problems is the mining of our supposedly renewable agricultural resources, for example, agricultural practices that are causing rapid erosion of our topsoil, the crisis of salinization on irrigated land, and the draining and polluting of aquifers. Another problem is the faltering technology of pest control. Although these are matters of concern to agricultural scientists, many new agenda advocates focus their attack upon large corporations with the implicit assumption that they alone spoil agricultural resources. In fact, the loss of agricultural resources is a worldwide problem, acute in areas of small-farm primitive agriculture. In the past, attention to land and forest conservation was obtained by outspoken "insiders," such as Hugh Bennett and Gifford Pinchot, who institutionalized their concerns as administrators, respectively, of the Soil Conservation Service and the Forest Service. However, it was Rachel Carson, an outsider, who provoked the development of environmentally responsible pest control strategies.

It is in this context of addressing future concerns that one can discuss Garth Youngberg's chapter on organic farming groups whose central theme is "cooperation with nature" and whose subthemes include "nature is capital" and "soil is the source of life." Youngberg points out that, at this point, the growing organic farming movement is still nonpolitical in its orientation; spokesmen and philosophers for organic farming assume that others will ultimately be obliged to heed their example. Many agricultural scientists dispute the claims that organic farming saves the soil while yielding as much profit (if not as much per-acre productivity) as mainstream United States commercial agriculture which makes heavy use of inorganic chemicals. The major exemplar of organic farming—China—is perhaps a temporary practitioneer, attracted to the system because it fits China's present mix of available resources, emphasizing intensive human labor.

In any event, it is apparent that mainstream United States agriculture has developed severe—and over the long run perhaps intolerable—externalities. Sociologist Philip Olson (Chapter 21) explores this question: "Why is it that our vast knowledge systems have not yet been successfully directed toward control of the changes (resulting from technological expansion) in the American social and value structures through the formulation and implementation of public policy?" Olson maintains that social scientists have tended to avoid authentic policy research, which (quoting Etzioni) "deals with values and seeks to clarify goals and the relations among them as well as among goals and sets of means . . . " and is "inevitably critical." Olson cites rural sociologists Nolan and Hagen who assert that by "building issues into and drawing relevant implications from the research process, (t)he researcher is thus taking an activist's role." Political scientists may be interested in Olson's explanation as to "why social research has not been successful in affecting policy outcomes of technological advances."

In a small way, this book seeks to remedy the failure of policy research in agriculture, not only by exploring changes in the agricultural policy process but also by exploring, in the following pages, the issues which this policy process must address.

12 A New Agenda for Agriculture

Don Paarlberg

Conventional wisdom has it that when a person or a party or a political coalition has long dominated public affairs, a change should be made. My purpose is to examine this piece of folk wisdom, not just with regard to people and parties, but more especially as it relates to the farm policy agenda.

It is, of course, absolutely necessary that there be a policy agenda and that responsibility be lodged somewhere for drawing it up. There is an almost infinite number of possible public policy issues. They cannot all be addressed. The alternative to a policy agenda is chaos. The need for an agenda and an agenda committee is so great that the function is supplied formally or otherwise, in every family, in every community, and in every deliberative body.

People think the central matter of public policy is the choice between alternative solutions to issues that are on the agenda. The *real* question is whether the issues on the agenda are the relevant ones. This critical determination is in the hands of the agenda committee.

Control of the agenda is the central issue, for control of the agenda connotes the ability to keep items *off* the agenda, that most potent of all powers, the one the public seldom sees.

Who is on the agenda committee? The power elite, always. With sure instinct they move in to take over this most important role of all.

Control of the agenda is achieved by bringing together economic, political, and bureaucratic power in support of the mutual self-interest of these groups, described by John Gardner as the "unholy trinity." Control involves legitimizing and institutionalizing the power structure. The way it operates is to put on the agenda those undertakings which the members of the power elite consider desirable, the favorable outcome of which is felt to be ensured, and to keep off the agenda those issues which, if enacted, might be hurtful.

The effort is made to convince the public that the items on the policy agenda are, by definition, the issues that should be there, that they have arisen spontaneously, as an expression of the textbook functioning of representative government, and conversely, to convey the idea that those items which do not appear on the public policy agenda are absent because they are lacking in importance, relevance, or merit.

How does an issue get off the agenda, once it has been put on? One way is by solving it, of course. But some issues cannot readily be solved. When the agenda makers find this to be the case, they deescalate the issue and thereby convey the idea that since the problem no longer appears in the media, it has been solved. Thus we "solved" the problem of the farmer who produced so little for market that the government's commodity programs were of negligible help. It is simple, but subtle. The role of the agenda committee in governing these matters is always downplayed. They are a group of wire-pullers.

This can be said of the agenda makers: They want to keep the agenda closed, except for their own items. They defend the status quo.

But the agenda committee does not have perpetual power. There comes a challenge—some unmet need, some felt injustice. The instinct of the agenda makers, of course, is to keep the new issue from being discussed. How can the challengers get their subject before the people? One way is by some bizarre event, which will capture the public interest and force the opening of the agenda:

> Some years ago a group of Illinois farmers drove their tractors to Washington to get their economic problems on the agenda.

> A hatcheryman drowned his chicks, on national television, to win reconsideration of price controls.

> The poor people established Resurrection City in Washington, to put their felt needs on the public policy agenda.

Obviously, these undertakings do little, in themselves, to solve problems. That is not their intent. The purpose is to get the issues on the agenda, an absolutely necessary first step.

The agenda committee instinctively resists these challenges, not only because the subject matter is anathema to them, but, even more important, because the challenge questions the legitimacy of their agenda-making role. To preserve that role, they will fight to the last. They deny that these bizarre events are intended to get an issue on the agenda. They characterize them merely as publicity stunts, which they are. Or they treat them on their merits, which of course are few. "How will drowning chicks change anything?"

These challenges often fail. The old single-taxers of the nineteenth century never got their issue on the agenda. Nor did the land tenure reformers of the 1930s. More recently, the drive to get farm bargaining power on the agenda came close but never really succeeded. The Greenback Party of post-Civil War times got their issue on the agenda, but could not get action.

Some drives do succeed. They have to overthrow the old establishment in order to win; it is that tough.

And what happens then is that after a time a new power elite develops; a new establishment is set up. Economic interest, political power, and bureaucratic zeal are gathered around a new nucleus. The new establishment, which was born out of an effort to open up the policy agenda, organizes itself to close the agenda and fight off challenges. It retains the old rhetoric and tries to keep its original image.

Replacement of the old agenda makers is rarely total; some division of power may occur, with the new and the old eyeing each other warily. The old power elite, which has experienced a diminution of its influence, will contend that nothing has changed. Diminution of the agenda-making power is ignominious, and everything possible will be done to convince the public that things continue as they were. These efforts can be so persuasive that they fool even those who try to bring them off.

None of this is new, of course, to a group of political scientists. After these introductory remarks, I shall try to review the farm policy agenda within this context and to come to a judgment as to where we are in this cycle.

During the middle of the nineteenth century, the nation's power elite (the establishment, the agenda committee, the power structure, the agenda makers—I am using these words as if they were interchangeable) consisted largely of the industrialists, the politicians, and the professional class. The farmers, by far the most numerous group, had very little agenda-making power. They mounted an assault on virtually all phases of the establishment—the educational establishment, the government establishment, and the establishment of the business world. And they won. They got their issues on the agenda. And they won on the issues. They got the land-grant college system, over the protests of the prestigious Eastern schools. They got a Department of Agriculture, over the resistance of those who already had departmental representation. They got the Homestead Act, which set up the family farm system, despite the opposition of financial and speculative interests that preferred large-scale farming units. To this string of victories was added, over the years, the experiment stations, the Extension Service, Vocational Education, the Farm Credit Administration, and other notable services.

So what happened? Some great things, of course: increased production and a better and more economical food supply, of which the consumers were the major and unintended beneficiaries. The level of living rose, for both farm and nonfarm people. The status of farm people rose. The result was so good that the architects of the reform institutionalized it. The victors consolidated their victory.

Special interests moved in—the larger farm operators, who were in best position to take advantage of the new government services. Those farmers who *could* not or *would* not or in any case *did* not adopt the new farm practices were disadvantaged by the increased volume of production that flowed from those who adopted the changes, causing reduced prices of farm products. Political power coalesced around these new programs. The government bureaucracy quickly joined the team. The architects of the reform—fairly affluent, production-oriented, entrepreneurial, and white—became the new agenda makers, and they fashioned policies in accordance with their perceptions. Kept off the agenda were problems for which research and education were not thought to be the solution. A movement which had opened the agenda closed it on the issues that had won.

This was the state of affairs during the early 1930s, when the Great Depression struck. Obviously, here was a situation for which research and education were *not* the solution. Relief, recovery, and reform were the mood of the times, and the then agricultural establishment could provide none of these. At least, it did not. Farmers, needing help, undertook a number of desperate acts, including the threatened hanging of an Iowa judge. They got their issue on the agenda. And they got their agenda items enacted: farm price supports, production controls, emergency credit, the Soil Conservation Service, the Rural Electrification Administration, and many others. Members of the old power elite were partly replaced, partly eclipsed. A potential overthrow of the enterprise system was averted. Good farmers survived, who otherwise would have gone under.

The new power structure was quickly consolidated. It was a new group of people, but they were drawn from the same old sources. Leading the campaign were the big farm operators, who had most to gain from the commodity programs and who were sophisticated enough to know how to go after the benefits. Joining the push for power were the bureaucrats associated with the new ventures and the politicians who served (or exploited) the new cause. These people formed what was then the new power structure, and produced what was then the new farm policy agenda. The old agenda makers had to give up much of their power. Some stayed around, making the most of a reduced role.

Quickly forgotten were the people who operated the small farms, where the real low-income problem existed. Neither the agenda makers of the nineteenth century nor those of the 1930s had much interest in these poor people.

Being institutionalized, the new programs continued long after the Depression had vanished. The new agenda committee estimated how much public goodwill the farmers enjoyed. They put a price tag on this goodwill and sold it for $3 or $4 billion a year. Not surprisingly, as the asset was sold off, the remaining stock was reduced.

The old rhetoric continued, of course. The programs were said to be in behalf of the poor farm people, but in fact they were strongly regressive. Of the available money 90 percent went to half the farm operators, those on the larger farms whose incomes were already above the farm and nonfarm average.

Neglected were not only the problems of the small farmers but also the problems of hired farm workers, minority groups in rural areas, rural nonfarm people, and the consumers. But for thirty years the new power structure was successful in keeping the issues of these people off the agenda.

What had begun as a movement to open the agenda soon congealed into a policy as closed as any experienced in agriculture during the last hundred years.

Beginning in the 1960s and continuing to the present, a new challenge is being issued. This comes from the poor, the rural nonfarm people, hired farm workers, minority groups, consumers, and environmentalists. They maintain that farm policies of the past have done little for them, and in a large measure they are right. They have challenged the farm policy agenda makers and have succeeded in getting their issues on the agenda, over the bitter objections of the power elite. Not only did they get their issues on the agenda, they got many of their programs passed, as an examination of congressional action will reveal.

In some cases, this fight to get issues on the agenda is waged second-hand, not directly by the disadvantaged groups which lack the needed sophistication. Instead, the causes are led by well-motivated well-to-do people working in behalf of this new clientele. Whether it is possible for the affluent to interpret accurately the needs of these disadvantaged people, "not having walked in their moccasins," is a hard question indeed.

In any case, the new issues got on the agenda. And things happened. People who had been dealt out of the agenda-making process were now dealt in. Some needy people improved their diets. Some ecological practices improved.

The coalition that sought and achieved these changes, true to the historic pattern, is now consolidating its position. Special interests, like the purveyors of cafeteria equipment, are moving into positions of power in our school lunch programs. The better-informed, the more astute, and the politically sophisticated groups are writing up the requests for federal grants under these various programs and are getting them. The bureaucracy is digging in, supporting the programs in which it has an interest. Political power is congealing around these new programs. If this new cycle runs true to form, we can expect a new power elite to develop, to set up and control a new policy agenda, and to exclude any issue that might be a challenge to its power. We can expect the bulk of the benefits to go to those in the upper ranges of eligibility. And we can expect to hear repeated, long after its meaning is diminished, the rhetoric that was so effective in getting the new issues on the agenda.

Agenda-making power in agriculture is now shared, unequally, by three groups:

Group 1: The remnants of the research and education movement of pre-Depression days

Group 2: The New Dealers and their heirs, badly shopworn, with their price supports and production controls

Group 3: The new, zealous coalition with its food stamps, environmental controls, consumer issues, and the like

Group 3 now has the broadest based support and wins the largest appropriations. They are presently the most powerful members of the farm policy agenda committee.

What might one conclude from this review?

First, labeling a person as liberal or conservative cannot be done by determining his or her position on a given issue, because an issue changes as it goes through its life cycle. Liberalism and conservatism are attitudes of mind rather than positions on issues. The liberal looks with favor on being liberated from the forms of the past; the conservative wishes to conserve what he has come to think of as worthy. The conservative worships a dead liberal; a liberal wants to overthrow what an earlier liberal established.

The research and education movement, launched by the Republicans, was liberal when it started and turned conservative. The commodity programs, started by the Democrats, began as a liberal movement and became conservative. The new farm policy agenda, like every new movement, has liberal connotations. But if it runs true to form, it will harden into a conservative mold.

Second, one can learn to beware of the rhetoric that surrounds agenda making, knowing that the rhetoric tends to be repeated long after the objective facts have changed.

Third, it can be established as a principle that when government undertakes to assist some special group, the chief beneficiaries will turn out to be those in the upper ranges of eligibility. Leadership of the program tends to be captured by those who are more aware, more aggressive, and more politically sophisticated. These are also the ones who are more affluent.

Finally, one is led to concur (at least I do) with the folk wisdom that when a person or a party or a political coalition has long dominated public affairs, a change should be made. How frequently do we need a change? We have had three changes in a little more than 100 years. A liberal would think this too few. A conservative would think it too many. Perhaps one can characterize his own position as liberal, conservative, or moderate based on whether he thinks three fundamental changes in a century are too few or too many . . . or, as with Goldilocks in the story of the three bears, "just right!"

13 Inside-Access Model for Representation of New Groups in Agricultural Policy Making

Joseph Hajda

Seasoned political strategists know that a vital time to influence American public policy is in the formative stage in the executive branch of government and that the two most important questions are, Who is making the decisions and what interests are being served? A major problem, then, is to discover how and why specific decisions are made.

A place to influence the formative stage of policy making is at the highest level—in the decisive traffic intersections of the message flows and communication streams of government. These strategically located intersections of the decision system are controlled by key government officials and serviced by specialists from the upper and middle levels of bureaucracy.

By "public policy" I mean the sum and substance of political authorities' views, objectives, decisions, actions, and methods selected in a political entity, indicating the main trends of development and the conditions, means, and methods of attaining the chief aims. Seen as a stream of all such public activities or outputs that are produced by the political authorities, public policy is made by government agencies, along with those quasi-government and nongovernment agencies whose public actions are authoritative, binding, and intentional.[1]

Public "agenda building" refers to the process through which demands of various classes of groups are translated into issues that vie for the attention of decision makers and the public. We think of formal public agenda as the agenda of decision makers in a political entity, while the informal public agenda refers to issues in the domain of public discussion but not part of the formal agenda.[2]

Looking at the various components of government structure, we can distinguish policy making among the highest, middle, and lower levels of government. An issue may potentially appear on many agendas of the various levels. An issue may be on the formal agenda of one, two, or all three branches of national government.

While recognizing the constraints on what can be feasibly put on the Presidential agenda, we should not minimize the opportunities for action at that level. The President acts with the support and cooperation of key individuals and groups in the executive office, the federal bureaucracy, Congress, and the private establishment—constituted by the more important businesses, banks, law firms, foundations, and media.[3] The way major issues are treated at the highest level is crucial. Key food and agricultural policy questions call for decisions at the highest level, decisions that fall into the category of vital policy questions.

Inside Access Model

Three basic models help in understanding the way the different groups participate in policy formation.[4]

(1) The outside initiative model describes classes of groups with minimal prior access to decision makers. The model accounts for the process through which issues arise in nongovernment groups and are expanded to reach the nonformal public agenda and (perhaps) the formal agenda.

(2) The inside-access model refers to direct representation of classes of groups in policy-making structures, or to groups' close contact with decision makers. The model describes issues that are placed on the formal public agenda and whose supporters do not try to expand them to the nonformal public agenda.

(3) The mobilization model describes how decision makers attempt to obtain public support for their perception of public issues. The model accounts for the ways decision makers implement a policy by expanding an issue from the formal to the nonformal public agenda.

The focus here is on the inside-access model. Persons articulating a group's policy demands generally feel that one has to cultivate access to individuals located at strategic intersections, and that one must create a situation favorable to maintaining control over an issue—hence the need for making "private decisions within the government."[5]

When the inside-access pattern operates, national policy making becomes the art and science of creating and maintaining domestic and international order, not by way of open and responsible settlements, but by means of power or the balancing of material interests among the politically powerful groups.

Inside Access in Recent Years

A look at vital decisions pertaining to food and agriculture in recent years reveals that many decisions emerged from choices specified by those with inside access. Vital decisions were made in relatively private settings; in some cases the attentive public was only dimly aware that these issues were on the formal public agenda, and the mass public was only dimly aware that these issues were on the formal public agenda, and the mass public was totally unaware of their existence. Groups characterized by concentrations of wealth and status succeeded in maintaining an order conducive to balancing material interests among themselves. When attempts were made to establish various coordinating mechanisms for the fragmented food policy apparatus, no effort was made to include representatives of working farmers, farm workers, and consumers. It would be difficult to argue that their interests were served well by the policy outputs.

Because it was recognized that food and agricultural policy making in the 1970s became a complex affair that affected productivity, efficiency, human welfare, national security, foreign policy, and domestic tranquility, several attempts were made to provide for a high-level mechanism for policy coordination. Briefly the relevant institutional structures were the following.

(1) The Cost of Living Council was assigned the responsibility in 1973-1974 for reviewing actions affecting food supplies and prices with the view of progressively reorienting agricultural policy to the needs of the 1970s. Chaired by the Secretary of the Treasury and composed of eight members (including four cabinet officers, but not the Secretary of Agriculture), the Council was terminated in June 1974. The substructure of the Council provided from January 1973 to May 1974 for a food industry advisory committee, composed of 16 representatives of the food industry.[6]

(2) From September 1974 to January 1977, the executive committee of the Economic Policy Board was the central clearinghouse for Presidential policy on all economic and financial matters, including key food and agricultural issues. Composed of nine members, four of whom were cabinet officers (Secretaries of the Treasury, State, Labor, and Commerce, but not the Secretary of Agriculture), this top elite committee also was chaired by the Secretary of the Treasury.[7]

(3) From November 1974 to March 1976, the International Food Review Group was given the task of coordinating followup to the World Food Conference. It was chaired by the Secretary of State, with the Secretary of Agriculture as vice chairman, and was assisted by a working group at the assistant secretary level.

(4) From September 1974 to March 1976, the Food Committee under the National Security Council and the Economic Policy Board provided a forum for food policy review. Composed of ten members, five of whom were cabinet officers (including the Secretary of Agriculture), the committee played an important role during the U.S.-U.S.S.R. grain negotiations in formulating instructions to the United States negotiators. Secretaries of State and Treasury served as cochairmen of the ten-member committee. Staff-level assistance was supplied by the Food Deputies Group of the Economic Policy Board, which had a slightly different composition and was chaired by a member of the Council of Economic Advisors.[8]

(5) From March 1976 to January 1977, the Agricultural Policy Committee was assigned the central role in developing and directing food policies.[9] Replacing the International Food Review Group and the Food Committee, the Agricultural Policy Committee was composed of eleven members, four of whom were cabinet officers (Secretaries of Agriculture, State, Commerce, and the

Treasury), and seven represented agencies in the executive office of the President. Chaired by the Secretary of Agriculture, the committee was formed to consolidate agricultural policy making into one group reporting directly to the President and advising him on formulating, coordinating, and carrying out all agricultural policy—both domestic and international.[10] The Food Deputies Group became the Agricultural Policy Working Group (APWG). Chaired by an assistant secretary of agriculture, the APWG provided staff assistance to the Agricultural Policy Committee by monitoring agricultural developments and preparing status reports and other materials on selected policy issues.[11]

The biographical and journalistic data pertaining to the members of the relevant institutional structures show that the key decision makers were drawn disproportionately from groups at the top of the socioeconomic hierarchy; that they worked closely with their peers in the private establishment; that they maintained key affiliations in upper-status segments of the society; and that they expected to move into corporate jobs.[12] Accustomed over the years to working closely with representatives of the most powerful economic segments of the private establishment for common objectives, the high-level policy makers served those segments well.[13] Observable policy outputs of recent years provide ample evidence about which private establishment values were fostered, in what form, for whom, and in what amounts.

While policy outputs are observable, policy inputs at the highest level must be inferred, except for partial glimpses revealing particular inputs into the policy process. The situation is complicated by the fact that in recent years the food and agricultural concerns were dispersed within the national government among scores of political entities. A study by the staff of the General Accounting Office[14] found that the 1976 structure for making decisions within the national government included no less than 30 congressional committees and 26 executive departments and agencies sharing responsibility for setting various aspects of food and agricultural policy. The study identified seven congressional committees—four in the Senate and three in the House—and 17 departments and agencies sharing major policy-making responsibility. Several of these political entities were responsible for policy issues other than food and agriculture. In addition, numerous suborganizations, committees, and commissions were responsible for various elements of policy input.

Agendas and minutes of the coordinating mechanisms can illuminate the nature of the decision process at the highest level and can provide partial glimpses of particular policy inputs. I examined agendas and minutes of the International Food Review Group; the Food Committee; the Food Deputies Group; the Agricultural Policy Committee; and the Agricultural Policy Working Group. My efforts met with partial success. First, I received a statement from the State Department listing the agendas of the International Food Review Group. But I was informed that the State Department records "do not reveal any formal meetings or agenda of the ... food committee."[15] No mention was made of the Food Deputies Group. Second, I received a statement from the Department of Agriculture listing the agendas of the Agricultural Policy Working Group and the minutes of its four meetings. But I was informed that the Agricultural Policy Committee held only two meetings and that no minutes of these meetings were kept.[16] No mention was made of the agendas.

The International Food Review Group held 18 meetings between November 22, 1974, and July 22, 1975, including 15 by its working group and 3 by its principals.[17]

The Agricultural Policy Working Group held 10 meetings between April 22, 1976, and December 21, 1976. I wish to point out that eight of the ten meetings were held between April 22 and October 13—that is, before the Presidential election.[18]

After scrutinizing the agenda items for all 28 meetings held by the two groups and the minutes of the four meetings held by the Agricultural Policy Working Group (held between April 22 and August 11), I submitted a list of major issues *not* included on their formal agendas: the various food and nutrition programs; agriculture and ecological questions; rural poverty; rural development; land-use questions; agriculture and civil rights of nonwhite males and women; world hunger and malnutrition; and farm labor organizing. The record shows that grain and soybean export issues, meat import policy, food price outlook, and peanut policy were listed on the agenda of at least six meetings of the Agricultural Policy Working Group.

The formal agendas plainly reflected the viewpoint that issues affecting the interests of dominant groups should be the concern of key decision makers.

Aside from excluding less privileged groups, the orientation[19] that pervaded the decision structure was decisive in another way. None of the attempts to establish coordinating mechanisms was designed to plant the seeds for democratic, indicative planning in the United States. In a time of rapid change, no national institution proved capable of a systematic approach to food and agricultural affairs, an incapacity most conspicuous in failure to institutionalize planning such as the national security agencies have long since achieved.

Needed: New Inside-Access Patterns

The voices of working farmers, farm workers, and consumers have enlarged and sharpened the public debate on food and agricultural issues in recent years. But because they had less developed working contacts with top decision makers, they found it difficult to move issues of vital importance to them onto the formal agenda (although this does not mean that no policies were initiated to assist the economically less powerful segments of the society).[20]

What can be done to change the way that different classes of groups might participate in formal public agenda setting at the highest levels within the framework of a high-level coordinating mechanism that could devise medium-term and long-run viable strategies? I suggest the establishment of a National Food and Agricultural Council which would have the central role in developing and directing public policies—both domestic and international. The council would report directly to the President and would advise him on all central domestic and international issues of food and agricultural policies.

Representatives of working farmers, farm workers, and consumers should have seats on the council[21] along with government officials from appropriate executive branch departments and agencies, and share responsibility for developing public policy recommendations pertaining to food and agriculture.[22]

The council would not supplant existing agencies. It would not suppress the alternative suggestions and interests of other agencies and organizations; nor would it supplant the institutional structures for informal agenda setting. It would provide opportunity for government officials and representatives of the people most directly concerned with food and agricultural affairs to have a voice in formal public agenda building at the highest level. It would ensure that alternative policy proposals reach the top of the decision-making system instead of being suppressed or merged in the search for consensus.[23]

The council could provide a mechanism that would give the United States an alternative to the fragmented approach to world food problems in recent years. By exposing key policy makers to a broad range of viewpoints, the council could play a vital role in examining, analyzing, appraising, and recommending policies relative to managing national agricultural resources. The council would need a mandate to make significant contributions to indicative, economic planning and social planning—euphemistically called by some persons "balanced national growth and development."

Under indicative planning, the council would refrain from mandatory statements but would attempt systematically to coordinate public actions so that they could contribute as efficiently as practicable to achieving democratically determined national goals.[24]

The two most important steps in planning are forecasting and determining the economic and social goals to be sought. Neither goal-setting nor forecasting functions would require any radical change in the government's role. Both functions are performed on an extensive scale. But when goals are set and forecasts made without planning, there is often a danger that the pursuit of one goal will frustrate the attainment of others and that there will be little effort to achieve consistency for the totality of all forecasts.[25] The council would examine proposed goals and forecasts, for consistency and coherence, and would consider the totality of the goals and forecasts in relation to the availability of resources. Various classes of groups represented on the council would be empowered to offer alternative plan options.

In addition, representatives of working farmers, farm workers, and consumers would be instructed to prevent secrecy of information or decision making.[26]

Testing the Quality of Political Life

Establishing good government from reflection and choice is essential for the benefit not only of working farmers, farm workers, and consumers, but also of the whole society in the United States and in friendly lands. Assuming a shared concern of American people with the people in other lands for a greater measure of human dignity, we need to translate the concern into measures aimed at achieving a meaningful degree of participation by all classes in the shaping of the basic values—such as well-being and power.

Seen in this context, the issue of greatly broadened representation in food and agricultural policy making at the highest level of government is, in essence, a test of the political worth of the United States as a democratic polity among various types of polities. Surely, it is a fair test of the quality of our national political life.

Notes

1. Mark V. Nadel, "The Hidden Dimension of Public Policy: Private Governments and the Policy-Making Process," *Journal of Politics,* February 1975, p. 2.

2. Roger Cobb, Jennie-Keith Ross, and Marc Howard Ross, "Agenda Building as a Comparative Political Process," *American Political Science Review,* Spring 1976, pp. 126-127.

3. Samuel P. Huntington, "The United States," in Michael Crozier, S.P. Huntington, and Joji Watanuki, *The Crisis of Democracy* (New York: New York University Press, 1975), p. 92.

4. Cobb, Ross, and Ross, "Agenda Building," pp. 127-128.

5. Ibid., pp. 135-136.

6. When we refer to more important businesses, we mean the galaxy of a few very large corporations constantly expanding their share of total assets. Both food manufacturing and food retailing are highly concentrated, and concentration is on the rise.

7. Donald Smith, "Elite Committee Forms Economic Policy," *Congressional Quarterly Weekly Report,* February 28, 1976, pp. 475-477.

8. "Formulation of Foreign Agricultural Policy," Department of State News Release, January 22, 1976, p. 2.

9. "Test of Remarks by the President to Be Delivered at a Farm Forum, Springfield, Illinois," White House News Release, March 5, 1976, p. 3.

10. "Fact Sheet on Agricultural Policy-making Reorganization," White House News Release, March 5, 1976, pp. 1-2.

11. The Food Deputies Group that became the Agricultural Policy Working Group included representatives of the Departments of Agriculture, Treasury, State, and Commerce, Office of Management and Budget, Council of Economic

Advisors, Council on International Economic Policy, Domestic Council, National Security Council, Special Representative for Trade Negotiations, and Council on Wage and Price Stability.

12. Similar findings can be found in a much broader study of Robert D. Putnam, *The Comparative Study of Political Elites* (Englewood Cliffs, N.J.: Prentice-Hall, Inc., 1976).

13. For an example pertaining to the Department of Agriculture, see Don Hadwiger, "The Old, the New, and the Emerging United States Department of Agriculture," *Public Administration Review,* March/April 1976, pp. 155-165. Hadwiger refers to "an enduring national coalition of commercial producers which imposed its economic interests upon practically every activity of the USDA" (p. 157).

14. *Food and Agriculture Issues for Planning,* April 22, 1977.

15. According to Gerard D. Forcier of the Bureau of Public Affairs, July 21, 1977, letter.

16. According to Assistant Secretary of Agriculture Dale E. Hathaway, May 2, 1977, letter.

17. "Meetings of the International Food Review Group," Department of State document.

18. "Agricultural Policy Working Group: Dates and Agenda for Meetings," Department of Agriculture document.

19. By orientation I mean that a class of groups is approaching a set of goals.

20. The notion of being excluded was especially voiced by representatives of wheat farmers. President of Great Plains Wheat, Inc., Kenneth Kendrick in a letter to President Ford, March 8, 1976, complained that no provision was made for "farmer input into deliberations" by the Agricultural Policy Committee and stated that "farmers should have a definite voice in determining the disposition of their production."

21. Representatives of working farmers, farm workers, and consumers would be appointed by the President from lists of nominees submitted by the major organizations of each of the groups they would represent on the council. The appointments would be subject to the advice and consent of the Senate.

22. Peter H. Schuck, "Public Interest Groups and the Policy Process," *Public Administration Review*, March/April 1977, pp. 132-140, makes the case for inside access of various citizen groups in policy making on the grounds of administrative efficacy, social equity, and public confidence.

23. This pattern of policy making and group interaction can be described as "public pluralism" as contrasted with such varieties of pluralism as laissez-faire and corporate pluralism. See William Kelso, "Public Pluralism: A New Defense of an Old Doctrine," *Social Science,* Winter 1977, pp. 16-30.

24. "Additional Views of Commissioner Weinberg on Indicative Planning" (Published by the National Commission on Supplies and Shortages, December 1976) is a concise statement explaining how indicative planning would work.

25. "Additional Views of Commissioner Weinberg," p. 2.

26. The need to drastically circumscribe the definition of government secrecy has been advocated by a variety of experts. For an example of a former government official see Charles Yost, *The Conduct and Misconduct of Foreign Affairs* (New York: Random House, 1972), pp. 173-175.

14 Food Stamps: The Recurring Issues

Jeffrey M. Berry

On the day after his inauguration in 1961, President John F. Kennedy began to make good on his promise to do something about the problem of hunger in America. His first executive order instructed Secretary of Agriculture Orville Freeman to expand the quantity and variety of food available to the needy through the commodity distribution program. Kennedy had spoken eloquently during his campaign of the want and deprivation he had seen during his travels around the country. He knew, however, that the commodity distribution program had been an ineffective means of alleviating hunger. Within a few weeks another directive was sent to the Agriculture Department, this time requesting pilot studies of a food stamp program.

Food stamps were not a new idea; they had been used during the Depression between 1939 and 1943. Although World War II put an end to the program, the idea was kept alive in Congress by Senator George Aiken and, later, Representative Leonor Sullivan.[1] The distinguishing feature of the food stamp plan was that unlike other forms of welfare, it would be a self-help program. When it passed the Congress in 1964, it was conceived of as a method by which government helped people help themselves. The law required that participants devote a portion of their income for the purchase of their stamps. In return for their money, they would receive an equivalent amount of stamps plus a "bonus" amount of free stamps that would enable the user to increase his or her food purchases.

From its humble beginnings as eight pilot projects in 1961, the food stamp program has grown to a point where it is now used throughout the United States at a cost to the federal government of roughly $5.5 billion a year. The nature of the program began to change early in its life to become in many ways exactly what it was not supposed to be. Food stamps were specifically intended to provide supplementary food purchases, not general income relief. Food stamps were born with the idea that hunger and malnutrition were problems that could be treated separately from poverty itself. Nevertheless, because of the substitution of bonus stamps for cash dollars that recipients would otherwise spend on food, the program is one of income support as well as food supplementation. It is the welfare program it was designed not to be.

The disagreement and confusion over the goals and objectives of the

This chapter is part of a larger research project on the evolution of the food stamp program sponsored by a grant from the Ford Foundation. The views expressed here are author's alone. I would like to thank Deborah Manning for her assistance.

151

program have had significant implications for food stamp policy making. The same issues concerning the proper role of food stamps have arisen over and over since the pilot projects were initiated in 1961. Three basic, recurring questions have been central to the ongoing debate over the food stamp program. First, how effective has the program been in reaching its target population? Second, what should be the proper ratio of payments to benefits? In other words, to what extent are participants responsible for paying for the stamps they are to receive? Third, what is the legitimate scope of the program? What are the boundaries of the target population?

The purpose here is to examine these issues as they have developed over time. Incremental changes have brought about a program dramatically different from that of the Kennedy years. Beyond reforming the food stamp program, these changes have significantly affected our entire welfare system.

Food Stamps: A Multidimensional Program

In the early years, little serious thinking was done on how food stamps fit into the larger welfare system. Originally, the food stamp program was intended both to feed hungry people and to expand consumer demand for surplus farm commodities. Even though the farm surpluses soon began to disappear, the early conception of food stamps as a farm and feeding program tended to isolate it in people's minds as something independent of other welfare programs. Yet it was the inadequacies of existing income support programs that made food stamps necessary in the first place.[2]

The importance of food stamps within the welfare system became more apparent during the struggle over the Nixon administration's Family Assistance Plan. By 1971 over 10 million Americans were receiving food stamps in peak months, and the Congress and the administration had liberalized benefits to make the program significantly more attractive. In political terms, this made it more difficult to produce an acceptable income maintenance system. Liberals wanted a program with benefits generous enough that they would at least match what recipients could get from a combination of Aid to Families with Dependent Children (AFDC) and food stamps. Conservatives resisted a level of benefits that would truly accomplish this. Compromise failed, and the Family Assistance Plan died.[3] George McGovern proposed a more generous $1000 per person guaranteed annual income during the 1972 campaign, but it was treated with popular scorn and surely contributed to his defeat.

The sentiment of the Carter administration is to replace food stamps and other basic welfare programs with their own proposed negative income tax. It should be noted that the food stamp program already approximates the characteristics of a negative income tax system in many ways. Benefits are paid out according to family size on a sliding scale based on available income.

Eligibility is open to the working poor as well as to those unable to work. There is a liberal benefit reduction or "tax" rate of 30 percent so that the incentive to work is maintained. The critical difference, of course, is that food stamp payments are in coupons rather than cash. Individuals cannot live on food stamps alone, but the program does help to fill the gaps of our welfare system. The full range of benefits and functions of the food stamp program can best be understood through brief descriptions.

(1) Food stamp payments have become an *income transfer* of substantial proportions. A recent study by the Congressional Budget Office estimates that on the average only 57 percent of the food stamp bonus is spent on extra food. The remaining 43 percent is substituted for cash that would have been spent for food in the absence of the stamps.[4]

(2) Food stamps are a form of *welfare supplementation.* Roughly two-thirds of all food stamp households receive income from AFDC, SSI (Supplemental Security Income), or state general assistance.[5]

(3) Food stamps are a means of *welfare equalization.* Unlike food stamps, which use national standards of eligibility and payments, AFDC standards are set by each individual state. Wide disparities exist between the states because of differing attitudes toward welfare and available resources. The use of the sliding scale, however, allows AFDC food stamp recipients in low-paying states to pay less for their stamps. Food stamps do not eliminate the inequities in AFDC, but can reduce them by $50 or more in the most extreme cases.

(4) Food stamps can be used as *supplemental social insurance.* Those relying on the two primary social insurance programs, social security and unemployment compensation, frequently discover that the cash allowances are inadequate. Food stamps can be particularly useful to those on unemployment with large families since coupon allotments are based to a greater degree on family size than is unemployment compensation. The importance of food stamps to older Americans is demonstrated by the fact that one out of five food stamp households receives income from social security.

(5) Food stamps are occasionally utilized by the government to provide *disaster relief.* Under a provision of the law, the Secretary of Agriculture can provide free food stamps to victims of disasters regardless of their prior eligibility status. They are likely to be used as compensation for loss of income resulting from some type of disaster or emergency. During the terrible winter of 1977, for example, free food stamps were distributed in Buffalo, New York, after numerous blizzards had shut down the city's economic life.

(6) Finally, while the emphasis here has been on the other benefits and functions of food stamps, it should not be forgotten that it is a *supplemental feeding program.* All coupons must be spent on food. The total amount of bonus coupons for fiscal year 1976 was close to $5.3 billion, of which roughly $3 billion can be considered additional food demand created by the program. Although research has shown that food stamps do not significantly improve

recipients' diets in terms of nutritional quality, those in the program do at least purchase more food.[6] The expanded demand for food that results from the program does, of course, benefit grocers and, to a marginal degree, farmers.

Although the food stamp program was not developed in direct coordination with other welfare programs, its evolution over time has constituted what Richard Nathan describes as "unintended welfare reform."[7] Still, questions remain about the food stamp program itself. For purposes of analysis these interrelated issues will be addressed separately.

Program Participation

Concerns about whether the program reached potential participants arose out of the very first pilot projects.[8] After five months' experience, participation in the food stamp program was less than half of what it had been for commodity distribution. The drop in enrollment was particularly pronounced in Detroit, the only large city among the first eight projects. Although they acknowledged that the purchase price was a disincentive to some, program administrators did not regard the price structure as a major impediment to participation. The purchase price was designed to represent a family's "normal" expenditures, so there seemed to be no reason not to charge people for what they would spend on food anyway.[9]

As the program expanded into more pilot areas, surprisingly low rates of participation were again evidenced in the large urban areas, this time St. Louis and Cleveland. In St. Louis, the home district of Congresswoman Leonor Sullivan, who was the most important sponsor of food stamps, participation dropped to a fraction of what it had been under the commodity program. The reason for low participation in Cleveland and St. Louis was obvious to welfare workers in both cities. A combination of high rents and low welfare payments left many of the poor in these two cities without the amount necessary to pay for their stamps. The solution was an "excess shelter deduction" from income (and purchase price) for families who spent above 30 percent of the family's total income for rent and utilities.

The shelter deduction was a critical development in the program because it marked a change in the definition of income. *Disposable* income—what was left over after essential expenses other than food—became an important policy guide.[10]

The purchase price began to come under attack in 1967 with the emergence of hunger as a major political issue. Well-publicized findings by doctors of acute malnutrition in rural areas of the South, and Robert Kennedy's trip to Mississippi to study hunger first-hand, drew national attention to the failure of government feeding programs to reach many of the truly needy. Later the CBS television documentary "Hunger in America,"[11] the Citizens' Board of Inquiry's

Hunger, U.S.A.,[12] and Nick Kotz's book *Let Them Eat Promises*[13] all generated more criticism of the food stamp and commodity distribution programs.

The Department of Agriculture initially resisted the pressures from activists and liberal congressmen who wanted a reduction or elimination of the purchase price so that more poor people could participate. The self-help aspect of the program, embodied in the purchase price, was still favored by conservatives on the agriculture committees in Congress and by some officials in the Agriculture Department. The compromise that resulted was that the purchase price was reduced to the nominal sum of 50¢ per person for those at the lowest monthly income level (then $0 to $20). But liberals who wanted wholesale reform pressed their demands for increased coupon allotments; extension of feeding programs into counties that had neither food stamps or commodities; an effective "outreach" effort to find and educate nonparticipants about the benefits of food stamps; and total elimination of the purchase price for the poorest recipients.

The controversy over the food stamp program was at its peak when Richard Nixon came into office in 1969. Sensitive to the hunger issue, the new Secretary of Agriculture Clifford Hardin moved within his first month in office to initiate two pilot studies of a zero purchase price. By May the administration proposed legislation that would set a zero purchase price for those at the lowest income level. A year and a half later Congress acted to pass an amended food stamp law that gave the poorest of the poor free stamps. A family of four became eligible for a zero purchase price if its income was less than $30 a month.

Between 1970 and 1971 national participation jumped from a monthly average of 4.3 to 9.4 million individuals. This increase was primarily brought about by program expansion into new areas and more generous coupon allotment schedules. Hardin's successor, Earl Butz, felt that the program's huge costs reduced money available for real agricultural programs and therefore budgeted no money for outreach until obliged to do so as a result of a 1974 court decision.[14]

The latest stage in the struggle over program participation has been the effort to make stamps free for all participants. Liberals mounted a major attempt to eliminate the purchase price in 1975, but conservatives in both houses beat back this proposal. After a congressional supporter of this proposal, Bob Bergland, became Secretary of Agriculture, the purchase requirement was removed in the omnibus farm bill of 1977.[15]

One reason that the argument over whether to adopt policies to increase participation has gone on so long is because there has never been any agreement as to what is an "adequate" participation rate.[16] There is no way of knowing what eliminating the purchase price will do to the participation rate. Since removing the purchase price was the last step in making food stamps an in-kind negative income tax, conservatives view this reform as the forerunner of a comprehensive guaranteed annual income. Indeed, the next phase in the attempt to reform the program is to give people full discretion over how they spend their income subsidy, through a "cashing out" of food stamps as envisioned by President Carter's welfare reform plan.

The Payment-Benefit Ratio

The food stamp purchase price is relevant also to the entire payment-benefit structure. The ratio between the amount paid in (or deducted) and the value of the stamps received is a factor in determining the net welfare benefit, whether the payment is in coupons or in cash.

Initially the payment-benefit ratio was based on research in the area of food consumption. Using survey data, economists in the Department of Agriculture devised a ratio that took into account what people spent and ate. Thus, participants at the lower end of the income scale were not given the full complement of stamps because it was thought that this would distort rational economic behavior. For the very poorest, even the amount of coupons necessary for the department's minimally nutritious economy (later "thrifty") food plan was far in excess of their usual consumption. If the poor were given "too many" stamps, there was the danger they might blackmarket some of them. Also a primary goal of the payment-benefit ratio design was to prevent the program from supplementing income through a substitution of coupons for cash that would otherwise be spent for food.

As the program began to come under more and more scrutiny in the late 1960s, the inequity in the allotments became a subject of sharp criticism. Although the poorer family paid a much smaller percentage of their income for their stamps,[17] their coupon allotment was still short of the amount needed to purchase USDA's lowest cost, economy diet. In December 1969, Secretary Hardin announced that the department was equalizing allotments at the level of the economy food plan. Some liberals have continued to argue that the allotments are insufficient and ought to be raised across the board.[18]

In recent years, most of the discussion of the payment-benefit ratio has revolved around the percentage of income recipients should pay, not how much they receive in return. The Ford administration initiated two major efforts to require that most recipients pay the full amount by law, 30 percent of (net) income. The moves by the Ford administration came within a vastly different political context than that of Nixon Presidency. Hunger and malnutrition were no longer the burning issues they had been when Nixon took office. When Gerald Ford became President, the food stamp program was fully national, with relatively generous benefits. Moreover, a new concern regarding the size and the cost of the program had begun to emerge. Adverse stories in the press citing high numbers of errors in the certification process and the presence of people in the program with annual incomes well above the poverty line fueled public discontent.

Both endeavors by Ford to raise the purchase price to 30 percent through administrative regulation ultimately failed. The first Ford effort to raise the purchase price, as part of a series of governmentwide budget cuts announced by the administration in 1974, was frustrated by a congressional enactment.[19] The second effort, justified as a curb on the growth and misuse of an unpopular social program and strengthening Ford's image as a conservative for his battle with Ronald Reagan in the 1976 Presidential primaries,[20] was blocked by a successful law suit.[21]

Throughout the life of the program, the payment-benefit ratio has been the target of liberal and conservative reformers. In the past, liberals would point out that it is unfair to make food stamp participants pay 30 percent of their income for food while the average American pays much less. Conservatives would respond that when total cash income is considered, food stamp recipients pay 18 percent for their food, only slightly above the national average of 17 percent.[22] With the elimination of the requirement for a cash purchase price in the 1977 law, the deduction "price" for the stamps has been set at 30 percent of income. Liberals were more than willing to let the standard be set at 30 percent as part of the tradeoff for a zero purchase price. As always, beneath the theoretical justifications, the selection of the ratio was really an arbitrary choice of giving people a little more or little less money.

Program Scope

Defining who is a poor or needy person is a problem that all welfare programs face. For a program where income is the primary eligibility factor, a line must be drawn somewhere which says, in effect, that anyone earning $1 more than the given figure is no longer poor. To make this type of decision more rational, the government has developed indices to measure the cost of certain goods over time. The cost of the amount of goods deemed to be minimally adequate constitutes a poverty line. The official government or Office of Management and Budget (OMB) poverty line was developed by Mollie Orshansky of the Department of Health, Education, and Welfare in 1964. In 1971 the food stamp program began to use its own poverty index based exclusively on the cost of food. Both the OMB poverty line and the food stamp line were initially constructed with formulas based on USDA's economy food plan.

Prior to 1971, the states set their own eligibility standards in concert with state standards for federally aided public assistance programs. As a consequence, the income eligibility line varied widely from state to state. Amendments to the food stamp law in 1970 directed the Secretary of Agriculture to set national standards, with income eligibility still to be determined by net income after allowable deductions were taken out. These deductions were for significant medical costs, mandatory payroll deductions, unusual disaster expenses, child care, and the hardship shelter allowance. Liberal activists and congressmen were able to persuade program administrators to adopt two more deductions before the regulations were finalized: educational costs (tuition and fees) and a work incentive that disregarded the first 10 percent (up to $30) of income derived from work or a training program.[23]

Despite their importance in extending the scope of the program, the deductions were not a major issue during this time. Excessive program participation was not viewed as a potential problem.

In 1974 conservatives began to voice increasing criticism of the program, the central issue being the rising cost and participation. It was the deteriorating economy, of course, that stimulated the dramatic increase in participation from a monthly average of 12.9 million in 1974 to 18.5 million in 1976. However, it was frequently claimed that the system of deductions was allowing large numbers of high-income families to qualify for stamps.

Although subsequent research has shown the number of high-income recipients to be exaggerated, the very presence of a small number of families in the $7000-$9000 income range angered a good many congressmen.[24] It was also assumed that higher-income families were making unusually large deductions.[25] The solution to this and the terrible problem of computational errors by case workers was a standard deduction that would replace the set of itemized deductions. The version of the standard deduction enacted into law in 1977 was a compromise between conservatives and liberals. Every family, no matter what their legitimate deductions under the old system, will now receive a flat deduction of $60 per month. In addition, there are separate shelter, child care, and work expense deductions. The shelter and child care deductions can be utilized up to a combined total of $75 beyond the standard deduction. The work expense allowance is limited to 20 percent of gross earned income. The shelter deduction, which is permitted when shelter costs exceed 50 percent of monthly net income, was especially important to Northern urban liberals who wanted some provision made for the higher housing and heating costs of the Northeast.

The standard deduction plus the limits on the three itemized deductions finally puts a cap, albeit a liberal one, on the amount that can be subtracted from gross income when benefits are determined. The other part of establishing a stricter basis of eligibility was redefining the food stamp poverty line. As one of the concessions for the elimination of the purchase price in 1977, the OMB line was designated to replace the higher food stamp poverty line, which will pare approximately 1.1 million people off the program. While these higher-income people are disqualified, the elimination of the purchase price will bring more poorer families into the program. Taking the two changes together, net participation is likely to increase.

The disagreement over where the cap on deductions should be placed, the validity of different poverty lines, and the general method of determining income are part of the larger question that is yet to be answered. Who is a poor person? There is still no consensus, no all-purpose operational definition that is satisfactory. The OMB method is not a logically superior means of defining who is poor; it is simply a cheaper one.

A related issue is the degree to which the program should encompass the working poor. Defining the working poor is probably even more difficult than defining those who are just plain poor. Through the use of various deductions and a liberal marginal tax rate, the food stamp program has preserved a strong work incentive. Those who receive income from working, however, are often found in the higher range of the income scale; consequently, the change in the eligibility standard will strike hardest at the working poor. Everyone wants to help the working poor, but no one agrees on where to draw the line. One person's "working poor" is another person's high-income recipient.

Conclusion

The food stamp program has undergone enormous changes in both scope and purpose since it was begun during the Kennedy administration in 1961. The relationship of food stamps to our general system of welfare has also changed remarkably during this period. When it was first proposed, the food stamp program profited greatly from being conceptualized as something separate and distinguishable from "welfare." As a feeding program, food stamps was a policy people could easily back. In 1961 it was a realistic route to providing more aid and greater coverage than trying to reform cash assistance.

In looking back over the history of food stamps, it is clear that the program has served as a surrogate for broader-scale reform. Surely some type of reform of basic cash allowances would have been instituted had the food stamp program never been created. But how much "reform" and how soon it would have come is difficult to say. Nevertheless, while a seemingly endless debate over comprehensive welfare reform has dragged on in Washington, changes in the food stamp program have brought about tangible benefits for the needy. By filling many of the gaps in our welfare system, the existence of the food stamp program may have the unfortunate effect of lessening the pressure for a national guaranteed annual income. On the other hand, the incremental changes that have made food stamps benefits more generous have made a switch to a guaranteed income less costly and possibly more acceptable to some of its critics.

With another cycle of welfare reform at its beginning stage, the policy issues discussed here are of critical significance. When and if the food stamp program is converted to a separate cash payment or made part of another cash assistance plan, its final form will still be shaped, in part, by decisions made concerning the present system. It is within this context that changes in food stamp policy relating to accessibility, benefits, and program scope take on added importance.

Notes

1. The best history of the program prior to its revival in 1961 is contained in *Food Stamp Act of 1976*, H. Rept. 1460, 94th Cong., 2d Sess. (1976), pp. 390-495. On the passage of the legislation in 1964, see Randall B. Ripley, "Legislative Bargaining and the Food Stamp Act, 1964," in Frederic N. Cleaveland and Associates, *Congress and Urban Problems* (Washington: Brookings Institution, 1969), pp. 279-310.

2. On the overlap between food stamps and other welfare programs, see *National Survey of Food Stamp and Food Distribution Program Recipients: A Summary of Findings on Income Sources and Amounts and Incidence of Multiple Benefits*, prepared by the Subcommittee on Fiscal Policy of the Joint Economic Committee, 93d Cong., 2d Sess. (1974).

3. See generally, Daniel P. Moynihan, *The Politics of a Guaranteed Income* (New York: Vintage, 1973); and Vincent J. Burke and Vee Burke, *Nixon's Good Deed* (New York: Columbia University Press, 1974).

4. Congressional Budget Office, *The Food Stamp Program: Income or Food Supplementation?* (January 1977), pp. 37-39.

5. Ibid., p. 26.

6. On the nutritional quality of food stamp recipients' diets, see J. Patrick Madden and Marion D. Yoder, *Food Stamps and Commodity Distribution in Rural Areas of Central Pennsylvania* (University Park: Pennsylvania State University, 1972). On gross food consumption, see U.S. Department of Agriculture, Consumer and Marketing Services, Food Stamp Division, "The Food Stamp Program: An Initial Evaluation of the Pilot Projects" (April 1962), pp. 25-29.

7. Richard P. Nathan, "Food Stamps and Welfare Reform," *Policy Analysis* 2 (Winter 1976):64.

8. See Julius Duscha, "New Food Stamp Plan Causing Some Hardship in Detroit Area," *Washington Post,* December 10, 1961, p. A2; and Julius Duscha, "Food Stamp Plan Cuts Total of Aid Applicants," *Washington Post,* December 11, 1962, n.p.

9. "The Food Stamp Program: An Initial Evaluation of the Pilot Projects."

10. The definition of income has always excluded mandatory payroll deductions. It was around this time that deductions for emergency and medical expenses were formalized and a deduction for child care was added.

11. CBS Reports, "Hunger in America," broadcast May 21, 1968. Reprinted in *Hunger and Malnutrition in the United States,* Hearings before the Subcommittee on Employment, Manpower, and Poverty of the Senate Committee on Labor and Public Welfare, 90th Cong., 2d Sess. (1968), pp. 55-64.

12. Citizens' Board of Inquiry, *Hunger, U.S.A.* (Washington: New Community Press, 1968).

13. Nick Kotz, *Let Them Eat Promises* (Englewood Cliffs, N.J.: Prentice-Hall, 1969).

14. *Bennett v. Butz,* 386 F. Supp. 1059 (USDC D. Minn., 1974).

15. P.L. 95-113.

16. For varying estimates of the participation rate, see Harold Beebout, "Estimating the Population Eligible for Food Stamps," Library of Congress, Congressional Research Service (February 1975); *Report on Nutrition and Special Groups, Appendix B to Part I—Food Stamps,* prepared by the Senate Select Committee on Nutrition and Human Needs, 94th Cong., 1st Sess. (1975); Maurice MacDonald, "Why Don't More Eligibles Use Food Stamps?" University of Wisconsin, Institute for Research on Poverty (July 1975); Fred K. Hines, "Factors Related to Participation in the Food Stamp Program," U.S. Department of Agriculture, Economic Research Service, Agriculture Economic Report #298 (July 1975); and Douglas L. Bendt, Warren E. Farb, and Charles Ciccone, "Analysis of Food Stamp Program Participation and Costs, 1970-1980," Library of Congress, Congressional Research Service (April 1976).

17. Prior to 1970 there were separate schedules for the North and the South. These figures are from the Northern tables and are reprinted in *Food Stamp Program and Commodity Distribution,* Hearings before the Senate Committee on Agriculture and Forestry, 91st Cong., 1st Sess. (1969), pp. 34-40.

18. There have been a number of unsuccessful efforts in Congress to raise allotments to the Department of Agriculture's low-cost diet. Instituting the low-cost plan would increase allotments an average of 29 percent.

19. P.L. 94-4. For an account of the legislative struggle over food stamps in the 94th Congress, see Henry C. Kenski, "The Politics of Hunger: The 94th Congress and the Food Stamp Controversy (A Preliminary Report)," paper delivered at the annual meeting of the American Political Science Association, Chicago, September 1976.

20. Ford's own food stamp proposal introduced in the 94th Congress had disappointed conservatives who felt it did not go nearly far enough in reforming the program. Conservatives backed the legislation introduced by Senator Buckley and Representative Michel (S. 1993, H.R. 8145).

21. See *CNI Weekly Report,* June 24, 1976, pp. 1-2.

22. See the testimony of Edward J. Heckman, *Food Stamp Regulation Proposals,* Hearing before the House Committee on Agriculture, 94th Cong., 1st Sess. (1975), pp. 9-33.

23. *Nutrition and Human Needs—1971, Part 3—Food Stamp Regulations,* Hearings before the Senate Select Committee on Nutrition and Human Needs, 92d Cong., 1st Sess. (1971).

24. Surveys by both the Department of Agriculture and the House Agriculture Committee showed that slightly over 5 percent of all participating households have gross incomes of $560 per month or more ($6720 a year). Income eligibility is, of course, related to family size, and the "average" family

at the upper-income levels is likely to have five or six members. *Food Stamp Program Profile, Part I* and *Part II—Appendix,* prepared by the Senate Select Committee on Nutrition and Human Needs, 94th Cong., 2d Sess. (1976).

25. See *Food Stamp Program Profile, Part I,* pp. 8-11; and *Part II—Appendix,* pp. 14-15. See also Janice Peskin, "The Shelter Deduction in the Food Stamp Program," Department of Health, Education, and Welfare, Office of Income Security Policy, Technical Analysis Paper #6 (August 1975).

15 The Fire Ant Controversy: Pesticides and the Public Interest

Ardith Maney

Interest in food and agricultural policy is part of the increased concern that environmentalists share with other nontraditional, but increasingly well-organized, constituencies of the U.S. Department of Agriculture (USDA) including consumer groups, labor unions, churches, civil rights organizations, and groups organized around food and hunger issues. Similar groups sometimes influenced agricultural policy in the past—conservation groups were interested in the activities of the Forest Service and the Soil Conservation Service; churches, unions, and civil rights groups lent support to the New Deal's farm policies and to post-World War II surplus commodity distribution and Food for Peace programs. But seldom before the late 1960s did such groups, outside the USDA's traditional farm constituency, work with one another to influence USDA policy making on a continuing basis.

Each of these new influences on the Department of Agriculture deserves serious, separate attention by anyone seeking to understand the substantial changes taking place in American farm and food policy in the 1970s and 1980s. The impact of environmental groups has been especially dramatic, and presents a useful introduction to the activities of other groups as well. Although several of the concerns that environmental groups have had with farm policy are already well known, these need to be reexamined in a systematic fashion in order to understand the dimensions of the environmentalist critique of USDA policy and the impact that these groups have had on how USDA officials see themselves and their missions.

Agricultural policy has been described in the past as one of the political systems most impervious to increased participation or penetration by outsiders—a series of loosely linked, specialized subsystems organized around functional areas, crops or products, and departmental missions,[1] each virtually a closed shop in which consumer, environmental, or other outside groups who might try to become involved would be severely disadvantaged. Indeed, agricultural policy, if it showed signs of major system change, could be a particularly useful vantage point from which to examine conditions leading to increased participation in public policy and the kinds of policy changes which result—in short, how national political institutions respond to demands for political change.

Many commentators have cited the period surrounding the first celebration of Earth Day on April 22, 1970, as the highpoint of official acknowledgment of the public's interest in environmental issues in the United States. Shortly over a year of official activity around 1970 brought about the following important actions: the enactment of the landmark National Environmental Policy Act (NEPA) of 1969 which required that government agencies prepare statements detailing the impact of any programs that would adversely affect the environment; a declaration by the President of the United States pledging the 1970s to be the decade of the environment; and the creation later in 1970 of a major new federal regulatory agency, the Environmental Protection Agency (EPA), with broadranging responsibilities over the health and safety of the nation's natural and human resources.[2]

This national outpouring of concern could have been expected to affect the programs of all the major departments and agencies of the federal government, in due course. However, important effects of the movement for environmental protection were immediately felt on the USDA; for example, the creation of the EPA included the transfer of responsibility for regulation of agricultural chemicals from the USDA to the new agency, followed in 1972 by legislation strengthening the registration and regulation of these products by the EPA. Other effects, including the EPA's banning of several of the best-known and most widely used of the persistent pesticides—DDT, aldrin, and dieldrin—and cutbacks in important USDA pest control programs occurred soon after.

Indeed, the Department of Agriculture had been a major target of environmental groups for some time before they achieved these victories. They succeeded in striking directly at the department's preeminence in the federal government's formulation of food and agriculture policy, by challenging the use of chemicals used in agricultural production—especially pesticides. This chapter will consider aspects of the objectives, strategies, tactics, and impacts of environmental groups on one of their major targets—the USDA pest control program against the imported fire ant—which illustrate the environmentalists' effects on the department over time and over the whole spectrum of departmental pesticide policy including operation of cooperative federal-state pest control programs, research on the effects of pesticide use on agricultural production and on wildlife, encouragement of farming practices which included extensive pesticide use by farmers, and regulation of pesticides while this was a responsibility of the USDA.

The use of persistent pesticides has been the issue central to the environmentalists' critique of the USDA. Environmentalists had, as their objective, to end what they saw as the indiscriminate use of the relatively inexpensive and extremely effective pesticides which came onto the market shortly after the end of World War II. There chemicals quickly skyrocketed in use as farmers switched over from other means of pest control. Conservation and wildlife groups (the new term *environmental* to describe these groups and others did not come into general use until the late 1960s) first became concerned about short-term effects of fish, bird, and small animal kills immediately following aerial spraying. Later, roughly paralleling the scientific findings of the persistence of these chemicals in the tissues of fish and wildlife and evidence that pesticide residues increased in quantities in the tissues of other animals along the food chain, these and new critics extended their concern to the long-term impact of pesticide use on wildlife, human food, and humans.

Intensive use of pesticides and other agricultural chemicals (e.g., herbicides, fungicides, fertilizers, growth regulators, etc.) to increase production had been supported by virtually all the farm and agribusiness organizations, a unanimity which also extended to long-time congressional supporters in the House and Senate. At the same time, the Department's Agricultural Research Service received praise from conservationsists as well as from farmers and the scientific community for some of its alternative strategies against insect predators such as the successful use of sterile males to control a major pest of cattle, the screwworm fly. However, solutions applied to one insect do not necessarily apply to others: the USDA was pursuing control programs against a number of other important insect pests using the new persistent pesticides. These programs attracted the attention of conservationists because of their size and visibility; the USDA was one of the major users of persistent pesticides in the nation.

Moreover, the USDA was the most influential user, since it clearly encouraged farmers to use pesticides on their own. Its emphasis was on the contribution pesticide use would make to increased production. Former Secretary of Agriculture Earl Butz represented the position of support for what science and technology had brought to agriculture. He often referred to a "technological package" of fertilizers, pesticides, seed, and equipment which had been agreed to by farmers, the USDA, and agricultural science and on which the postwar development of monoculture farming rested. Chemical pesticides such as heptachlor, dieldrin, and mirex—which were successively used against the fire ant—were a main ingredient of this new technology and the part of that package which, along with DDT, first attracted a general audience and widespread concern. Farmers grew more dependent on pesticides even while some chemicals were being removed from the market by the federal government.

Statistics issued by the USDA continued to show substantial increases in pesticide use including a doubling of production in the nine years ending in 1974. At that time, the domestic pesticide market was estimated in the following proportions: 55 percent was being used in the agricultural sector; 30 percent by industrial, institutional, and government users; and 15 percent was destined for home and garden use.[3] Pesticide use had been legitimized and promoted by the USDA officials who were also responsible for its regulation. Speaking before a major audience of industry leaders in 1972, the National Agricultural Chemical Association, Secretary Butz bluntly set out the importance to food and agriculture policy of the efforts of agricultural researchers, government officials, and admonished both heavenly and earthly pesticide critics as follows:

The plain truth is, of course, that the ecology of nature is pretty severe on man, and man is constantly trying to modify it. Let's be honest. God put the worm in the apple; man took it out. God put the cockroach in the cracker barrel; man took it out. . . .[4]

Agricultural researchers and other departmental officials were recognized by the USDA to be playing an important role in providing the nation's food supply, and pesticide use was a substantial ingredient in food production.

The job of changing departmental pesticide policy was in turn influenced by several important organizational characteristics of the environmental groups themselves and the government decision makers they opposed. With these background factors about the political and organizational 'environment' of pesticide policy in mind, it will be possible to examine the various phases of environmental group/USDA conflict over pesticide use. First, there are several points to be made about USDA decision making which influenced the chances for success of the department's environmental critics.

Departmental decision making appeared closed and monolithic from the outside. The environmental groups interested in USDA pesticide policy were not knowledgeable about departmental and agency missions, procedures, or decision-making styles. Unlike the farm and agribusiness groups who pushed for and supported pesticide policies, environmentalists knew few USDA officials well and were unfamiliar with federal and state agricultural scientists who also had doubts about pest control campaigns such as that against the fire ant. Once they had made the USDA their target within the government in order to influence pesticide policy, they were bound to be at a considerable disadvantage as outsiders, vis-à-vis a department known for having especially strong clientele support at the grass roots and resourceful and influential friends in Congress.

However, the environmental critique hit the department especially hard because it called into question a benevolent self-image which USDA officials drew on for support as they went about their work. Officials were accustomed to believing that economic concerns (e.g., increases in agricultural production and continued prosperity for producer and consumer) would continue to take precedence over the aesthetic and recreational interests which they associated with conservation groups. Also, officials were proud of the department's long history of concern about environmental issues, notably in the soil conservation area. They held strongly to the view that the department acts in the broad public interest, especially the belief that by definition the agriculturalist's mission to feed the nation already implies a concern for the prudent management of natural resources. Thus, they were unprepared for the economic, health, and safety arguments advanced by environmentalists and increasingly accepted by influential publics.

At the same time, department officials held varying opinions on pesticide policy, and these were reflected in departmental and agency decision making. The pest control programs (which comprised the largest share of the department's budget committed to pesticide use) had been at first entrusted to the

Agricultural Research Service (ARS), the department's primary research arm. Even without attention from environmentalists, ARS faced multiple and conflicting demands when it considered questions related to pesticide use. Its workload was largely determined by producer interests and their supporters in Congress, who often were more interested in action (i.e., control or eradication of insect predators) than research. So, even in the absence of outside critics, ARS continually would be expected to seek to maintain a balance within its ranks between its scientists' claims for research support and clientele pressure for action. Moreover, the close ties that ARS had with scientists in the country's land-grant colleges working on the agency's pest control programs would increase the representation of different scientific perspectives and opinions considered in the decision-making process on pesticide use.

Assignment of program development and management to a scientific and research agency made the pest control programs especially difficult to analyze by those seeking to influence public policy. This conveyed some clear advantages to ARS officials in countering the attacks of outside critics among the environmentalists and others (e.g., ARS officials controlled much more of the information about the operation of pest control programs than similarly situated USDA administrators in other program areas). But it also increased the burdens that ARS faced in apprising supporters of progress and problems encountered along the way. For example, program officials had continuing difficulty convincing farmers of the dangers of returning animals too early to fields which had been treated with dangerous chemicals. It was also difficult to explain complicated treatment strategies to producer groups and state legislators whose support was needed for funding and program administration. At other times it was difficult to explain scientific constraints to senior departmental officials, the White House, and friends and foes in Congress.

Implementation of the various ARS pest control programs, including the campaign against the fire ant, depended on the continuing concurrence, or at least indifference, of an especially large number of significant political actors. Within the congressional agriculture committees and subcommittees, the chairmen and a few ranking members of both parties settled differences among themselves and wielded most of the power, presenting a united front to the outside world. And the usual situation was indifference by most of the other members of Congress, weak party leadership and sanctions, and infrequent and inconsistent White House attention. ARS was accustomed to pressure from program supporters, but it was not accustomed to the spotlight of public scrutiny when it came later.

The federal-state nature of the pest programs introduced other important political actors whose cooperation was crucial to programmatic success. For example, in the fire ant program, congressional program supporters were successful in delivering their share of federal funds, but the states and the other participants in the affected areas in the South where the program was in

operation—presumably the areas which had most to gain from the program—
were much more erratic in their financial support. Nonfederal support varied by
year, depending upon both the seriousness of the threat of fire ant infestation
and the strength of local program opponents. While the USDA and its agencies
had probably had more experience with cooperative programs than any other
federal department, the operation of a pest control program waged against the
fire ant placed special burdens of cooperation with landowners and producer
groups and state, county, and municipal governments and agencies that the
program's opponents were successfully able to exploit.

Some points are important to note about the challengers. Almost from its
beginning, in 1957, opposition to the fire ant program was spearheaded by two
important conservation groups and their local affiliates: the National Audubon
Society and the National Wildlife Federation. Strong opposition also soon
developed among national and state wildlife agencies. Later these and other
opponents were joined by the Environmental Defense Fund, whose lawsuits,
under NEPA's mandate for environmental impact statements, led to EPA's
deregistration proceedings against the principal fire ant pesticide—mirex.

At the key points in the controversy, opponents were also aided by dissent
among agricultural scientists in the Southern land-grant universities, by government studies showing inefficiency and management problems in the program,
and by an increasing body of independent scientific evidence of the dangers to
humans and the environment resulting from continued use of persistent
pesticides in agriculture. In the case of the fire ant campaign and other programs
using persistent pesticides, opponents had the advantage because there were so
many groups to be coordinated or at least placated. It was difficult to obtain
compromises because there were strong emotional and ideological commitments
on both sides. Thus controversies over government endorsement of pesticide use,
whether DDT, aldrin, dieldrin, heptachlor, or mirex, would be characterized by
charges and countercharges of bad faith, ad hominem attacks, suspicion, and
mistrust, rather than by bargaining and mutual accommodation.

Many of the outside groups seeking to influence agriculture policy—environmentalists included—differ from the USDA's usual clientele of producer groups
and their allies. Some producer groups opposed pesticide use for narrow
economic interest—beekeepers and dairymen suffered from pesticide use by
neighboring farmers. However, most of the opposition came from self-styled
public interest groups, a term also increasingly used by political scientists for
groups which base their demands on a general public interest, not a narrow
personal or economic interest. Recent literature contrasts private and public
interest groups and provides a background for considering differences in
resources, strategies, and tactics and their relative chances for success in
bureaucratic politics.[5] Significantly, the environmental groups most active in
curbing the fire ant program, the National Audubon Society and the Environmental Defense Fund, are representative of these public interest activities

generally. Moreover, their actions present a commentary on the growing political sophistication of the environmental movement in the 1960s and 1970s.

Finally, although environmental groups sometimes did not recognize potential allies among bureaucrats in state and federal agriculture departments and agencies, they profited by grass-roots ties of their own. Conservation groups such as the National Audubon Society had close ties to officials in state and federal wildlife agencies; access to independent, competent scientific expertise outside ARS and the state agencies cooperating with USDA programs; and a communications channel to government officials and sympathetic publics through the press, radio, and television.

Few opportunities existed for interests which were later adversely affected by the fire ant program to be involved in the policy process setting up the program. From 1957 to 1961 environmental critics mostly concentrated on trying to influence the USDA and the Agricultural Research Service directly. In the second period, from 1962 to 1969, they sought in varying ways to invoke the sanctions of other official decision makers on the agency; while it was a frustrating time for these critics, this period was crucial in forming public awareness of environmental concerns. Then, beginning in 1969, environmental and other critics of the program sought and later succeeded in removing decision making from the USDA. This accomplished, they set about seeking to influence the new decision makers.

In the end, the fire ant controversy shows evidence of the participation of public interest groups, the courts, Congress, and the White House in important areas of agricultural policy. Environmental groups were ultimately successful in redefining the costs and benefits of agricultural chemical use. Immediate economic benefits to producers and consumers from full production must now be weighed against long-range harmful effects on the environment.

The old pesticide policy subsystem has been expanded, but similar policy subsystems may still be intact for many policy issues with which ARS is concerned. The subsystem members involved (departmental and agency officials; researchers in ARS, the USDA, and the land-grant schools; members of Congress specializing in agricultural policy; producer groups; state and local politicians) remain important as continuing participants and still share a perspective about agricultural research and action that stresses increased production and confidence in the answers which technology provides. In the matter of pesticides, however, and particularly in the case of the fire ant controversy, these subsystem members are subject to a number of new controls exercised by institutions of the larger political system: a new bureaucratic rival, the Environmental Protection Agency, is able to ban agricultural chemicals or starve departmental programs such as the fire ant campaign; and the White House or the Congress settles disputes between the USDA and the EPA. If appeals are directed to the White House or Congress, however, they are bound to widen the scope of conflict still further and stimulate counterorganization by environmentalists and other groups.

Environmental questions about agricultural chemicals can no longer be settled within the friendly confines of the congressional agricultural appropriations subcommittees but involve cross-jurisdictional committees like Government Operations, governance committees like Budget, and competing subject matter committees.

The notion of subsystem or subgovernment which is often applied to agricultural policy implies stability and an ability to settle disputes among a small group of members holding a common point of view. It also implies a lack of scrutiny by wider publics. As an agency within the U.S. Department of Agriculture, a department long known for its effective support from producer groups and Congress, the Agricultural Research Service used the subsystem format when it organized the fire ant program. The fire ant controversy put the agricultural research community on notice that other programs and priorities may be challenged in similar ways in the future.

Notes

1. This is part of a larger study of new influences on food and agricultural policy which has been supported by the Iowa State University Summer Research Grant Program and the National Science Foundation. Much of the data come from internal records of the USDA, the Agricultural Research Service, and its operating agencies, the Entomological Research Division and the Plant Pest Control Division in the National Archives. Wherever possible, these sources were supplemented by interviews with participants and other official documents and records. An excellent account comparing ARS efforts in four USDA pest control programs including the fire ant campaign can be found in William L. Brown, Jr., "Mass Insect Control Programs: Four Case Studies," *Psyche* 68 (1961):75-106.

The concept of the policy subsystem is described in J. Leiper Freeman, *The Political System* (New York: Vintage, 1964), and Grant McConnell, *Public Power and American Democracy* (New York: Vintage, 1966) and has been widely applied to agricultural policy making by political scientists and others. Cater, a journalist and former White House official, described these subsystems as "subgovernments" in his *Power in Washington* (New York: Vintage, 1964). The following quote from his book accurately outlines the congressional and producer group support for the USDA pest control programs before they drew the attention of environmentalists and other critics.

In one important area of policy after another substantial efforts to exercise power are waged by alliances cutting across the two branches of government (executive and legislative) and including key operatives from outside. In effect, they constitute subgovernments of Washington comprising the expert, the interested, and the engaged. These subgovernments are not to be confused with factions. Within them, factions contend to greater or lesser degree. The power balance may be in stable or highly unstable equilibrium. But the subgovernment's tendency is to strive to become self-sustaining in control of power in its own sphere. Each seeks to aggregate the power necessary to its purpose. Each resists being overridden (p. 17).

2. Among others, Walter A. Rosenbaum's *The Politics of Environmental Concern* (New York: Praeger, 1973) and J. Clarence Davies' *The Politics of Pollution* (New York: Praeger, 1973), 2d ed., have described the rise of the environmental movement and analyzed its achievements. Many of the prominent environmental critics directed attacks at the USDA's fire ant program including Rachel Carson in *Silent Spring* (Boston: Houghton Mifflin, 1962) and Harrison Wellford in a Ralph Nader-sponsored study, *Sowing the Wind* (New York: Grossman, 1972). For a defense of pesticide use by a prominent subsystem member, see Jamie L. Whitten, *That We May Live* (New York: D. Van Nostrand, 1966).

3. The figures are from *The Pesticide Review,* 1975, quoted in U.S. Senate Subcommittee on Administrative Practice and Procedures, *The Environmental Protection Agency and the Regulation of Pesticides,* Committee Print (Washington: GPO, December 1976), p. 1.

4. Earl Butz, Secretary of Agriculture, "Greater Dimensions for Agriculture," a speech delivered before the National Agricultural Chemicals Association, October 2, 1972.

5. In *The Semisovereign People* (New York: Holt, Rinehart and Winston, 1960). E.E. Schattschneider distinguished between groups seeking public and private goods, and Jeffrey M. Berry has recently published the results of an extensive survey he did of public interest groups in Washington in *Lobbying for the People* (Princeton, N.J.: Princeton University Press, 1977). What happened in the interim since Schattschneider's book appeared has been a proliferation of groups who openly identify themselves as public interest groups and see a commonality in strategy and tactics, approaches, and organizational resources. For an insider's discussion of these groups and their activities, see Peter Schuck, "Public Interest Groups and the Policy Process," *Public Administration Review* 37 (March/April 1977):132-39.

16 Implementing Federal Nondiscrimination Policies in the Department of Agriculture, 1964-1976

William C. Payne, Jr.

The primary concern of this book is agricultural policy—the process by which it is made and its effect upon people. This chapter looks at this question from the perspective of federal civil rights policies and their implementation in the Department of Agriculture in the period from 1964 to 1976.

Any examination of this subject must begin with the fact of overt discrimination against minority groups living in rural areas from the colonial period to the recent past. From expansionist wars against native Americans to the enslavement of blacks, from the annulment of Spanish land grants in the Southwest to the internment of Japanese Americans in World War II, the history of minority relations in this country included ties to the land and therefore to agricultural policy.

One of the singular phenomena of the social history of the United States has been the tide of black migration away from the rural South. In 1920, there were over 900,000 nonwhite farm operators in the region. By 1969, that figure had dropped to just over 85,000. Preliminary indications from the 1974 census of Agriculture suggest that this figure is now below 50,000. In 1910, blacks owned 15 million acres of land in the United States. By 1969, that figure had dropped to less than 6 million acres.

This virtual disappearance of the black farmer has been a result of an agricultural policy that was rooted in slavery and, later, a social and economic structure that denied equality of opportunity to minorities. In general, minorities have been bypassed by the revolutions in agricultural technology, mechanization, plant and seed biology, pesticides, fertilizers, conservation practices, communications, and the benefits of knowledge provided through the land-grant college system. Minorities have been denied equal access to education, to credit, to information, and even to food, shelter, and medical treatment. Blacks among the rural minorities have been treated unfairly, first as slaves, then as sharecroppers and tenants. Many of those fortunate enough to own land have been defrauded or otherwise forced to give up their land by circumstances beyond their control. In short, minority persons in rural areas have been victimized by an agricultural policy whose effects, if not intent, have been to deny minorities the alternatives that were and are available to nonminorities and to preclude minorities from the control that nonminorities have over the forces that influence and shape their lives.

173

Why? For one thing, agricultural policy is controlled by interests whose treatment of rural minorities has helped create such conditions. For another, an acquiescent federal government has permitted the effects of such policies to continue without enforcing the nondiscrimination provisions of the law.

While it is idle to speculate what might have been the history of this country had discrimination against rural minorities not occurred, it is a truism that neither agricultural history nor agricultural policy can be portrayed accurately without considering the prominent role played by rural minority group people.

Civil Rights Enforcement Mechanisms in USDA

Title VI of the Civil Rights Act of 1964 established a policy of nondiscrimination in federal programs. Regulations implementing the law were published in the Department of Agriculture in late 1964. Formal efforts to implement the law began in February 1965, with the appointment of an Assistant to the Secretary of Agriculture for Civil Rights and a small staff. Lending support to these efforts was the publication in the same month of a year-long study of discrimination in agricultural programs in the South by the U.S. Commission on Civil Rights.[1] The Commission's report concluded:

As the group most depressed economically, most deprived educationally, and most oppressed socially, Negroes have been consistently denied access to many services, provided with inferior services when served, and segregated in federally financed agricultural programs whose very task was to raise their standard of living. The Commission's analysis of four major U.S. Department of Agriculture programs has clearly indicated that the Department has generally failed to assume responsibility for assuring equal opportunity and equal treatment to all those entitled to benefit from its programs. Instead, the prevailing practice has been to follow local patterns of racial segregation and discrimination in providing assistance paid for by Federal funds.

President Johnson demonstrated executive-level concern by personally writing Secretary of Agriculture Orville Freeman and requesting a report of actions taken to correct abuses revealed in the Commission's report. This initial impetus was instrumental in making the Department—an old, decentralized, and highly bureaucratic agency—one of the most active federal agencies in civil rights matters in the mid- and late 1960s whether it wanted to be or not.

Title VI of the Civil Rights Act of 1964 covered only those federally assisted programs that passed through state and county entities on their way to individual beneficiaries. USDA added to its regulations a prohibition against discrimination in programs where the benefits passed directly to individuals. A Citizens Advisory Committee on Civil Rights was established. Guidelines for the collection and evaluation of data on minority group participation in USDA programs were issued, as were guidelines on the integration of previously segregated office facilities. By mid-1965, USDA had dispatched teams of investigators to determine how widespread were the problems revealed by the Civil Rights Commission. Almost immediately, it seemed, segregated offices began to disappear, employment of minorities increased, and minority program participation expanded.

These changes continued on their own momentum through 1967. In 1968, the death of Martin Luther King, the Poor Peoples Campaign encampment in Washington, a hearing on rural problems in Alabama by the U.S. Commission on Civil Rights, and an internal Commission report on the USDA structure for civil rights enforcement provided additional pressure on the civil rights program in USDA. When added to a 1969 letter from the Attorney General to the Secretary of Agriculture urging more effort in the civil rights area, these forces resulted in a USDA policy statement by Secretary Clifford Hardin covering agency compliance programs, training, evaluation, employment opportunities, and program reviews. This eventually resulted in the development of stronger programs for the collection and evaluation of minority program participation data, targeting program benefits, outreach, and, in November 1971, the establishment of a separate and substantially enlarged Office of Equal Opportunity (OEO) to coordinate civil rights matters in USDA.

In 1973, the USDA regulations were amended to prohibit discrimination based on sex or religion in direct assistance programs. In 1974, a task force was established to improve the delivery of program services to American Indians. In 1975, a division was created in the Office of Equal Opportunity to promote minority business enterprise assistance in USDA procurement programs. In 1976, a civil rights impact assessment and review procedure was established to survey the civil rights implications of certain types of policy actions before decisions on them are finalized.

Despite the apparent soundness of its organization and management mechanisms, the civil rights program in USDA is only marginally effective. This conclusion is supported by looking at the record in areas like employment, access to participation in decision making, and distribution of program benefits.

Minority Employment

Minorities have constituted approximately 20 percent of the federal government workforce since 1970. In the Department of Agriculture, minorities constitute only 10.8 percent of all permanent, full-time employees. The Department of Agriculture's minority employment percentage is the lowest of any major federal department or agency except for the National Aeronautics and Space Administration.

Part of the failure to achieve a higher minority employment ratio can be attributed to the fact that the Department's agencies and programs are highly decentralized. The Department has over 15,000 offices throughout the country. This decentralization contributes to low overall minority employment. Table 16-1 shows selected states, the 1970 minority rural population of working age, and the proportion of minority USDA employment in 1975. Each of the states listed had over 10 percent minority rural population aged 21 to 65, yet only two of the states had over 10 percent USDA minority employment. Generally speaking, the USDA minority employment rate was half or less than that of the working-age rural minority population.

Certain USDA agencies have poor minority employment records and thus tend to pull down the Department's average. Three of the largest agencies— Forest Service (6.1 percent), Soil Conservation Service (SCS) (6.8 percent), and Farmers Home Administration FmHA) (8.8 percent)—account for half of the employees in USDA, yet all had less than 10 percent minority employees in 1975. Other agencies, like Food and Nutrition Service (23.7 percent) and Animal and Plan Health Inspection Service (14.5 percent), had comparatively high rates of minority employment.

Many agencies have only apparently satisfactory minority employment records because there are many minorities employed at the clerical levels but few minorities employed at the professional levels. For example, in 1975 the immediate Office of the Secretary had only one minority professional and no Hispanic employees whatsoever. In the Office of General Counsel, only 5 of 189 professionals were minority, and there were no minority hires at any level during

Table 16-1
USDA Employment in Selected States, 1975

States	Percent Rural Minority Aged 21 to 65	Percent USDA Minority
Alabama	18.9	4.4
Arizona	34.0	7.5
Arkansas	12.6	5.9
California	17.3	9.8
Colorado	10.5	5.6
Florida	13.7	7.1
Georgia	17.9	5.8
Louisiana	24.6	8.9
Mississippi	31.5	5.1
New Mexico	60.7	20.7
North Carolina	19.8	7.2
Texas	20.7	10.8
Virginia	17.7	8.5

the year. In the Economic Research Service only 1 of the 57 professionals hired during the year was minority. In the Agricultural Research Service only 1 of 78 professionals hired during the year was minority. None of the professionals in the Farmers Cooperative Service was a minority person.

Employment of nonfederal employees in federally assisted agricultural programs is also a concern. In the Agricultural Stabilization and Conservation Service (ASCS), minorities accounted for only 3.2 percent of more than 8600 county-level employees in 1975. In the Cooperative Extension Service, minorities accounted for only 7.2 percent of more than 17,000 county- and state-level employees.

Another component of USDA's poor minority employment picture is the underrepresentation of minorities in certain occupational and skill classifications. For example, only 1 percent of all USDA foresters, 2.7 percent of all USDA engineers, 5.6 percent of all USDA commodity grading specialists, and 6.6 percent of all USDA soil conservationists are minority persons.

Even where minorities are employed, they are usually found at the lower grades. In 1975 only 29 of the 1391 USDA employees in the four highest grades (G.S. 15 through G.S. 18) were minority persons—2.1 percent. Similarly, none of the 164 foresters, none of the 65 soil conservationists, and only 2 of the 289 engineers in the four highest grades were minority persons.

Still another factor in the minority employment picture is the failure to hire available minorities or to aggressively pursue minority recruitment. For example, although minorities comprise 6.0 percent of USDA professional employees, only 33 of 847 professionals hired in 1975 were minority persons (3.9 percent). Although minorities comprise 9.3 percent of USDA administrative/technical employees, only 84 of 1311 administrative/technical employees hired in 1975 were minority persons—6.4 percent. With such negative replacement rates, a decrease in overall minority employment would be expected to, and did in fact, occur in 1975 as overall minority employment dropped from 11.1 to 10.8 percent.

At the rate established between 1970 and 1976, it will be 20 years—1997—before USDA achieves the minority employment percentage that the rest of the federal government has had since 1970. Clearly, one area where agricultural policy can be influenced more favorably toward minorities is in equal employment opportunity.

Participation in Decision Making

A key measure of the extent to which minorities have achieved access to decision making in agricultural programs is the proportion of minorities serving on advisory boards and committees that have been established to provide grass-roots input into agricultural policy. Thousands of persons serve on these groups. As shown in Table 16-2, with few exceptions, minorities are underrepresented. As can be seen, minorities comprised less than 2 percent of the members of REA cooperatives' boards of directors, ASCS county committees, and soil and water conservation district boards.

In 1975 USDA adopted a policy that minorities and women would be represented on committees in reasonable proportion to the degree that they are affected by the work of the committee. This was interpreted to apply only to national public advisory committees and not the local boards and committees, many of whose members are determined by election.

Minority Participation in USDA Programs

The real test of discrimination in agricultural policy is whether minorities are participating in USDA programs to the degree one would expect in a nondiscriminatory environment. When the U.S. Commission on Civil Rights reported on equal opportunity problems in farm programs in early 1965, it was stated that minorities were denied access to participation in many programs and segregated and otherwise discriminated against in many others. Judged by a test of equitable participation in some agricultural programs today, it appears that equal opportunity in agricultural programs has yet to be realized for many rural minorities.

Rural Housing

Although minorities occupy less than 10 percent of all rural housing units, they account for over 30 percent of all substandard nonmetropolitan housing units in areas serviced by the Farmers Home Administration (FmHA). For blacks, the figures are 6.1 percent of the housing units and 25 percent of the substandard

Table 16-2
Minority Persons on Agriculture Boards and Committees, 1975

Group	Percent Minority
REA-Assisted electric cooperatives Boards of directors	1.9
ASCS county committees	1.2
SCS district soil and water conservation boards	1.7
FmHA county committees	11.2
Extension councils and committees	unknown

housing. With such measures of need among rural minorities, it might be expected that they would comprise a primary target group for federal housing policy in rural areas. Yet, as shown by Figure 16-1, FmHA rural housing loans to blacks have been decreasing dramatically. In 1965, when the FmHA rural housing loan program was comparatively small, blacks received 9.3 percent of the loans (1430). By 1971, when the program reached new loan highs, blacks received 19.4 percent of the loans made (21,573). By 1976, however, the proportion of loans to blacks had dropped down almost to its 1965 level—9.5 percent (10,823).

Decreasing population does not appear to be the reason for this decline. Black rural households actually increased between 1969 and 1974 by 150,000. The reasons appear to be economic. In 1969, the practical lower income limit for FmHA rural housing borrowers was approximately $3000. By 1974, this limit had risen to approximately $5000. Whereas the effective income limit denied loans to approximately 24.7 percent of rural white households and 36.2 percent of the rural black households in 1969, by 1974 the effective income limit applied to approximately the same proportion of rural white households—

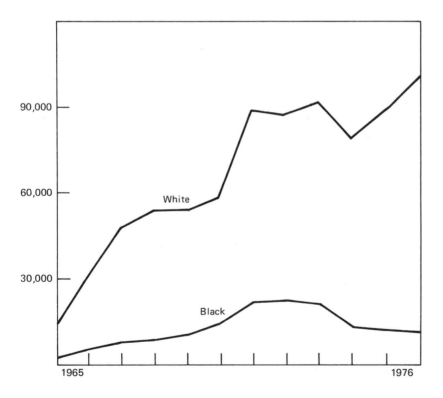

Figure 16-1. Farmers Home Administration Rural Housing Loans, 1965-1976.

24.7 percent—*but was excluding 50.3 percent of the rural black households.*[2] These facts clearly suggest the need for an altered government policy that will include a greater number of lower-income persons in rural housing loan programs.

Farm Ownership

Paralleling the rapid and continuing decline of black and other minority farm operators has been a similar decrease in Farmers Home Administration loans to minorities for farm ownership purposes. As shown in Figure 16-2, loans to blacks in 1966 totaled 810, or 5.7 percent of all loans made. By 1976, there were only 166 farm ownership loans to blacks, or 1.5 percent of the total loans

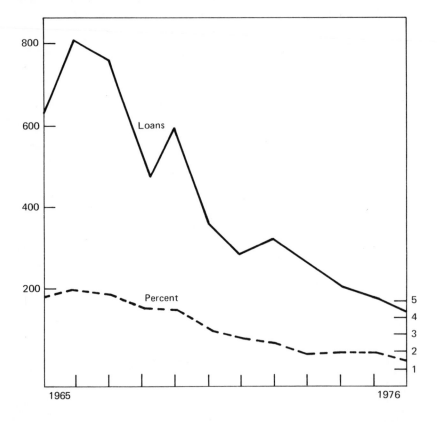

Figure 16-2. Farmers Home Administration Farm Ownership Loans to Blacks, 1965-1976.

made. It is apparent that the federal government is doing very little to preserve the opportunity for rural blacks to farm.

Loans to other minorities have been equally low such that in 1976 only 277 of the 11,140 farm ownership loans made—2.5 percent—went to minority borrowers.

Soil Conservation Cooperators

The Soil Conservation Service (SCS) is the agency of the Department of Agriculture through which technical assistance to landowners and operators for soil and water conservation purposes has been given since the mid-1930s. Prior to the Civil Rights Act of 1964, technical assistance in the soil and water conservation programs, like other USDA programs, was provided in a discriminatory manner. In 1966, in the South, 51 percent of the white operating units were SCS cooperators. Among black operating units, only 28 percent were cooperators. Ten years later, in 1975, the percentage of eligible black operating units that were SCS cooperators had increased to 40 percent while the eligible white operating units that were SCS cooperators had increased to 59 percent.[3] The disparity in the rates of participation for black and white operating units had been only slightly reduced over the 10-year period. An even greater disparity in rates of participation is found among American Indian operating units. In 1975, in 13 states surveyed, 60 percent of the white operating units but only 35 percent of the American Indian operating units were SCS cooperators.

Despite the disparity in rates of participation in SCS programs, it appears that the rates of technical assistance provided to those who do participate are very close and in some instances actually favor the minority cooperators.

4-H Clubs

At the time of the passage of the Civil Rights Act of 1964, minority participation in the youth-oriented 4-H club program of the Extension Service was generally segregated and limited mainly to those counties having minority agents. 4-H club enrollment—black and white alike—dropped significantly in states like Arkansas, Mississippi, and North Carolina in response to pressure to integrate services. A 1969 study showed that in Mississippi, black 4-H club enrollment was definitely related to whether a black extension agent was assigned in the county. By 1975, segregation in 4-H club activities had been reduced, but one out of five clubs in integrated environments was still segregated.

Family Food Programs

In contrast to other USDA programs where minority participation appears disproportionate with nonminority participation when measures of eligibility are compared, the family food assistance program administered by the Food and Nutrition Service is one in which minority participation compares favorably with eligibility. Whereas minorities constituted 42.9 percent of all persons in poverty in 1975, they constituted 51.7 percent of all persons participating in the family food assistance program that year.

Policy Implications

The data as well as the history related above make it apparent that minorities do not participate in or benefit from many agricultural programs to the extent one would expect in a nondiscriminatory situation. The same observation applies for participation in decision-making boards and committees and for USDA employment. It is hard, therefore, to escape the conclusion that discrimination still exists in agricultural programs and policies.

Several factors may account for this—a history of discrimination against minorities, the conservative influence of major constituency interest groups (agribusiness, the land-grant system, and farm organizations), the role of congressional committees, and the inertia of an old-line bureaucracy. All these factors have joined to create the conditions under which rural minorities suffer today.

Another factor in this situation is the character of leadership given to the civil rights enforcement effort in the federal government. In the 12-year period since the passage of the Civil Rights Act of 1964, enforcement of federal nondiscrimination law and policy in USDA has been characterized by a failure of leadership among some top USDA officials and administrators. Most recently, from 1972 to 1976, the USDA civil rights enforcement program suffered from outright attempts to circumvent enforcement action against programs found to be out of compliance; the USDA civil rights office was permitted to go without a permanent director for more than two years during the period; staff initiatives to improve existing civil rights mechanisms were discouraged; an open attempt was made to abolish the USDA civil rights office. Such actions clearly communicated to agency officials the low priority accorded civil rights matters in USDA, and they responded accordingly. The results of such policies and leadership attitudes are reflected in the minority participation data cited earlier. The implications of this situation are that minorities will continue to experience discrimination in agricultural programs unless past directions are reversed.

It is significant to note that USDA progress in civil rights since 1964 nearly always has been the result of external pressures. The structure of decision making in the Department—with its heavy reliance upon the White House, Southern-dominated congressional committees, the conservative leanings of the agribusiness-land grant-farm organization combination of interest groups, and the inertia of its own bureaucracy—has usually worked to defeat liberalizing moves favoring advancement of civil rights except for brief periods following embarrassing public pressure exerted through lawsuits or through media-augmented protests or inquiries. In terms of understanding the barriers to effective civil rights enforcement in agriculture programs and in terms of dealing with the policy implications of these events, it is important to note that many of the same barriers and the same problems that existed in 1964 remain today.

If conditions are to be changed with a view toward both correcting for the effects of past and current discrimination and providing equitable treatment for rural minorities, the following actions should be taken:

1. It must be made clear, through personal example and leadership by top USDA officials, that civil rights is a departmental mission and that civil rights will be fully incorporated into all USDA policy planning and program management matters.
2. As a sign of change, there must be a significant increase of minorities and women employed in USDA, particularly in management positions.
3. Persistent discrimination must be immediately rooted out, using the remedies available under the law.
4. In order to correct for the effects of past discrimination, affirmative action to achieve equal opportunity should be implemented in all phases of USDA operations.

Notes

1. U.S. Commission on Civil Rights, *Equal Opportunity in Farm Programs,* 1965.

2. Memorandum, Ronald Bird, Leader, Housing Program Area, Economic Research Service, to Percy R. Luney, Chief, Program Planning and Evaluation Division, Office of Equal Opportunity, USDA (March 15, 1977).

3. In the course of examining the participation data, the USDA civil rights staff determined that the highest rates of black participation occur in the four states where a minority conservationist has been assigned to the state staff to concentrate on technical assistance matters for low-income farmers.

17 The Politics of Collective Bargaining in Agriculture

Isidro D. Ortiz

Introduction

On June 5, 1975, California Governor Edmund G. Brown, Jr., signed into law the California Agricultural Labor Relations Act of 1975. This act granted farm workers in California the right to select unions to represent them in bargaining with their employers. Representing one of Brown's initial major legislative achievements as governor, the legislation was hailed by many because it brought the prospect of an end to labor strife and instability in California agriculture. Several months after its implementation, however, the nation's first collective-bargaining legislation covering farm workers had become embroiled in a storm of controversy. It was under attack from agricultural producers and unions. Funding ran out for the agency empowered to administer the legislation; the agency began to close some of its offices and lay off its staff. Measures authorizing additional appropriations were stalled in the legislature. The peace which had been brought to California agriculture threatened to evaporate in the face of renewed strife.

This chapter examines the role that Governor Brown played in the development of the nation's first collective-bargaining legislation in agriculture, as well as the obstacles encountered by Governor Brown in his efforts to effectively implement the legislation and institutionalize collective bargaining in California agriculture. The chapter begins with a brief overview of the efforts to organize farm workers and establish collective bargaining prior to the advent of Governor Brown. Next, it examines the ways in which Governor Brown forged the legislation in order to break a serious legislative impasse. It then describes the obstacles to the successful implementation of the nation's first collective-bargaining law covering farm workers. Last, the chapter concludes with a discussion of the lessons to be learned from California's experience in trying to bring peace and stability to labor-management relations in agriculture.

The Background

The signing of the Agricultural Labor Relations Act of 1975 climaxed a long history of bitter and violent strife in California agriculture between farm workers and agricultural producers. The principal bone of contention in this strife was the question of collective bargaining. For agricultural producers, the establish-

185

ment of collective bargaining was a development which would bring mixed blessings. In contrast, for farm workers and their allies, the establishment of collective bargaining was a vital and necessary step toward improved working conditions. Consequently, in the early part of this century, organizing efforts among farm workers had designated the elusive goal of collective bargaining as one of their central objectives. Most of these efforts failed, however.[1] Labor strife continued to plague California agriculture.

In 1939-1940 a solution to the strife appeared temporarily on the horizon when Senator Robert La Follette chaired a series of hearings on "Violations of Free Speech and Rights of Labor." The La Follette committee investigated the history of violations of the constitutional rights of workers in several areas of California. After intensive study, the committee recommended the establishment of collective bargaining in California agriculture.[2] With the outbreak of World War II, however, the urgency for action to bring peace to California agriculture immediately disappeared. The principal concern became the mobilization of the nation for the war effort. After the war, efforts continued to establish collective bargaining, albeit with no success.

In the mid-1960s these efforts received a new impetus with the advent of Cesar Chavez. Chavez experienced unmatched success in organizing farm workers.[3] From 1962 to 1973 Chavez built the first viable union of farm workers in California's agricultural history and secured contracts with grape and lettuce growers. By 1973 membership in the union, the United Farmworkers of America (UFW), AFL-CIO had grown to approximately 53,000 workers. It held contracts with approximately 350 growers throughout California.

However, in 1973, the Teamsters Union, after a six-year jurisdictional agreement giving the UFW the right to organize field workers, broke its agreement with the UFW. As contracts between the growers and the UFW were beginning to expire, the Teamsters began renegotiating the contracts with the growers amid charges of a conspiracy between growers and the Teamsters. The Teamsters' actions effectively undercut the UFW's membership and strength. By 1975 the UFW's membership had drastically declined to about 12,000 workers. The UFW had lost most of its contracts with major growers.

The Teamsters' actions immediately precipitated a bitter and bloody jurisdictional conflict involving the Teamsters, the UFW, and the growers. During the summer of 1973, the UFW declared a series of strikes against the growers and resisted numerous arrests and intimidation by the Teamsters and the growers throughout the summer. However, during the summer, two UFW members were killed while working on the strike. To prevent additional violence, Chavez ended the strikes. He then sent 50 families throughout the country to lead revived lettuce boycotts and launch a new boycott against the country's largest wine maker, Gallo Winery.[4]

The Advent of Governor Brown

During the California gubernatorial campaign of 1974, the strife in the fields and the boycott became one of the major issues dividing the candidates. Edmund G. Brown, Jr., the Democratic candidate, proposed that farm workers be given the same rights as workers in industry as a way of ending the strife. Central among these rights was the right to secret elections. His Republican challenger, Houston Flourney, Jr., denounced the boycott and activities of Chavez and his union.

In November 1974, Brown was elected governor in a Democratic landslide victory. On January 5, 1975, the Governor revealed his plans to introduce legislation giving farm workers the right to secret elections. In his inaugural speech, the Governor declared,

... It's time that we treat all workers alike, whether they work in the city or toil in the fields. ... I also believe it's time to extend the rule of law to the agricultural sector and establish the right of secret ballot elections for farm-workers. The law I will support will impose rights and responsibilities on both farmworker and farmer alike, and I expect that an appropriate bill that serves all the people will not fully satisfy any of the parties to the dispute, but that's no reason not to pass it.[5]

Immediately after, the Governor authorized several members of the California Agriculture and Services Department to draft a bill calling for secret ballot elections for farm workers.[6] On April 10, 1975, Governor Brown sent this bill to the California legislature. Entitled the Agricultural Labor Relations Act, the bill called for secret ballot elections for farm workers, allowed secondary boycotts in selective circumstances, banned strikes to win union recognition, and ostensibly invalidated contracts between growers and unions which had not been won through elections. The bill also called for the creation of a five-member Agricultural Labor Relations board with regional offices to administer the law. The board would be appointed by the Governor.

Brown's bill joined two other measures. By April 1975, the former Teamsters and growers had joined to support a bill sponsored by Democratic Senator George Zenovich of Fresno. Chavez and the UFW, on the other hand, were sponsoring a bill authored by Democratic Assemblyman Richard Alatorre of Los Angeles.

Intended as a compromise measure, Brown's bill immediately came under fire from Cesar Chavez and the UFW. They called the bill "deceptive" because it threatened to validate the Teamster-grower contracts and limit the use of secondary boycotts, one of the UFW's most potent weapons. The Teamsters and the growers, in contrast, refrained from criticism but expressed apprehension about the implications of the proposed bill for their contracts. Undaunted by the criticism from the UFW, Brown set out to secure a compromise acceptable to the various participants. Such a compromise could be reached, Brown was told by his Secretary of Agriculture, if the various groups could be made to negotiate. These groups included the growers' organizations, the Teamsters, Chavez and the UFW, the AFL-CIO, and the legislature.

Brown subsequently ordered the Secretary of Agriculture to meet with the growers and representatives of the UFW and attempt to reach a compromise among them. When it appeared that a compromise was on the horizon, Brown began to meet and negotiate with them on specific issues, e.g., the size of the bargaining unit, the legality of existing contracts, and the use of secondary boycotts. After negotiating for three weeks with the growers and the UFW representatives, Brown conducted a dramatic all-night session on the night of May 5, 1975. This session concluded with the adoption of 26 amendments to the initial proposed bill. Personally drafted by Brown and representing a "synthesis" of the conflicting positions heard by Brown during the three weeks of negotiation, the amendments were intended to facilitate a compromise between the UFW and the growers. As drafted by Brown, the amendments represented concessions to the growers and Chavez and the UFW. For example, one amendment imposed greater restrictions on the use of secondary boycotts—a proposal favored by the growers. Another amendment prohibited growers from banning elections because of preexisting contracts with another union—an amendment favored by Chavez and the UFW, who feared that the growers would deprive the workers of elections because of prior contracts with the Teamsters.[7]

Although the amendments were adopted, the Teamsters opposed the compromise, claiming that existing contracts would be invalidated on the date the new law would become operative (the Governor's assistant, Rose Bird, reassured them that this would not happen). They also opposed the requirement that representation elections must not be held under the proposed law until 50 percent of the workers employed at peak seasons were actually working.

The AFL-CIO building trades expressed fear that the new law would permit farm workers instead of building tradesmen to be hired for construction jobs on farm.

On May 19, 1975, Brown negotiated another compromise, giving the Teamsters and the tradesmen the necessary concessions. He also promised Chevez that the bill would be placed on the legislature's special session call in order that the new law might take effect for the 1975 fall grape harvest rather than on January 1, 1976.

Brown's intervention occurred at a critical time. As a result of the expression of apprehension by the Teamsters and building tradesmen, as well as the massive lobbying campaign by the Teamsters, the bill had become bogged down in the California Senate Finance Committee. With the necessary compromise aside, the bill quickly moved through the legislature. On May 29, 1975, the final legislative hurdle was passed when the California Assembly passed the bill by a 64-10 vote three days after the Senate passed it by a 31-7 vote.

On June 4, 1975, Governor Brown signed the legislation. In so doing, he called it a "beginning" toward an end to the strife and turmoil in California agriculture. As passed by the legislature and signed by Governor Brown, the Agricultural Labor Relations Act of 1975 granted farm workers the right to choose by secret elections which union, if any, would represent them. It limited secondary strikes and created a five-member board to be appointed by the Governor to administer the law—the Agricultural Labor Relations Board (ALRB). Its purpose, as declared in its preamble, was "to insure peace in the agricultural fields by guaranteeing justice for all agricultural workers and stability in labor relations."[8]

Implementing the Legislation

The passage of the legislation, as noted above, was hailed as a major watershed in California agricultural history and a legislative coup for Governor Brown. Immediately after its passage, the preparations for its implementation began in earnest. On July 1, 1975, Governor Brown appointed the five members of the Agricultural Labor Relations Board (ALRB). Shortly thereafter, the board began hiring a staff. Immediately after, the ALRB's chairman predicted that the board would be supervising as many as 150 elections per day.

On August 28, 1975, the law became effective amid much speculation about its success. Three months after its implementation, however, charges increasingly emerged that the law was "not working."[9] The board appointed to administer the legislation was embroiled in intense and bitter controversy; it also began to run out of funds. Several months later, in February 1976, the board's funding ran out; the board began to shut down its offices and lay off its staff. Efforts to secure additional funding were stalemated in the legislature. The Agriculture Labor Relations Act of 1975 was no longer being implemented. The next section of this chapter examines the obstacles to its implementation.

Obstacles to Implementation

Three factors stymied the implementation of the nation's first collective-bargaining law covering farm workers. These were (1) deficiencies in the administrative system created to administer the legislation, (2) the resistance of key participants to providing funds necessary for the implementation of the law, and (3) the lack of gubernatorial support for a compromise to facilitate the implementation of the legislation.

Administrative Deficiencies

In order for those entrusted with the responsibility for implementing a directive to discharge their responsibilities, as Barnard[10] and others have pointed out, they must understand the directive as well as be capable of carrying it out. In the case of the administration of the Agricultural Labor Relations Act, these conditions were not adequately fulfilled. The administrative officials entrusted with the responsibility for administering the legislation found themselves under extreme time pressures; they confronted a heavy caseload and complex law, and they lacked the experience and competence necessary to discharge their responsibilities effectively.

In attempting to implement the Agricultural Labor Relations Act, the ALRB was breaking new ground. Its efforts were unprecedented. Given this lack of precedence and hence experience upon which to build, one would have thought that the ALRB would have been provided sufficient time to prepare adequately for assuming its responsibilities. The board was not provided such time, however, as a result of the timing of the legislation's effective date and the scheduling of the first secret ballot elections. Because the legislation became effective on August 28, 1975, the ALRB and its staff had less than one week to prepare for conducting the first secret ballot election on September 2, 1975, and for the deluge of elections it had to conduct immediately after.

During the first month of its existence, the board conducted more than 200 elections; at the same time, it also found itself having to investigate at least 200 complaints from growers and the unions regarding some aspect of the implementation of the law. To carry out its responsibilities, during its initial month of existence the board also had to quickly hire approximately 91 employees and train them for administering the law. In addition to conducting elections, these employees also had to investigate complaints, hold hearings on contested ballots, and issue findings. Most, however, lacked the kind of experience needed to facilitate the implementation of the farm labor law.

The Resistance of Key Participants

In the absence of intense concerns about the implementation of the legislation, these administrative deficiencies might have proved harmless. The implementation of the Agricultural Labor Relations Act was not a process marked by the absence of such concern, however, for the stakes involved in its implementation were too high. Consequently, the deficiencies assumed a greater significance than might have been the case. Specifically, the deficiencies generated dissatisfaction with the ALRB among the UFW and, more importantly, precipitated intense resistance against additional funding for the ALRB on the part of the growers and their allies.

The UFW's Dissatisfaction with ALRB. The UFW's dissatisfaction with the board surfaced immediately after it began operation, stemming from the view that the board's operations under its general counsel, Walter Kintz, had perpetuated the collusion between the growers and the Teamsters Union.

By late September 1975, 26,433 votes had been cast. The UFW had won 45.5 percent of the votes; the Teamsters had won 29.4 percent. Of the workers 14 percent had voted for no union. The UFW's margin of victory, although satisfying to Chavez and the UFW, was considered to be 15 to 20 percent less than they would have received under experienced and competent administration. Combined with unfair labor practices on the part of the growers, the ALRB's inexperience and incompetence—Chavez and the UFW charged—had undermined the administration of the legislation to such an extent that many farm workers no longer felt they could "obtain justice through the electoral process."[11]

In late September 1975, Chavez and the UFW called for the dismissal of the ALRB's general counsel, Walter Kintz. Kintz—Chavez and the UFW charged—was the person most responsible for perpetuating the collusion between the growers and the Teamsters by failing to adequately enforce the law. They urged Governor Brown to replace Kintz with a general counsel and staff who would enforce the law without bias.

Governor Brown did not dismiss Kintz. Instead, he ordered an aide to investigate the relationship between Kintz and the ALRB. In early October, in an attempt to dissipate some of the hostility against the ALRB, Kintz created a "special enforcement force" within his office "to ensure compliance with the law and protect its integrity."[12]

These actions did not eliminate Chavez's and the UFW's dissatisfaction with Kintz. Approximately one month after these actions were taken, several members of the UFW staged a three-day sit-in outside Governor Brown's office and demanded both the restoration of jobs for 1800 farm workers allegedly fired for participating in union election activities and the dismissal of Kintz, whom they charged with not acting quickly enough to investigate and prosecute unfair labor practices by growers. Governor Brown refused to accede to their demands.

The Teamsters' and Growers' Dissatisfaction with ALRB. In contrast to dissatisfaction of Chavez and the UFW, the Teamster Union's and growers' dissatisfaction with the ALRB stemmed from their perception of the ALRB as being biased in favor of Chavez and the UFW.[13] This bias, they charged, was a result of Governor Brown's appointments to the board. When announcing his plans to appoint the ALRB's members, the Governor, they argued, had declared he would appoint competent, unbiased people. Instead, they maintained, he had appointed individuals whose previous associations biased their decisions in favor of Chavez and the UFW.

For the growers, one decision in particular reflected the ALRB's bias. This was the ALRB's administrative ruling on August 28, 1975, allowing union organizers to enter fields without the permission of growers to talk to workers for an hour before and after work and during the lunch hour. This ruling, the growers argued, was illegal, violating the property rights of the growers and the rights of workers who may not have wanted to be placed in the position of having to speak to a union representative but were forced to do so as a result of the ruling. Moreover, the growers argued, the ruling was unnecessary because the unions had sufficient opportunities to contact workers during nonworking hours.[14]

The growers did more than resort to protests against the ALRB's ruling. In San Joaquin County in early September 1975, a number of growers organized a vigilante group—the "Posse Commitates"—to patrol their ranches and prevent farm union representatives from gaining access to workers in their fields. Others took their grievances to the courts and met with initial success. On September 3, 1975, U.S. District Court Judge M.D. Crocker, at the request of a group of table grape growers, issued a restraining order preventing farm union representatives from entering the fields without the permission of the growers. One week later a Fresno County Superior Court judge, as a result of a suit filed by the Nisei Farmers League and Western Tomato Growers and Shippers Corporation, issued a similar order declaring that the access law violated the property rights of growers and prohibiting union representatives from entering the fields to talk to workers.

These orders were appealed immediately to the California State Supreme Court by Chavez and the UFW. On September 18, 1975, the court suspended the two lower court rulings pending a review of the access law by the United States Supreme Court. The court's decision, needless to say, constituted a setback for the growers. Rebuffed by the court, the growers shifted the focus of their efforts to the state legislature, where they immediately garnered the support of a coalition of Republican and Democratic legislators from rural districts sympathetic to the growers. Encouraged by the growers, these legislators began to press for changes in the composition of membership of the ALRB, whom they accused of being biased toward Chavez and the UFW.

To secure these changes, the legislators moved to build a sufficient number of votes to halt additional appropriations for the ALRB. This was an extremely effective vehicle for obstructing the implementation of the collective-bargaining legislation. To facilitate the operation of the ALRB, the California legislature initially appropriated $1.55 million; however, by early December 1975, this funding had begun to run out as a result of the heavy caseload which the board found itself processing during the critical months of its operation.

In mid-December a measure authorizing the appropriation of an additional $3.8 million to keep the ALRB in operation until July 1, 1976, was introduced in the legislature by legislators sympathetic to the ALRB. The measure immediately evoked the opposition of the legislators sympathetic to the growers. By early January the legislators had gathered sufficient support to pose a serious threat to the continued operation of the ALRB.

In early January 1976, the ALRB announced that unless funding was provided for its operations, it would have to dismiss its staff; and it notified its 200-member staff of possible termination.[15] On January 16, the ALRB voted to terminate a part of its activities and began to plan for the complete termination of its operations. Approximately two weeks later, on January 27, 1976, the California Senate, as a result of the efforts of the coalition of Republican and Democratic legislators, failed to approve the measure appropriating additional funding for the ALRB. The Senate voted 20-15 in support of the appropriation, but a two-thirds majority (27 votes) was needed for the measure to pass.

Gubernatorial Intransigence

The defeat of the measure in the Senate, needless to say, represented a setback for Governor Brown's efforts to institutionalize collective bargaining for farm workers. Consequently, the Governor immediately initiated negotiations with legislators supporting or opposed to the ALRB. On January 28, 1976, Governor Brown convened several pivotal legislators and members of his staff in an attempt to find a solution to the legislative impasse. The negotiations were unproductive, however; a compromise solution could not be found. A major factor in this failure to find a compromise solution was Governor Brown's refusal to yield to the demands of the legislators sympathetic to the growers.

Prior to and during the negotiations, Governor Brown warned that changes in the collective-bargaining labor legislation would "paralyze" the efforts to resolve labor-management strife in California agriculture. In January he declared,

To now try to start changing this or that is to open up a Pandora's box. I'm not really sure that's what the legislature wants to do. I think it would be a real step backward if we were now to let [the board] fall by the wayside and get back to the jungle. I really can't believe that the farmers and farmworkers or anybody else really wants to turn the clock back.[16]

Governor Brown's refusal to yield to the demands were praised by those sympathetic to the ALRB. However, his refusal to compromise prevented the passage of the emergency appropriation measure for the ALRB. By early February, the ALRB had exhausted most of its funds. On February 6, it held the final secret ballot elections. The emergency appropriation measure remained moribund in the legislation. The nation's first collective-bargaining law for farm workers was no longer being implemented.

The Aftermath: The Rise and Fall of Proposition 14

In the succeeding months, the efforts to revive the operations of the ALRB continued. The focus of these efforts became the budget for the succeeding fiscal year. Having failed in their efforts to secure passage of the emergency appropriation measure, the supporters of the ALRB mobilized to secure passage of a budget with appropriations for the ALRB. Some of them also mobilized to support the passage of a special "initiative" measure conceived by Cesar Chavez and the UFW.

In April 1976, Chavez and the UFW began to circulate petitions to place the collective-bargaining law on the November 1976 general election ballot. Within a record 28 days, the UFW and its supporters gathered 728,000 signatures—enough to qualify the measure for the November ballot. As conceived by the UFW, the initiative (proposition 14)

1. Wrote into law the access rule adopted by the ALRB in September 1975
2. Allowed, but did not require, the ALRB "in appropriate cases" to assess treble damage against a union or a grower found guilty of unfair labor violations
3. Required the ALRB to make an employer's list of employees available to any union that filed a notice of intent to petition for an election when the notice of intent was accompanied by a "reasonable showing of interest" by the workers
4. Declared that a minimum of 50 percent of an employer's workers had to petition for a decertification election before the ALRB would hold a decertification election
5. Required the legislature to appropriate in the annual state budget sufficient funding to allow the ALRB to implement the law
6. Required the Governor to appoint a new ALRB

If adopted, the initiative would not be subject to legislative amendments. It could be changed only by another vote of the electorate.

The initiative immediately evoked opposition from the growers. They quickly realized that if the initiative passed, effective changes in the collective-bargaining legislation would become extremely difficult. The growers initiated a two-pronged strategy to defeat Proposition 14. First, they reversed their position on funding for the ALRB, which they regarded as more favorable to their interests than the initiative. Instead of opposing funding for the ALRB, they promoted its inclusion in the budget. As a result of their reversal, the obstacles to appropriations for the board were substantially reduced. In late June, the remaining obstacles were removed when Governor Brown appointed three new members to fill vacancies on the ALRB. These appointments had been demanded by legislators opposed to funding for the ALRB. All were satisfactory to the growers, whose representatives said the appointments would produce a more impartial board. With the appointments secured, the growers focused their attention on the other half of their strategy—a statewide media campaign against the farm worker initiative.

Through their chief spokesman, Harry Kubo, president of the Nisei Farmers League, in their media campaign the growers charged that (1) the initiative was no longer needed because the legislature had appropriated funds for the ALRB in the annual budget and (2) the initiative violated the constitutional right to private property by codifying the ALRB's access ruling.[17]

These contentions were challenged by the UFW and Governor Brown. In response to the first contention of the growers, the UFW argued that the initiative was needed in order to guarantee the rights of farm workers from the capriciousness of the growers. If it had not been for Proposition 14, funding to implement the collective-bargaining legislation would not have been provided by the legislature. If Proposition 14 were not passed, they argued, the legislation would be stymied in the future. In response to the second claim of the growers, the UFW pointed out that the access ruling was "very limited and very specific" and applied only to election situations in agriculture. Moreover, the legality of the ruling had been affirmed by the California State Supreme Court.[18]

Governor Brown supported the UFW and the initiative. The initiative, the Governor argued in speeches and a series of special television commercials, would remove the farm labor law from politics and bring stability and peace to California agriculture. It also would permit state officials to concentrate on other issues confronting California. These issues, he contended, had been neglected because of the controversy over the farm labor law.[19]

In response to the Governor's contentions, the growers initiated an intense advertising campaign against Brown. In a series of full-page ads the growers accused the Governor of dishonesty in his support of Proposition 14. In late October, the growers also staged a demonstration in the Governor's office and accused the Governor of "lying to the people of California," when he declared in his speeches that Proposition 14 gave secret ballot elections to the farm workers. This declaration, the growers argued, falsely implied that California farm workers did not have such rights under the California Agricultural Relations Act of 1975.

In reply to these allegations, Governor Brown retorted that the growers in collusion with the major oil companies were attempting to "sabotage" the collective-bargaining law. On October 28, 1976, the Governor, at a special press conference, urged others "not to be fooled by the propoganda of corporate growers and oil companies, such as Getty Oil, Standard Oil, Superior Oil and others who are trying to sabotage the work of the California legislature." The oil companies and large corporate farms were "in the farming business and making good profits" and wanted to keep it that way, he charged, by defeating Proposition 14.[20]

The bitter debate over Proposition 14 continued into election day, November 3, 1976, with varying degrees of intensity. On November 3, the voters went to the polls. Much to the dismay of Chavez, the UFW, and Governor Brown, the initiative was rejected by the electorate by a 2-1 margin. The final tally showed that 2,880,215 votes were cast for the measure; 4,773,577 votes were cast against it.[21]

After the defeat of the proposition, the implementation of the nation's first collective-bargaining legislation continued. Today the law is still being implemented; the legislation remains surrounded in controversy. I will not examine the current implementation process, for this aspect is beyond the scope and purpose of this chapter. Rather, I will discuss the lessons of the California experience for future efforts elsewhere to institutionalize collective bargaining in agriculture.

The California Experience and Its Lessons

What does the California experience tell us about the utility, feasibility, and viability of efforts to institutionalize collective bargaining for farm workers? More specifically, does it suggest that such efforts are not worth pursuing, administratively impossible to carry out, and/or unlikely to succeed even in the face of strong executive efforts to facilitate these efforts? The answers to these questions suggested by the California experience, I believe, are negative. As this chapter has attempted to demonstrate, the efforts to establish collective bargaining are likely to be extremely controversial and frustrating. Nevertheless, they are worth pursuing if for no other reason than that, as has been the case in California, they may bring an end to violent strife in agriculture. Moreover, these efforts may succeed, especially if they are based on (1) an awareness of the problems likely to arise as a result of the efforts to establish collective bargaining for farm workers and (2) appropriate planning and provision for the personnel and funds necessary to administer the legislation.

Conflict between labor and management remains today in California. However, it is not the same form of conflict which characterized this relationship prior to the advent of the nation's first collective-bargaining legislation covering farm workers. Dissatisfaction and disagreement over aspects of the administration of the law exist among some of the participants.

As the California experience suggests, efforts to establish collective bargaining must be preceded by efforts to secure personnel with the qualifications necessary to understand and carry out their responsibilities. Those entrusted with the responsibility of implementing the legislation also must be provided sufficient funding to discharge their functions effectively. Such funding combined with the appropriate personnel and awareness of potential problems may not be sufficient to successfully institutionalize collective bargaining, especially if vital participants offer resistance. Without the funds and personnel, however, the process is likely to be more difficult; temporary nonimplementation may become permanent nonimplementation.

To avoid nonimplementation, efforts must also be made to secure the incentives necessary for securing and maintaining the cooperation of the various participants. In some cases the discovery of such incentives may be difficult. Nevertheless, the search is worth undertaking. As the California experience suggests, the prospect of an end to the strife which has plagued agriculture is a goal worth striving for.

Notes

1. For a discussion of these efforts see, for example, John G. Dunne, *Delano: The Story of the California Grape Strike* (New York: Farrar Strauss and Geroux, 1967), and Joan London and Henry Anderson, *So Shall Ye Reap* (New York: Thomas Y. Crowell Company, 1970).

2. London and Anderson, ibid., p. 37.

3. See Peter Matthieson, *Sal Si Puedes* (New York: Random House, 1969), and Jacques Levy, *Chesar Chavez: Autobiography of La Causa* (New York: W.W. Norton and Company, 1975).

4. For an extensive discussion of these activities, see Levy, ibid., pp. 475-527.

5. Quoted in "Governor's Inauguration Speech," *California Journal,* February 1975, p. 59.

6. This discussion of the ways in which the farm labor compromise was developed draws extensively from Charles Bowman, "Brown's Farm-Labor Coup," *California Journal,* June 1975, pp. 190-92, and the account presented by California Secretary of Agriculture and Services, Rose Bird, at the Symposium on California Farm Labor, San Francisco, September 1975.

7. This negotiating session concluded with a dramatic telephone call from Governor Brown to Cesar Chavez, whose representatives had been involved in the negotiations. At the instigation of the growers, who wanted to determine whether Chavez accepted the compromise, the Governor connected his telephone to loudspeakers in his office and called Chavez. Chavez agreed to the compromise and promised that the UFW would abide by its terms.

8. For an analysis of the legislation and its similarities and differences with the measures proposed by the growers and Chavez and the UFW, see Bowman, "Brown's Farm-Labor Coup," p. 192.

9. For an extensive discussion of this assessment of the status of the legislation, see "Why Farm Labor Law Isn't Working," *Los Angeles Times,* November 17, 1975.

10. Chester Barnard, *The Functions of the Executive* (Cambridge, Mass.: Harvard University, 1938).

11. The criticisms leveled against the Agricultural Labor Relations Board and its general counsel are reported in "Chavez: Collusion between Growers, Teamsters," *Los Angeles Times,* November 11, 1975.

12. Quoted in "Enforcement of Farm Law to Be Tightened," *Los Angeles Times,* September 30, 1975.

13. "Chief of Farm Labor Group Calls It a Case of Too Much, Too Soon," *Los Angeles Times,* November 11, 1975.

14. Ibid.

15. This warning represented an attempt on the ALRB's part to place pressure on the California legislature to secure funds. It was unsuccessful, however.

16. Quoted in "Emergency Aid for Farm Board Denied," *Los Angeles Times,* January 28, 1976.

17. "Arguments Obscure Prop. 14's Basic Points," *Los Angeles Times,* October 31, 1976.

18. The case made by the UFW for the passage of Proposition 14 is summarized in the UFW's leaflet, "Proposition 14: The Farm Worker Initiative."

19. "Brown Assails Oil Firm on Farm Law: Charges Alliance with Growers to Sabotage Statute," *Los Angeles Times,* October 29, 1976.

20. Ibid.

21. "Election Results," *California Journal,* December 1976, p. 409.

18 The Politics of Farmland Preservation

J. D. Esseks

Preserving farmland has become an agenda item for policy makers in many state and local governments. The threat or actuality of urban sprawl has driven farming, environmental, no-growth, humanitarian, and other groups to champion "Farmland Preservation" or "Save Our Farms" as a means to protect their varying interests which sprawl endangers.

From the experiences of several jurisdictions, this chapter develops hypotheses about the politics of farmland preservation. More specifically, it is concerned with how certain preservation techniques become agenda items, what political interests support and oppose them, and what conditions lead to their adoption and renewal (in the sense of policy makers and those who influence them judging a technique to have "succeeded" or "failed"). Four techniques (or approaches) are examined: (1) the incentive of basing property taxes on farm value rather than land market value, (2) the package of incentives represented by agricultural districts, (3) public sector purchase of development rights, and (4) restrictive zoning.

The political stakes in the adoption or rejection of these techniques can be high. Depending on the alternative chosen, costs may include significantly reducing a county's or township's revenues, increasing tax burdens for nonfarmland owners, depriving land developers or speculators of handsome profits, preventing elderly farmers from converting their land into "pensions" for retirement, or budgeting public funds for purchase of control over farmland.

On the other hand, once developed, farmland is likely never to be returned to farming; it is a nonrenewable resource. Scores of counties, many substate regions, and even some entire states (New Jersey) which face seemingly unending urbanization pressures may witness the end of farming as a significant economic and physical phenomenon in their midst by the close of this century. Unless they adopt public-policy preservation measures and/or are affected by shortages of mortgage money, gasoline for commuters, and other resources that fuel urban sprawl, they may see the elimination or severe reduction of the supply of locally produced fresh fruits and vegetables, the employment and investment opportunities provided by agriculture (for agribusinesses as well as for farming), the amount of green open space that is maintained privately rather than by tax-supported park agencies, and the health and aesthetic benefits of open space.

199

Farm-Value Assessment

In terms of state-level actions aimed at farmland preservation, the most widely used approach is farm-value assessment (also called "use-value assessment"). Between 1956 and early 1974, 42 states authorized assessment of farmland on the basis of its vlaue for farming purposes rather than on its apparent real estate market value, which for many parcels in or near the urban fringe reflects the land's potential for residential, industrial, or commercial uses.[1] A common practice has been for assessors to base per-acre market value of farmland on the recorded sales prices for similar parcels recently sold in the same area.[2] For example, we are told that in Connecticut the sale of "a tract of land at a high unit value for development purposes results in a similarly high unit value for assessment for all nearby tracts."[3] In contrast, under farm-value assessment (FVA), a parcel's tax liability would be derived from its cash rent value, a rating of its soil's productivity (the most common basis), or some other indicator of its worth in farming.[4]

A problem for many or most owners of farmland to which assessors ascribe development potential is that the eventual development sale may be years in the future. Urbanization tends to spread along existing transportation routes (which facilitate commuting and the location of new businesses). However, the farmland lying between the resulting "fingers" of sprawl may be ignored for some time by developers and speculators. Alternatively, speculator interest may not be strong enough to produce acceptable bids, that is, ones sufficiently high to satisfy the retirement needs of older farmers or to justify the economic and psychological costs of younger farmers moving their operations to a different county or state. But during the wait for acceptable offers, the farmer may be responsible for property taxes which the land's current earning capacity cannot support.

Where increasing property taxes wipe out or reduce farmers' profits, the result is likely to be a greater willingness, if not a sense of necessity, to sell the land. Other things being equal, the farmer's acceptance price declines and the chance of a sale to a developer or speculator increases. Speculator-held land may remain in farming on a lease basis, although the new owner or lessee will probably not invest in maintaining the land's long-run productivity. Where tax difficulties contribute to a farmer's selling at a relatively low price, developers may pick up the land for immediate building even if it is miles from existing urban areas. The lower land costs may make the distant location marketable. To discourage such "premature" conversions out of agriculture as well as sales to speculators who neglect farmland's productivity is an explicit objective of several state's farm-value assessment laws.[5]

Why have so many states (42) adopted farm-value assessment (FVA)? In 19 states, between 1960 and 1973, adoption included passage of constitutional amendments which permitted deviations from the norm of uniformity in levying property taxes. Their state constitutions had prohibited preferential treatment in assessments. FVA legislation has been politically so successful probably because of the following factors:

1. The concerted support of farming interests—they can agree on tax benefits,[6] whereas they tend to divide over zoning and government purchase of development rights.
2. The plausibility of their injustice arguments, e.g., many farmers would "literally be unable to pay them [the high taxes resulting from market value assessment] and would be involved in a forced sale of farmland or serious deficit financing."[7]
3. The related association by the public of farmland owners with actual farmers, rather than the banks and other investors who in fact own much or most of the farmland near urban areas and many of whom can afford "deficit financing" for the period until the land is developed.
4. The significant support in many states (such as Connecticut, California, New Jersey, and Pennsylvania) given by open-space advocates and environmentalists.[8]

To persuade New Jersey nonfarmers that they had a direct stake in FVA, the organizers of the 1963 referendum campaign to amend the state's constitution, so as to permit FVA, adopted the theme "Save Open Space in New Jersey."[9] California supporters of FVA also saw the political advantage of marrying the two causes: open-space conservation and farmland preservation. They advocated extension of the principle of assessment according to present use, rather than development potential, to recreational land (e.g., camp grounds, golf courses), and in so doing they broadened the base of support for the successful 1966 constitutional referendum on assessment reform.[10]

The major political opposition to FVA has tended to come from local governments, especially from tax officials. They complain of the greater administrative costs of farm-value assessment over market-based assessment,[11] and they warn of the sizable revenues lost to the jurisdiction because of FVA and the probable need to increase the tax burden on nonfarmland owners in order to compensate for the losses. Particularly attracted to this last argument should be the nonfarmer residents of jurisdictions with relatively limited urbanization where farmland still represents a large proportion of total assessed value, so that a drop in farmland assessments impacts significantly on tax receipts. Kolesar and Scholl report that, following the enactment of FVA in New Jersey, "in some heavily agricultural municipalities, the tax rates were inflated as much as 60 percent because of the loss in farm ratables."[12] In California for the 1974-1975 year eight counties lost revenues or experienced tax burden shifts amounting to 4 to 10 percent of total revenues; in three the tax difference (loss or shift) exceeded 10 percent, and in one it was 22 percent.[13]

The policy responses to such findings (or predictions before FVA is enacted) have not tended to be to defeat, repeal, or substantially weaken FVA legislation. One response, made in California and New York, is for the state to compensate local jurisdictions for part of the tax loss attributable to FVA. Another has been to reduce revenue losses by trying to exclude land speculators from the program. A study of 1973 recipients of farm-value assessment in the Chicago metropolitan area found that 40 percent were nonfarmers.[14] It is assumed that most nonfarmer owners of farmland near or in metropolitan areas will eventually either develop the land themselves, or sell at a profit to other nonfarmers. In the meantime, they can lease the land to farmers and charge rents which cover atast part of their mortgage and tax costs. Since farm-value assessment usually reduces the tax component of carrying costs, it probably encourages speculation in many cases.

Among the methods adopted by states to discourage speculator participation in FVA programs are (1) requirements that try to restrict benefits to genuine farmers and (2) financial disincentives against converting enrolled land to nonagricultural uses. In Vermont, beneficiaries are supposed to earn no less than two-thirds of their total gross income from farming, in Alaska it is at least one-fourth, and in Texas farming must be the owner's "primary occupation."[15] The disincentives to convert include, for 21 states (as of 1974), mandatory repayment of the taxes saved, that is, the difference between what was actually paid out and what would have been assessed in the absence of FVA, with the repayment liability or "rollback" ranging from 2 to 20 years prior to the conversion of enrolled land; for 11 states, interest charges on the rollback taxes; and in a few cases, special monetary penalties in addition to tax repayments.

Does farm-value assessment have loyal defenders besides the direct benefiaries? In particular, are environmentalists and other groups who genuinely seek to preserve farmland or curb urban sprawl likely to defend FVA in legislative reviews? I hypothesize "yes" only where they see it as complementing other methods of farmland preservation. These interest groups are likely to be influenced by the evaluation studies now available which find FVA to be an inadequate preservation tool. That was the conclusion reached by separate studies of the New Jersey, Illinois, and Washington state programs and by two multistate evaluations.[16] The more extensive of the latter two studies concluded:

[D]ifferential assessment, by itself, is likely to be an ineffective deterrent to conversion of farmland. . . .

If preservation to agricultural activities is a legitimate social goal, intervention in both supply and demand processes must be undertaken. Preferential assessment addresses only a small part of the supply process. To be more effective, a comprehensive program should be designed to ameliorate economic and secondary disincentives to farming on the supply side and to channelize urban expansion to nonagricultural land on the rural-urban fringe on the demand side.[17]

The same study argues that FVA can significantly reduce the rate of farmland conversion only where both (1) the demand for development properties is "weak," that is, offer prices are low enough so that the increases in net incomes resulting from the tax breaks push the farmers' acceptance prices higher than those offer prices or high enough for other economic and, perhaps, psychological factors (such as connected with moving) to cause the offers to be rejected; and (2) the "economic conditions in farming" are "poor," that is, the value of the tax breaks are large relative to farmers' net earnings without them.[18] Parts of the country, such as the economically marginal dairy farming regions of the Northeast, meet these two criteria; and in some of those areas, the aggregate numbers of farmers helped by FVA may have been large. The Connecticut Conservation Association claimed in 1974 that "If Connecticut farmers were taxed on the market value of their properties, there would be but a handful left."[19] Similar claims were made for FVA in New Jersey; without it, "a large proportion of farmers would have had to go out of business."[20]

However, in many areas of the country with generally good farm earnings (such as the Corn Belt and California) and/or with strong development pressures, the tax savings from FVA are likely to be relatively too small to impact on land-sale decisions. If farm profits are high, a $20 to $30 per-acre break may be welcome but irrelevant to whether the land is sold. And if developers are offering $4000 to $5000 an acre; even a $100 saving per acre may weigh little.

Dissatisfaction with farm-value assessment has prompted many states and local jurisdictions to search for different methods of farmland preservation or for measures which, together with FVA, promise greater effectiveness. Among the state-level studies have been those by the Blueprint Commission on the Future of New Jersey Agriculture, which reported in 1973; the Maryland Commission on the Preservation of Agricultural (1974); the Connecticut Governor's Task Force for the Preservation of Agricultural Land (1974); the State Planning Office of Maine (1972); and the Illinois Farm Bureau (1975). None of these policy searches resulted in recommendations to repeal farm-value assessment; rather, all the studies urged the adoption of new tools to work in conjunction with FVA: state purchase of development rights (for New Jersey, Connecticut, and Maryland) and agricultural districts (Maine and Illinois).

Agricultural Districts

Farm-value assessment is a basic part of the preservation technique which involves creating "agricultural districts." Implemented on a state basis so far only in New York, but recently (April 1977) enacted in Virginia and being seriously considered in Illinois,[21] this technique calls for landowners voluntarily to form districts of at least 500 acres and to commit their land to farming for eight-year periods (in Virginia, four to eight years). If a district gains approval by the relevant local government (and by a state review agency, in the New York and Illinois versions), the land qualifies for a number of benefits.[22]

(1) Property taxes may be based on farm-value assessment.

(2) The land is protected from enforcement of nuisance ordinances. Sprawl-type development into rural areas frequently results in many nonfarming families living next to or near active farms; and such neighbors often induce local governments to pass ordinances against farming practices which are nuisances to them but important or essential to the success of the farms: applying chemical fertilizers or herbicides, cultivating with noisy tractors at night or early on weekend mornings, or driving slow farm vehicles on public roads.

(3) State agencies are committed to modifying, for districted land, those among their administrative regulations which hinder farming or drive up its costs, such as policies on farm-derived air and water pollution.

(4) Districts are supposed to be protected also against two kinds of government actions which lead to nonfarming development within the districts' borders: exercise of the right of eminent domain and use of the expenditure power to support (with grants or loans) non-farm-related construction. In the New York and Illinois versions, before a local governmental agency acquires land or provides financial support for public or private entities to build within a district, it must submit to a state-level review and the possibility of an injunction. In the Virginia case, local government does the reviewing of proposed actions by state agencies, special districts, or public service corporations.

(5) Yet another protection is against special tax assessments for non-farm-related amenities (street lighting, sewer and water lines) which public jurisdictions run through or near farmland in a district. Let us say that the review discussed above does not stop the building of a sewer line or nonfarm drainage facility. The adjacent farmland would not be assessed, even though such amenities enhance its development value.

In addition, if the districts are large enough, singly or in clusters, the farmers in them may be saved from loss of needed agribusinesses—those which supply inputs (fertilizers, seeds, machinery) and which process or market their outputs. In areas undergoing development, the number of farm customers may drop too low to support these service industries. Farm-value assessment may not be able to prevent such losses, because the enrolled farms may be too scattered. But agricultural districting, with its objective of grouping contiguous or nearby farms, may provide the needed "critical mass."

Finally, the district's eight-year time horizon may elicit relatively more farm investment. Where development pressures lead landowners to expect to sell within a few years, they understandably neglect investments for maintaining the productivity of their holdings. However, for the eight years of belonging to a district, whether the owner is a farmer or speculator, at least some investment makes financial sense; total neglect does not.

In summary, the agricultural districting approach to farmland preservation gives promise of a number of income-enhancing benefits (lower taxes, less regulation, a time frame conducive to investment) which may help farmers to resist purchase offers. The land's higher relative earnings tend to push the farmers' acceptance prices closer to or beyond speculators' or developers' offers. In addition, this approach commits local governments to refrain from encouraging development within the districts through their expenditures and use of the power of eminent domain.

What political interests are likely to promote adoption of agricultural districting? I hypothesize that farming groups will, as they have done in New York, Virginia, and Illinois. This approach offers them significant income benefits, and they are not effectively constrained from converting their land out of agriculture if they wish. The main cost is only that of paying rollbacks on property taxes.

The Farm Bureau and Grange strongly backed and contributed to the drafting of New York's districting legislation, which was introduced and passed in 1971.[23] The Farm Bureau also has been the principal backer in Illinois. One of the authors of the Illinois bill reported that he and his Farm Bureau colleagues chose this approach after becoming dissatisfied with farm-value assessment and being convinced that the added incentives offered by districts (or *areas*, as they are termed in the Illinois bill) could significantly slow the rate of conversion.[24] A cynical interpretation of farming groups' sponsorship of agricultural districting is that their primary concern is to win income benefits for their members and that the ostensible farmland preservation objective is more a means than an end, that is, a means to attract nonfarmer support to the legislation. Of course, nonfarming groups can suspect such motivation and still be attracted to the legislation because they believe it will, in fact, promote preservation.

What nonfarming groups are likely to oppose agricultural districting? Because this approach is more costly in concessions to farmers, it may attract a wider array of opponents than farm-value assessment. Environmentalists, for example, may balk at the provision for modifying state regulations which increase farm costs, if, as it seems likely, some such regulations will concern farm-derived air and water pollution. Local government officials may oppose districting because of its constraints on their freedom to shape their jurisdiction's development, namely, the restrictions on eminent domain and the location of capital improvements. During legislative committee hearings on the 1977 Illinois bill (H.B. 772), the Illinois Municipal League (speaking for a membership of 930 cities, towns, and villages) testified against it for that reason.[25] Similar opposition has surfaced in New York from "some community leaders who favor unrestrained suburban development and see limitations imposed by the law as a hindrance."[26]

For advocates of farmland preservation and open space whose continued support of a policy instrument requires some evidence of its effectiveness, the record on agricultural districting is *not yet* persuasive. Of course, it consists of only a single state's experiences. In New York the participation seemingly has been high. As of October 1976, there were 320 districts, comprising about 4.4 million acres, or close to half of New York's total land in farms.[27] But how many of the participating landowners would have converted their land out of agriculture in the absence of the districts? In mid-1976 about 28 percent of the districted acreage fell in SMSA counties, that is with considerable urbanization in at least part of the county; and 19 percent of the total acres "were located within 25 miles of an urban area over 50,000 in population."[28] It seems likely that, in such areas, many owners of districted land received purchase offers from speculators or developers or could have attracted offers if they had put parcels on the market. Much of the land was probably close enough to urban centers for building commuter housing or siting industries. However, whether and how many landowners rejected offers or did not seek them because of districting or invested more in their farming because of the benefits from districting and its time frame are questions which need to be answered by empirical studies.

Purchase of Development Rights

The farmland owners who may now respond to the incentives of farm-value assessment and/or agricultural districting are likely, in time, as urbanization draws closer to their land, to face irresistible purchase offers. A technique now being tried in New Jersey and New York which promises long-term preservation of farmland is government purchase of development rights. In September 1976, Suffolk County (New York) approved a $21 million bond issue to fund the first phase, about 3800 acres, of a three-part purchasing program, which in total is expected to transfer to the county government the development rights of 12,000 to 15,000 acres, or about 30 to 38 percent of the county's remaining farmland.[29] In January 1977, the state of New Jersey launched a pilot purchasing program, limited to $5 million in expenditure and to four townships in one county (Burlington), but with the possibility of considerable expansion if the pilot effort proves successful.

The Suffolk County and New Jersey programs appear to have essentially the same expectations regarding the sequence of (1) government actions, (2) land-owner responses, and (3) resulting private and public benefits. The government offers to buy development rights (or *easements,* as they are called in New Jersey) for the difference between the market and farm-use values of the land. Many farmers are expected to respond favorably because the program gives promise of fair compensation for surrendering their rights to develop the land; their property taxes would be permanently based on the land's value for farming (since no other use is legal); and their families would inherit the land at its lower farm-use value, lessening the need to sell land in order to pay death duties.[30]

Another expected farmowner response was to use some of the proceeds from the development rights sales to invest in improving their farm operations, such as by buying better equipment or acquiring additional land so as to realize efficiencies of scale.

The public benefits expected to flow from these private gains include both agricultural and nonfarming payoffs: securing supplies of fresh fruits and vegetables to local consumers, ensuring the survival of local agribusinesses, preserving open space which would be privately maintained and tax-paying, encouraging the tourist industry which was threatened by increased congestion on the landscape, and curbing urban sprawl and the associated increases in public expenditures.[31]

To push the development rights approach to agenda status and then to authorize and fund it appears to require more political resources than the same tasks for farm-value assessment or agricultural districting. Per-acre development rights on or near the urban fringe probably will be costly,[32] and purchase programs are likely to require a specific and rather large appropriations bill or bond resolution on which opposition can conveniently and dramatically focus. With FVA and districting, public costs tend to be in tax revenue foregone or tax burdens shifted, which are less easy to explain and dramatize.

To succeed, especially through the appropriations process, development rights schemes may require the active backing of the jurisdiction's chief executive. The New Jersey program had the support of Governor Brendan Byrne; and in Suffolk County the elected county executive, John Klein, was the program's chief patron within government and tireless advocate to the public.[33] In New Jersey crucial support came also from Philip Alampi, the state's Secretary of Agriculture for many years and someone skilled in winning backing in the legislature for farm programs. It was a study commission which he appointed and chaired that recommended the development rights approach to farmland preservation in New Jersey.[34]

Alampi's legislative task was eased by the decision to raise only $5 million. His study commission had recommended in 1973 that the state acquire up to 1 million acres of prime farmland, an amount which was expected to guarantee the viability of agriculture in New Jersey. But budgetary difficulties and politics precluded investing the several hundred million dollars required for so much land. Alampi compromised on a relatively small demonstration project which, with its $5 million, was expected to acquire from 6000 to 10,000 acres.[35] During legislative hearings in February and March 1976, the proposed pilot program was opposed by the New Jersey Farm Bureau on the grounds that it was too small in size and lacked complementary measures (e.g., relaxation of state regulations affecting agriculture) which would help keep farming viable. In other words, the program might preserve farmland but fail to preserve farming.[36] Other opposition came from the New Jersey Association of Realtors and the State's Builders' Association, with both groups apparently concerned about the antigrowth implications of the program. The authorizing legislation nevertheless passed in July 1976, and implementation began in early 1977.[37]

John Klein had the more difficult task of raising more money ($21 million) from a smaller jurisdiction (a county rather than an entire state).[38] For the two-thirds legislative majority required to approve a bond issue, he needed support from county legislators representing the more populous western part of the county. Of the 18 seats in the county legislature 16 were apportioned to the five western townships. However, the direct benefits of the program—the proceeds from development rights sales, the lower inheritance taxes, the rural vistas preserved—were to be concentrated in the five eastern townships. The remaining farmland in the county's western part was considered too expensive and scattered to be included in the program. Complicating efforts to secure support from "West End" legislators were the troubles of a large sewer district in the county's southwest corner, which imposed special assessments on its users and which, in 1976, neared default on its bond payments. County legislators from the district felt under constituent pressure to resist a new bond issue (for development rights purchases), which would mean more taxes and yet apparently no benefits for their area. In a vote taken on May 11, 1976, on the preservation plan, none of the six legislators representing parts of the sewer district voted for the bond issue; and the two-thirds majority was missed.[39] Twelve positive votes were needed (out of 18), but only nine were cast. In a second vote, on September 9, one of the sewer district representatives and three other West End legislators switched to the affirmative to carry the bond resolution.[40]

Between the two ballots, the sewer district's financial difficulties abated, and propreservation lobbying by environmental and civic groups intensified. In June these groups joined in the Save Our Farms Committee, which included about 30 environmental organizations, 6 local government bodies (village or town boards), and 28 civic associations.[41] Three of the local government and about 20 of the nongovernment organizations were from the West End. The committee's published objectives were to secure through the farmland preservation program "Clean Water, Clean Air, Agriculture, Balanced Economy, Lower Taxes, Sound Planning, Open Space, [and] Recreation."[42] These objectives had clear appeal to nonfarming groups in the East End—maintaining a pleasant environment of small towns, farms, and summer homes, with good well water and low taxes, among other benefits. For the many summer people and year-round residents who originated from New York City or congested suburbs, the preservation program promised to protect them from a life style from which they had escaped or were fleeing each summer.

But what did these objectives mean to West End residents? The program's potential growth-reducing or compacting effect could help them with their tax bills. The county government provides police and other services to all residents. If the farmland preservation program leads to less sprawl, there should be some savings in public service costs, since it usually costs less to serve a compact population than a scattered one. However, open space and recreation were probably the more important objectives for West Enders. Their part of the county was close to becoming wall-to-wall suburbs, so that only the East End offered considerable rural land to pass through on pleasure drives or to picnic or camp.[43] But would they not prefer to drive another half-hour or so, into another county farther from the city, letting their own county fill in with development but saving themselves from additional taxes due to development rights purchases? Citizens of the suburbanizing counties adjacent to Chicago may prefer that option; prairie farmland stretches for hundreds of miles to the west and south. But geography effectively denies that option to Suffolk County West Enders. To the north, east, and south is water (Long Island Sound and the Atlantic Ocean); and to the west are virtually solid suburbs and then New York City. A good part of the political success of the development rights approach in Suffolk County may be due to this unusual geographic context. Legislators and constituents may have valued the remaining farmed open space extraordinarily highly because it had no rivals within easy access.

On the other hand, scarcity is relative to the people doing the valuation. Those people may be willing to pay for the preservation of farmed open space near their homes, even if they have access to similar land after an hour's drive. The development rights approach may catch on in New Jersey and expand beyond the pilot project. It is on the agenda of Howard County, Maryland, which is situated between Baltimore and Washington. One of the county council's five members, Ruth Keeton, worked with farming and civic groups to develop legislation which she introduced early in 1977. As in Suffolk County, many nonfarming residents were supporting the program for its promise of limiting suburbanization and the resulting higher taxes and changes in life style.[44] Metropolitan Baltimore and Washington were expanding toward the county, and the superhighways already bisecting it threatened to spread development widely.

While government purchase of development rights preserves farmland from development, it may not preserve it for commercial farming. The prohibition on development of enrolled parcels may well attract to adjacent, nonprogram land housing developers who seek to capitalize on the open space and rural vistas provided by those parcels. The viability of farming on the latter may then be jeopardized by human and domestic-pet trespassing, disruption of drainage, nuisance suits, and other income-reducing consequences of the juxtaposition of farming and residential land uses. To avoid or moderate these problems, a jurisdiction could employ some combination of development rights purchases and agricultural districting.

Farming viability may be threatened also by the "critical mass" problem, that is when too much land in an area is converted out of farming or becomes idle and therefore leaves essential agribusinesses with too few clients to sustain themselves. Lesher and Eiler speculate that Suffolk County's development rights program will flounder on this problem.[45] They doubt that there will be sufficient political support to expand Suffolk's program beyond the initial stage of purchasing about 3800 acres; the cost in higher taxes seem too great. And they doubt also that "the needed mix of input suppliers and marketing services" would remain if only 3800 acres survived in farming.[46] However, as many or more acres outside the program may continue to be farmed. Locational problems or weakening market demand for buildable land may keep the bulldozers away for many years. Wall-to-wall suburbanization is not inevitable. Population growth or redistribution is unlikely to be great enough to fill in all the farmed open space now on the urban fringes of our cities.[47] Therefore, a modest-cost development rights program may provide a farming core which, along with nonprogram land, ensures the viability of commercial farming in an area for many additional years.

Restrictive Zoning

Since the restrictive zoning approach to preserving farmland relies on the police power, it may obviate the need for large public expenditures or complicated incentives programs. However, it tends to incur severe legal and political obstacles. The legal questions revolve mostly around the Fifth Amendment prohibition against taking of property without fair compensation. With the chance to sell or develop their land for a return of several thousand dollars per acre, farmland owners often challenge restrictive zoning ordinances before the relevant legislative body and then, if need be, in the courts, using the argument that denial of the right to convert their land out of agriculture is an unconstitutional "taking" of property, that is, taking away the opportunity for more profitable uses. The legal aspects of the "taking" issue are too complex to discuss here.[48] However, an important political factor is that many advocates of farmland preservation have become convinced, rightly or wrongly, that the "taking" argument will defeat zoning techniques for preservation and that, therefore, they have to look to other policy methods. This line of reasoning was apparently influential in New Jersey and Suffolk County.[49] It was found also in the state of Washington, where the introduction of agricultural zoning legislation was discouraged by the expectation that the state's supreme court would nullify it.[50]

Another discouraging factor in Washington and probably most other states was the expectation of strong political opposition. An earlier effort to direct Washington's local governments to protect agricultural land had met "violent opposition from a large segment of the population adamantly opposed to being told what to do with their land."[51]. State-imposed zoning has been considered unfeasible also in Illinois because of expected strong opposition both from local governments, guarding their land-use powers against state incursions, and from farmers, preferring to keep zoning controls at the local level where their potential for influence is greater.[52] The California zoning bill discussed at the beginning of the chapter passed the state Assembly in January 1976 but in August was defeated at the committee stage in the Senate. Its chief sponsor, Assemblyman Charles Warren (Los Angeles), mobilized impressive public support: from the state Bar Association, several environmental groups, major newspapers in the state, and also (after some watering down of the bill) the League of California Cities.[53] The opposition, however, was stronger, including the state chamber of commerce, building trades labor unions, contractors, and realtors who objected to the antigrowth implications of protecting prime agricultural land; fifteen county boards of supervisors which opposed at least in part because of the threat to their land-use powers; and major farming and cattle interests because of the threat to their freedom to dispose of the land how and when they wished.[54]

When the option is restrictive zoning by local governments rather than by the state, interjurisdictional conflict need not be a factor; but remaining will usually be opposition from development interests (realtors, builders, etc.). The growth businesses may oppose other farmland preservation techniques, as they did during New Jersey's consideration of development rights purchases. But zoning is a potentially greater threat to them because of its compulsory nature; landowners may not elect to escape its impact, as they can with the first three approaches discussed. However, against zoning, development interests usually have allies among local farmers who intend to develop their own land or who demand the right to sell to the highest bidder. The farmers' political resources may include considerable clout in local elections and the capacity to make persuasive "fair play" arguments before zoning authorities (e.g., "I need to retire and this developer offers me enough to make retirement possible").

Summary

This chapter offers hypotheses about four approaches to farmland preservation which are now being applied at the state and/or local level. They include the following.

(1) Restrictive zoning is likely to have limited effectiveness; adopting or strictly enforcing it tends to be discouraged by doubts as to its constitutionality and by intense economically based opposition, including from farmers.

(2) The other three techniques offer sufficient economic benefits for farmers to be centrally involved in efforts to promote them to agenda status, to enact them, and then to support them in subsequent legislative reviews.

(3) To be politically successful, the same techniques need nonfarming allies (environmentalists, advocates of no or slow growth), many of whom will require

evidence that the technique "works" in the sense of providing public benefits as well as private advantages (e.g., tax breaks to farmland owners).

(4) The farm-value assessment approach is unlikely to yield much evidence of producing such benefits by itself.

(5) The multifaceted approach of agricultural districting is more likely to justify itself, at least in stimulating greater investment in the land's agricultural productivity and, perhaps, in slowing the rate of sales to speculators and developers.

(6) Of the three, the development rights approach appears to be the most difficult politically to adopt. While it promises long-term preservation of farmland, its high cost seems to preclude applying it in many jurisdictions or on many acres in any one jurisdiction. However, special circumstances—geographic barriers, the intense preferences of recent immigrants from cities or suburbia— may combine to push the "political" value of agricultural space high enough for large expenditures to be acceptable. At stake are nonrenewable resources and life styles which many people may be deeply motivated to preserve.

Notes

1. Raleigh Barlowe and Theodore R. Alter, *Use-Value Assessment of Farm and Open Space Lands* (East Lansing: Michigan State University Agricultural Experiment Station, 1976), pp. 3-4.

2. Traditionally, assessed values for farms were held much closer to farm values than the present "highest and best use" philosophy permits. Assessors gave the benefit of any doubt about the ultimate urban demand for land to be the man who continued [to] farm, though once he started selling house lots, then his whole farm was judged to be worth house lot prices. In today's revaluations, a farmer need only be in an area where *someone* is selling lots to have housing considered the "highest and best use" for his land. Howard E. Conklin, "Agricultural Districts in New York State: Where and Why They Work," in *The Proceedings of the Conference on Rural Land-Use Policy in the Northeast,* October 2-4, 1974 (Ithaca, N.Y.: Northeast Regional Center for Rural Development, 1975), p. 174. See also Carolyn Sally King, "Use-Value Assessment of Farmland in Illinois," Thesis, Graduate College of the University of Illinois at Urbana-Champaign, 1976, p. 29.

3. Irving F. Fellows, "Use-Value Assessment in the Northeast," in *Proceedings of the Conference on Land-Use Policy,* p. 167.

4. Robert J. Gloudemans, *Use-Value Farmland Assessment: Theory, Practice and Impact* (Chicago: International Association of Assessing Officers, 1974), pp. 15-18.

5. See for examples, New York, Agriculture and Markets Law, Article 25; Delaware, Farmland Assessment Act of 1968; Delaware Code Ch. 83, Title 9;

and California Code, Ann. Rev. and Tax Code 402.1, 421-31, and Government Code 51240.

6. For example, the 1961-1962 campaign for farm-value assessment in California was supported by "eight leading California farm organizations," including the Cattleman's Association, the California Farm Bureau Federation, the state Grange, and the Council of California Growers. Race D. Davies, *Preserving Agricultural and Open-Space Lands: Legislative Policymaking in California* (Davis, Calif.: Institute of Governmental Affairs, 1972), p. 26.

7. Spencer Volpp, Illinois Agricultural Association legislative representative, quoted in the *Daily Chronicle* (DeKalb), April 19, 1977.

8. On Connecticut, see William G. Lesher, *Land Use Legislation in the Northeast: Connecticut* (Ithaca, N.Y.: Northeast Regional Center for Rural Development, 1975), p. 21; on California, Davies, *Preserving Agricultural and Open-Space Lands,* pp. 30, 33; on New Jersey, John Kolesar and Jaye Scholl, *Saving Farmland* (Princeton, N.J.: Center for Analysis of Public Issues, 1975), p. 6; and on Pennsylvania, Regional Science Research Institute, *Untaxing Open Space: An Evaluation of the Effectiveness of Differential Assessment of Farm and Open Space* (Washington: GPO, 1976), p. 108.

9. Kolesar and Scholl, *Saving Farmland,* p. 6.

10. Davies, *Preserving Agricultural and Open-Space Lands,* pp. 32-33.

11. They need to consult soil productivity maps or other indicators of the parcel's capacity to generate income from farming.

12. Kolesar and Scholl, *Saving Farmland,* p. 11.

13. Gregory C. Gustafson and L.T. Wallace, "Differential Assessment as Land Use Policy: The California Case," *Journal of the American Institute of Planners,* 41 (November 1975):318.

14. Ingolf Vogeler, *The Effectiveness of Differential Assessment of Farmland in the Chicago Metropolitan Area* (Springfield, Ill.: Department of Local Government Affairs, 1976), p. 67.

15. This discussion of eligibility requirements and financial disincentives comes mainly from Barlowe and Alter, *Use-Value Assessment of Farm and Open Space Lands,* pp. 4-12. The New York statute seeks to bar benefits to pseudo-farmers (e.g., owners of estates who plant a few acres) by requiring that preferentially assessed land gross an average of at least $10,000 in sales of agricultural commodities for the two preceding years. FVA must be applied for annually.

16. Kolesar and Scholl, *Saving Farmland,* pp. 28-9; Vogeler, *Effectiveness of Differential Assessment in the Chicago Area,* pp. 74-6; David W. Holland, *An Economic Analysis of Washington's Differential Taxation Program* (College of Agriculture, Research Center, Washington State University, 1974), pp. 9-10; Gloudemans, *Use-Value Farmland Assessment;* pp. 44-51, 54; Regional Science Research Institute, *Untaxing Open Space,* p. 63.

17. Regional Science Research Institute, *Untaxing Open Space,* p. 63.

18. Ibid., pp. 60-2.

19. Lesher, *Land Use Legislation in the Northeast: Connecticut,* p. 69.

20. Regional Science Research Institute, *Untaxing Open Space,* p. 159.

21. Oregon offers similar benefits for land zoned for farm use under county ordinances. Ibid., p. 203.

22. For the text of the New York statute, see "Article 25—AA—Agricultural Districts, Agriculture and Markets Law," in *McKinney's Consolidated Laws of New York—Annotated Book 2B* (St. Paul, Minn.: West Publishing Company, 1972); for the Virginia law, see "Agricultural and Forestal District Act," in chap. 36, (1977), Title 15.1, Code of Virginia; the relevant Illinois Bill in 1977 was H.B. 772, "Agricultural Areas Conservation and Protection Act."

23. Telephone interview with Howard E. Conklin, Department of Agricultural Economics, Cornell University, July 15, 1977, who participated in the drafting of the bill.

24. Interview with Herbert Klynstra, Illinois Agricultural Association (that state's Farm Bureau), Bloomington, March 4, 1977.

25. "We don't believe that farmers at the edge of town should do our zoning ordinances. With 500 or more acres, they can block the growth of cities." Telephone interview with an officer of the Illinois Municipal League, Springfield, July 15, 1977.

26. Regional Science Research Institute, *Untaxing Open Space,* p. 342.

27. W.G. Lesher and H.E. Conklin, *Legislation to Permit Agricultural Districts in New York* (Ithaca, N.Y.: Department of Agricultural Economics, Cornell University, 1976), appendix.

28. Letter to author from William G. Lesher, then of the Department of Agricultural Economics, Cornell University, March 17, 1977.

29. Suffolk County, Public Information, "News Release, September 29, 1977" (County Center, Hauppauge, New York).

30. Suffolk County, *Report of the Committee on Farmland Preservation* (Hauppauge, N.Y., 1974), p. 6; New Jersey, *Public Hearings before Assembly Agriculture and Environment Committee on Assembly [Bill] No. 1334, Held: February 23, 1976 and March 1, 1976* (Trenton, N.J., no date), pp. 29, 12x.

31. *Report of the Committee on Farmland Preservation,* p. 7; and *Public Hearings,* pp. 1, 2, 4, 2x.

32. As of September 29, 1977, Suffolk County had obtained landowner acceptance for bids on 1125 acres at an average per-acre cost of $2866. "Notice" from Suffolk County Public Information, September 29, 1977 (County Center, Hauppauge, N.Y.).

33. Klein reports that between 1972 and 1976 he spoke on behalf of his farmland preservation program to "hundreds" of Suffolk County audiences, including church groups, civic associations, and service organizations (Rotary, Lions). Interview in Washington, D.C., August 4, 1977.

34. Blueprint Commission on the Future of New Jersey Agriculture.

35. *Public Hearings,* p. 35x.

36. Ibid., p.

37. New Jersey, P.L. 1976, C.4: 1B-1 *et seq.*

38. For background on the Suffolk County program, see Tracy Kidder, "The Battle for Long Island," *The Atlantic,* 238 (November 1976):47-54.

39. Ibid., p. 52.

40. *Long Island Press,* September 9, 1976.

41. These classifications and the approximate quantities per class were taken from a full-page advertisement in *Newsday,* September 7, 1976, which listed the committee's advisory committee members and their organizational affiliations.

42. Ibid.

43. In John Klein's opinion, West Enders supported the program largely because "They wanted to be able to drive through farmland, show their children potato farms, and pick strawberries in roadside fields [where they could fill baskets on their own for so many cents per basket]. They didn't want to live in wall-to-wall suburbs." Interview of August 4, 1977.

44. Telephone interview with Ruth Keeton, Ellicott City, Md., July 18, 1977. For background on the proposed Howard County program, see *The Work Force for the Preservation of Howard County Farmland* (Ellicott City, Md.: Howard County Office of Planning and Zoning, n.d.).

45. William G. Lesher and Doyle A. Eiler, *Farmland Preservation in an Urban Fringe Area: An Analysis of Suffolk County's Development Rights Purchase Program* (Ithaca, N.Y.: Dept. of Agricultural Economics, Cornell University, 1977), p. 20.

46. Ibid.

47. Howard E. Conklin and William G. Lesher, "Use-Value Assessment of Farm Land—An Aid to the Preservation of Farming or to the Containment of Urban Growth?" (manuscript, department of Agricultural Economics, Cornell University, 1977), pp. 10-11.

48. See Fred Bosselman, David Callies, and John Banta, *The Taking Issue: An Analysis of the Constitutional Limits of Land-Use Control* (Washington: Council on Environmental Quality, 1973). For an optimistic view of the constitutionality of restrictive zoning to preserve farmland in Florida, see Dennis C. Dambly, "Preservation of Florida's Agricultural Resources through Land Use Planning," *University of Florida Law Review,* 27 (1974).

49. Interview with the Presiding Office of the Suffolk County Legislature, Floyd Linton, in *Pennysaver News,* July 12, 1976; see also the article by the Honorable Rosemarie Totaro, Assemblywoman, "The Transfer of Development Rights Concept as a Preservation Tool," *New Jersey Municipalities* 52 (November 1975):7.

50. Regional Science Research Institute, *Untaxing Open Space,* p. 252.

51. Ibid.

52. Telephone interview with an officer of the Illinois Agricultural Association, Bloomington, May 11, 1977.

53. Press release from office of Assemblyman Charles Warren, January 14, 1977. The supporting papers included the *Los Angeles Times,* the *Sacremento Bee,* and the *San Diego Union.*

54. Valerie C. Kircher, "Keeping 'em down on the Farm: The Legislative Battle over Preserving Agricultural Land," *California Journal* 7 (May 1976):156; *Los Angeles Times,* August 24, 1976.

19 The Scramble for Water: Agriculture versus Other Interests in Wyoming

John B. Richard

The international food crisis, energy requirements and shortages, "hit" lists on water projects, and the Western states' drought demonstrate the importance of adequate water resources throughout the nation and the world, especially in relation to agriculture and food supplies. Food and fiber needs and energy requirements place serious demands on the resources of the Western states, while at the same time new concern for the environment has developed which often conflicts with agricultural and energy policies.

Political Subsystems Related to Agricultural Water Problems

The political-administrative subsystem determining agricultural water policies exhibits the same characteristics utilized by many systems theorists and described by several authors.[1] The environment within which the political subsystem must operate provides important parameters for decision makers. In the natural environment of Wyoming, the land resource base is large; water supplies are both plentiful and scarce. The national government owns approximately 50 percent of the land, not counting Indian and state lands, and 72 percent of the minerals. Economic factors include energy, agriculture, and tourism. Social factors include a small rural-oriented population, low unemployment, and a faster growth rate than the nation's. The role of the scientist and expert is perhaps more important in the field of resource policy making than in many other areas of governmental concern.[2]

The legal environment in the West and Wyoming is very important in controlling and developing water resources—the "rules of the game." There are two general doctrines of water law which have been recognized in the several states. The common law riparian doctrine accords to the owner of land contiguous to a stream the right to use of the water in that stream. The appropriation doctrine, adopted by constitutional or legislative provision in all 17 Western states, is based on beneficial use and priority of application with the maxim "first in time, first in right" indicating who shall have the best right to the use of a particular watercourse or body of water. This doctrine gives no particular preference to the landowner simply because his or her land is contiguous to the water supply.

The legal basis for the federal government's involvement in water policies is found primarily in seven constitutional provisions: commerce, territory and property, war power, general welfare, treaty power, compact, and supremacy clauses. The commerce clause includes control over navigation and even nonnavigable waters, usually without the necessity of compensation.[3] The territory and property clause gives Congress control over public lands, but the essential question is whether sovereign control and ownership interests in water arising on public lands are maintained or whether the states have acquired control through development of the prior appropriation doctrine, various congressional statutes, Supreme Court decisions, or admission of states with constitutional provisions asserting state control. Recently, the United States was ordered by the Supreme Court to quantify its claims on the Eagle River in Colorado despite United States objections.[4] In Wyoming the legislature (1977) provided by statute for a general suit seeking adjudication of all water rights in the Big Horn River. Court decrees, interstate compacts, treaties, and thousands of pieces of land legislation also provide some of the general rules within which policy makers must operate.[5]

The administrative structure dealing with water resources is vast. The Hoover commission in 1955 found 43 national agencies directly or indirectly involved, and recent analysis in Wyoming indicates that this has not changed appreciably. Seven major cabinet departments including 22 separate bureaus or agencies and 7 additional independent agencies or commissions are directly involved in Wyoming. There is considerable competition among these agencies, they tend to emphasize individual projects, and frequently they create their own political subsystems. State administrative structure in Wyoming follows this national pattern of diversity. Sixteen agencies and seven advisory boards are involved. At the local level, water problems are handled by scores of municipalities and special districts.[6]

The Political Structure

The several studies referred to above have documented the close working relationship between the complex administrative structure and the political structure at the national level. Similar relationships are found at the state and local levels, and these structures in turn are closely aligned with the national policy-making structure. Agricultural interests are very strong at the state level. Conservationists hope to retain certain cultural and aesthetic values inherent in virgin forests and watersheds. Recreationists hope for large-scale development of recreational sites through either private or government development. Urban areas are rapidly expanding and increasingly in need of new or supplementary sources of water. Private power developers hope for economic expansion while public power advocates picture large-scale government development of available water resources. With the energy crisis, mining interests have expanded their activities in coal, and oil shale development is a possibility. Timber and grazing interests are also vitally interested. In short, as Wengert notes, the range of group activity concerning water resources policy is extraordinarily wide and diverse.[7]

Probably the most outstanding feature of the group activity involved in water policy making is the extent to which certain interests and groups have dominated policy making in this field. Agricultural uses of water have been quantitatively dominant over other uses, and the system of water law clearly favors agricultural uses. Agricultural groups in Wyoming also are tied directly to several agencies by various means. The state board of agriculture and conservation commission must be made up of individuals employed in agriculture. Members of other boards such as game and fish and economic planning and development have historically been drawn primarily from agriculture and related occupations. A survey of administrators involved in water also indicated agricultural backgrounds were predominant—55 percent.[8] Dominance in state legislative and administrative agencies by agriculture is now being challenged by conservation, industrial, and municipal groups.

The Governor of Wyoming has a strong hand in overall policy development if he chooses to use it. The legislature has been dominated by agricultural interests in the past, and there is still a strong attachment to agricultural values. Agricultural representation in the legislature in 1967 and in 1977 remained stable at 23.3 percent and 22.8 percent, respectively, far more than in the society at large. Business and banking increased slightly from 33 percent in 1967 to 35.9 percent in 1977.[9] The tendency in both the Governor's office as well as in the legislature has been to emphasize development, jobs, and the total economic picture.

Public interest and opinion in water resource matters are often not articulated. Individual opinions and values exist, but there is rarely a direct opportunity for expression, and individual preferences are often ambiguous or conflicting. This, of course, allows the political-administrative structure considerable discretion on specific issues. On general matters in Wyoming there is a fairly strong conservation feeling among the citizenry. A recent poll of over 1000 Wyoming citizens on political issues during the 1976 election indicated that there is strong feeling for preserving Wyoming's water.[10] See Table 19-1.

While public opinion is fairly coherent concerning water, considerable uncertainty about development of mineral resources exists. The tendency is toward conservation and preservation, but the pressure of jobs, money, and development is also strong. Overwhelming support is voiced for reclamation of strip-mined areas, but feeling is mixed on "rapid development"; shipping out coal or burning it in Wyoming; limiting construction of coal-burning plants; and nuclear power plants. On land-use planning the citizenry was completely divided.

Table 19-1

Wyoming Citizen Attitudes Concerning Water, 1976 (Percent)

Questions:

1. Should agricultural uses of water be given preference over mining and industrial uses in Wyoming?
2. Is the development of additional coal slurry pipelines using Wyoming water a wise policy for the state to follow?
3. Is diverting water from the Green River Basin to the Powder River Basin for mining and industrial purposes good water management?
4. Should state air and water quality standards in Wyoming be very high and strictly enforced?

Responses	Strongly Agree	Agree	Undecided	Disagree	Strongly Disagree	Don't Know
1	17.9	49.3	12.4	13.1	0.9	6.3
2	1.2	11.2	15.9	34.2	19.2	18.3
3	1.1	13.5	18.5	26.1	9.7	31.2
4	36.2	47.9	4.5	6.8	1.0	3.6

Source: Kenyon N. Griffin, *Public Policy Issues: 1976 Election Year Survey*, Center for Governmental Research, University of Wyoming, January 1977, tables 1-4, pp. 11-14.

Issues and Problems: The Scramble

The scramble for water in Wyoming and the West is in its infancy. Future needs of water and land are tremendous. The Westwide study, sponsored by the Bureau of Reclamation, states:

The role of Western water in meeting future high-priority energy needs is tied primarily to the development of large reserves of coal and oil shale, waste heat disposal from thermal electric and fuel conversion plants, supplying municipal growth directly associated with fuel production, and providing hydroelectric peaking power capacity. . . ."[11]

The report goes on to say that the great number of new and enlarged sites required for mining, processing, and energy conversion located in the Southwest, the Rocky Mountain region, and the northern Great Plains will have "important ramifications on both quantity and quality of water supplies." Potential uses of water for energy development in only one region of Wyoming are shown in Table 19-2. Over 70 percent of the country's strippable coal is found west of the Mississippi, and over 600 billion barrels of potentially recoverable oil in shale are found in Wyoming, Colorado, and Utah, although the feasibility of oil shale development is in doubt.

Further substantiating the importance of water is an environmental impact

Table 19-2

Estimates of Water Requirements in Northeast Wyoming, 1971-2000 (thousand acre-feet)

Water Requirements for	Probable Level of Development				Extensive Level of Development			
	1971	*1980*	*1985*	*2000*	*1971*	*1980*	*1985*	*2000*
Electric power	8.3	15.7	15.7	33.4	8.3	15.7	15.7	33.4
Synthetic natural gas	–	–	19.4	30.2	–	–	63.0	95.1
Export	0.6	9.2	12.2	17.6	0.6	9.2	23.6	82.7
Mining	0.4	3.5	6.0	9.2	0.4	3.5	13.3	36.1
Totals	9.3	28.4	53.3	90.4	9.3	28.4	115.6	247.3

Source: Adapted from U.S. Department of the Interior, *Westwide Study Report on Critical Water Problems Facing the Eleven Western States*, Bureau of Reclamation, April 1975, p. 419.

statement dated October 12, 1976, in which the Bureau of Reclamation proposed to make available for energy-related industrial purposes up to 1.0 million acre-feet of water annually from mainstream Missouri River reservoirs. The coal mining areas of eastern Montana, western North Dakota, parts of western and central South Dakota, and northeastern Wyoming would be the anticipated areas of water use. The water would be available from "storage capacities reserved for future irrigation development that will not be required for irrigation use during the time frame."[12] In the Platte River subregion of Wyoming, future coal development will require ". . . importation water, augmentation, or additional conversion of agricultural water supplies. Industrial supplies are now being obtained in part by purchasing irrigation water rights and transferring the water use to industrial use rather than developing new surface or ground water supplies."[13]

How shall scarce water resources be allocated and distributed among competing geographic, social, and economic interests in the society? Which of the sectors will receive priority in scarce periods and places or when population pressures make shortages commonplace? What Mann says of Arizona may well be applied to Wyoming: "Basic economic issues have a very real relationship to the issues concerning the management and utilization of the water supply. Whatever increases of water use occur in one segment of the economy will ultimately result in a deprivation of that water for use in another. . . ."[14]

Particularly evident in the policy-making system regarding these problems is the Balkanization of legal restraints and the incremental approach to decision making. So many agencies at all levels of government are involved with varying types of jurisdiction and degrees of authority that overall solutions are difficult to come by, even if they are available.

In general, agriculture has resisted overall recodification of water laws and administrative reorganization, but incremental changes are beginning to affect its position in the policy-making system. For example, in 1955, the legislature, at the urging of Pacific Power and Light and with the prospect of steam power plants, provided that steam power use of water was a preferred use although it was not given the power of eminent domain.[15] Through a complicated transfer of irrigation use to industrial water, the Dave Johnston steam electric plant was developed. Two years later the prospect of Columbia-Geneva Steel Company locating an iron ore mining and processing operation in Wyoming stimulated the legislature to provide for preferred industrial uses of water.[16] In 1974 the legislature made special provision for the use of Wyoming water in a proposed coal slurry pipeline to Arkansas.[17] In 1974, the state legislature also changed the procedures for approving transfers of water from one use or place to another.[18] The Board of Control may now consider economic losses caused by the transfer, the extent to which the loss is offset by the new use and whether other sources are available for the new use. Under these provisions the new billion-dollar basin electric plant near Wheatland, Wyoming, has petitioned the Board of Control for a change of agricultural use to industrial purposes. Finally, an important change in water law occurred when the state engineer was authorized to abandon water rights forfeited through nonuse.[19] Previously a right could be abandoned only upon initiation of proceedings by another water user.

In addition to these new legal tools for transfer of water, other incremental changes have been occurring. Small quantities of water for municipal use have been transferred in many areas of the state.[20] The city of Laramie is purchasing some first-priority rights on the Laramie River and has made several transfers from agricultural to municipal use. Cheyenne is attempting to add new municipal water to previously acquired agricultural rights in a complicated interbasin transfer. Major mining firms hold huge portions of water in Boysen and Yellowtail Reservoirs which could threaten proposed irrigation extensions. Fifteen firms reportedly purchased over 708,000 acre-feet of water from the Bureau of Reclamation in these two reservoirs.[21] In a related situation, water rights permit applications for future reservoirs by industries have been acquired. These water rights are contained in reservoirs not yet constructed and were originally intended for irrigation uses.[22] This may not actually be a loss to agriculture since it often involves supplemental or flood waters, but it does mean that new lands cannot be developed. The cost of water may have been too high for agriculture in any case. Finally, it appears that large mining companies are purchasing agricultural and ranching land with senior water rights. Vast amounts of land have been sold and in some cases leased back to the original owners. This may have a tremendous impact on agriculture if and when these "chips" are cashed in for industrial uses in the future.

It seems clear that "economics dictate," as one state legislator recently stated. Whoever pays the money gets the water. This incremental approach to development with no overall account being kept apparently does not disturb major groups. One single proposal for changing all this agricultural water to industrial or municipal use at one time would result in violent repercussions. The cumulative effect, of course, is just as serious.

In water policy making the principal technique for evaluating projects has been cost-benefit analysis (CBA). While it has often been politically manipulated, CBA is nevertheless important in the political arena. It is ironic that this "weapon," coupled with the concept of beneficial use from the prior appropriation doctrine, has had unintended consequences for agriculture and is now working to the advantage of industry. With stricter evaluation measures and a higher interest rate, the cost-benefit ratio no longer favors historical uses. Cost benefit favors change.

Professor Frank Trelease, water law expert, foresees considerable difficulty for agriculture. He indicates that many water laws now actually favor the shift of water away from irrigation to cities and industries, empowering administrators to move water off farms without full consideration of all consequences.[23] While Trelease is not sure that these changes constitute deliberate discrimination against agriculture, he is sure that agriculture is always the loser. The pressure to reallocate water usually means transferring water at hand (agricultural) to a more lucrative use. Trelease cites numerous examples both in the United States and in other countries in which water laws detrimental to agriculture have been enacted. Some laws allow transfer of water without compensation (Peru, Minnesota); short-term permits result in uncompensated transfer (Australia, Japan, Iowa, Florida); administrators can "squeeze out" the farmer without legally terminating his right (Florida); preferences to municipalities with right of condemnation might also include industrial and business uses within the city (California, New Mexico, Arizona, Taiwan, England, Kenya, and others). According to Trelease, food production decreases, physical water systems are rendered worthless, financial investments are deterred, and true compensation often does not result.

Summary

Briefly, several important points need to be explicitly reiterated about the policy-making subsystem and public policy related to agricultural water resources and uses. (1) Frequently there is a failure to recognize the relatedness of land, water, and other resources (water taken off prime agricultural land takes that land out of production just as effectively as urban development and surface mining itself). (2) Although the state has a potential monopoly on the power to act, the Balkanized legal controls over water resources allocation, use, and development have consequences for policy making. (3) The multiplicity of agencies and groups dealing with land and water policy making means fragmented and complex administrative approaches to policy making often frustrating rational reallocation of water resources. (4) The cumulative effect of incremental solutions may result in serious water losses for agriculture and gains for industry and municipalities. (5) The altering of water uses may have profound effects on style of life—social and aesthetic factors—in addition to the physical change. (6) Insufficient political "will" to regulate all water, surface and ground, in a comprehensive framework results in decision makers being tied to their economic constituencies, which makes it difficult to break traditional patterns and lets "economics dictate." (7) There is an emphasis on engineering, science, technology, and quasi-scientific techniques such as cost-benefit analysis which clouds political decisions. (8) It is evident that these problems exist not only in Wyoming but in many other places as well.

In the future policy making in water resources needs to take into account some of the following points. (1) Agricultural water policy needs additional goals which analysts ought to consider such as overall food and fiber policy, conservation, wildlife and recreational needs, quality of life, redistribution of income, and population dispersal. (2) Cost-benefit analysis cannot take the politics out of a water resource decision, since on an "old" project political costs may already have been "sunk," and it is not just a question of new lands being developed but of old lands being converted out of production. (3) Multiple-purpose programs will have to be proposed which discourage single-purpose uses whether agricultural, industrial, municipal, or recreational. (4) Standards of equity concerning use of a state's resources largely for another area's use and benefit will have to be developed. (5) Are there solutions to be found which can be exported to developing nations, most of which have arid conditions similar to those found in the West?

Notes

1. See Arthur Maass, *Muddy Waters* (Cambridge, Mass.: Harvard University Press, 1951); Roscoe Martin, *Water for New York* (Syracuse, N.Y.: Syracuse University Press, 1960); Arthur Morgan, *Dams and Other Disasters* (Boston: Porter Sargent Publishers, 1971); Grant McConnell, *Private Power and American Democracy* (New York: Alfred A. Knopf, 1966); Frank Moss, *The Water Crisis* (New York: Frederick A. Praeger, 1967); Norman Wengert, *Natural Resources and the Political Struggle* (Garden City, N.Y.: Doubleday and Co., 1955); Norris Hundley, Jr., *Water and the West* (Berkeley: University of California Press, 1975); Dennis Thompson (ed.), *Politics, Policy, and Natural Resources* (New York: The Free Press, 1972); Dean Mann, *The Politics of Water in Arizona* (Tucson: The University of Arizona Press, 1963).

2. Wengert, *Natural Resources*, p. 7.

3. *Gibbons v. Ogden*, 22 U.S. (19 Wheat.) 1 (1824); *Economy Light and*

Power Co. v. U.S., 256 U.S. 113 (1921); *U.S. v. Rio Grande Dam and Irrigation Co.*, 174 U.S. 690 (1899); *U.S. v. Appalachian Electric Power Co.*, 311 U.S. 377 (1940); *U.S. v. Chandler-Dunbar Co.*, 229 U.S. 53 (1913); *U.S. V. Twin City Power Co.*, 350 U.S. 222 (1956).

4. *U.S. v. Eagle County*, 91 S.Ct. 998 (1971).

5. See John B. Richard, *State Administration and Water Resources in Wyoming*, Unpublished dissertation, University of Illinois, 1965; and Paul Gates, *History of Public Land Law Development* (Washington: Government Printing Office, 1968); and the reports of the Public Land Law Review Commission.

6. See Commission on Organization of the Executive Branch of the Government, *Task Force Report on Water Resources and Power*, vol. 1 (Washington: Government Printing Office, 1955), pp. 59-61; Richard, *State Administration and Water Resources.*

7. Wengert, *Natural Resources*, p. 7.

8. Richard, *State Administration and Water Resources*, p. 143.

9. John B. Richard, *Government and Politics of Wyoming*, 3d ed., (Dubuque, Iowa: Kendall/Hunt, 1974), with current updating.

10. Kenyon Griffin, *Public Policy Issues: 1976 Election Year Survey*, (Laramie: Center for Governmental Research, University of Wyoming, January 1977), tables 1-4, pp. 11-14.

11. U.S. Department of the Interior, *Westwide Study Report on Critical Water Problems Facing the Eleven Western States* (Washington: Bureau of Reclamation, April 1974), p. 72.

12. Bureau of Reclamation, *Water for Energy: Missouri River Reservoirs*, Draft Environmental Impact Statement (Billings: Bureau of Reclamation, Upper Missouri Region, October 1976), p. i.

13. Department of the Interior, *Westwide Study*, pp. 419-420.

14. Mann, *Politics of Water in Arizona*, pp. 67-68.

15. *Session Laws of Wyoming*, 1955, chap. 227.

16. *Session Laws of Wyoming*, 1957, chap. 116.

17. *Session Laws of Wyoming*, 1974, chap. 25; *Wyoming Compiled Statutes*, 41-10.5.

18. *Session Laws of Wyoming*, 1974, chap. 23; *Wyoming Compiled Statutes*, 41-4 and 41-4.1.

19. *Session Laws of Wyoming*, 1973, chap. 176; *Wyoming Compiled Statutes*, 41-47.2.

20. Personal correspondence with Wyoming state official, April 5, 1977.

21. *Casper Star-Tribune*, Casper, Wyoming, March 18, 1976, p. 1.

22. Personal correspondence with Wyoming state official, April 5, 1977.

23. Frank Trelease, "Water for Food—Or for 'More Important' Purposes?" paper presented for International Association for Water Law, Second International Conference on Water Law and Administration, Caracas, Venezuela, February 8-14, 1976, p. 1, and following.

**Alternative
Agriculturists:
Ideology, Politics, and
Prospects**

Garth Youngberg

Introduction

In September 1975, Don Paarlberg, in his now celebrated speech entitled "The Farm Policy Agenda," declared that "the biggest issue of agricultural policy is this: Who is going to control the farm policy agenda and what subjects will be on it?" Concluding that "the agricultural establishment has, in large measure, lost control of the farm policy agenda," Paarlberg enumerated a wide array of new agenda items which "have been placed on the agenda over the protests of the agricultural establishment."[1] Many of the items cited by Paarlberg—food prices, USDA food programs, ecological questions, rural development, land-use issues, civil rights and collective bargaining for hired farm labor—relate in varying degrees to the alternative agriculture movement.

In general, alternative agriculturalists object strenuously to so-called conventional agriculture with its heavy reliance upon synthetic chemical fertilizers and pesticides, large-scale, expensive mechanization, nonrenewable fossil fuels, and the trend toward ever-larger farm units, especially the huge corporate farming operations which have emerged in recent years. Believing that conventional agriculture is destructive of both human and natural resources and therefore destined in time to destroy itself as well as the larger population, alternative agriculturalists are deeply committed to the reorientation of agricultural practices and techniques. The following analysis attempts to assess the ideology, politics, and policy prospects of this diffuse, dedicated, and growing movement. If, as Paarlberg said in 1975, "it would be well for those who teach agricultural policy to throw away their old lecture notes,"[2] then it seems highly appropriate—even urgent in light of the issues involved—for the student of agricultural policy to raise this question: To what extent will those new lecture notes include references to the ideology, policy objectives, and policy accomplishments of alternative agriculturalists?

Broadly conceived, the alternative agriculture movement includes a bewildering variety of members, agricultural practices, activities, and goals. For example, production methods mix and blend in countless variations depending upon farm size, the state of transition from chemical to organic practices, the availability of labor, microeconomic considerations, markets, ideological commitment, and the like. Still, at the risk of oversimplification, such producers may be roughly divided between organic and so-called ecofarmers. Organic farmers

227

normally manage smaller and much more labor-intensive operations and tend to eschew commercial soil amendments favoring, instead, compost and manures for organic matter. By contrasts, ecofarmers, although sympathetic to many traditional organic concepts, are far more willing to adopt various new soil amendments or natural "fertilizers" such as rock product minerals, humates, seaweed derivatives and bacterial soil activators,[3] and even limited amounts of synthetic fertilizers and pesticides. Large-scale farmers or those wishing to expand operations are drawn to these expanding sources of organic matter.

In an ideological sense, the smaller-scale organic farmer and especially the organic gardener are more attuned to the ideology of Robert Rodale of *Organic Gardening and Farming* magazine. Ecofarmers find greater wisdom and ideological guidance in Charles Walters, Jr., of *Acres, USA,* the man often credited with coining the term *ecoagriculture* to indicate that farming can be both ecologically sensitive and economically profitable. Because distinct analytic categories do not exist within the literature of organic agriculture, the terms *organic* and *ecofarming* will be used more or less interchangeably throughout this chapter.

Other elements of the organic movement include the designers of organic agricultural technology and alternative energy systems, the homemaker who refuses to purchase chemically produced food, a number of consumer groups, research and advocacy centers, university researchers, publishers, authors, books and periodicals. An increasingly sophisticated infrastructure of alternative agricultural farm suppliers, the organic foods wholesale and retail distributive system, and the growing number of food cooperatives and farmers markets are additional elements of the movement.

The Ideology of Alternative Agriculturalists[4]

Despite the lack of membership consensus, there are certain basic ideological themes which appeal strongly to a sizable cross section of the movement. The following deals with these underlying themes. The precise degree to which various members and elements subscribe to these themes must await a more thorough empirical analysis.

The Movement's Leading Spokesmen

According to Lane, most ideologies "have a body of sacred documents (constitutions, bills of rights, manifestoes, declarations), and heroes (founding fathers, seers and sages, originators and great interpretators)."[5] In the case of organic ideology, a complete listing of such sacred documents and heroes goes far beyond the scope of this analysis. Falling as it does within the broad outlines of various historical and contemporary conservation, environmental, and ecology movements, the ideology of alternative agriculturalists overlaps with and draws upon a complicated and elaborate ideological heritage.[6] Here, only some of the more prominent spokesmen of organic agriculture will be considered. These and other organic ideological seers and sages do, of course, share many of the broader concerns of ecologists and environmentalists.

The late E.F. Schumacher was one of the most influential contemporary exponents of the ideology of alternative agriculturalists in both academic and nonacademic circles. Indeed, the correspondence between the ideology of Schumacher's *Small Is Beautiful*[7] and the ideological orientation of various leading alternative agriculture groups is pervasive and unmistakeable. Schumacher himself was no doubt influenced by some of these contemporary groups as well as such historically important philosophies and religions as Gandhism, Zen Buddhism, and Christianity, plus Thoreau and the Luddites to mention just a few of the ideological strains which appear in *Small Is Beautiful.*[8]

Bits and pieces of the ideology of the alternative agriculture movement are also evident in the feature articles and editorials of a number of leading alternative agriculture publications. Here, Robert Rodale, editor and publisher of *Organic Gardening and Farming,* emerges as a principal figure, especially in relationship to the concept and ideology of organic agriculture. The following draws heavily upon the meaning and ideology of organic agriculture as enunciated by Rodale. While many in the alternative agriculture movement regard Rodale's purist ideology as unrealistic (one told me that it was fine for the little old ladies in white tennis shoes who want to garden in Des Moines, Iowa), as editor of the most widely read organically oriented publication (currently over 1 million people subscribe to *Organic Gardening and Farming*), his views take on special significance.

Unlike the legendary Pheonix of Greek mythology, Rodale's ideology did not spring forth full blown from organic matter. His father, the late J.I. Rodale, founder of *Organic Gardening and Farming,* was a major influence upon him. According to his own testimony, the work of at least three other men also greatly influenced Rodale's ideology. First, Charles Darwin's book, *The Formation of Vegetable Mould through the Action of Worms, with Observations on Their Habits,* published in 1881, is regarded by Rodale as a classic in the literature of organic agriculture. Second, in Rodale's view, F.H. King, former chief of the Division of Soil Management of the United States Department of Agriculture, made "even more direct contributions to the origins of organic farming theories and practices. . . ." Dr. King, observes Rodale, was "extremely impressed by the careful handling of organic materials by all oriental farmers—a direct contrast to the wasteful and destructive methods of many American farmers." King's book on oriental agriculture, *Farmers of Forty Centuries,* was apparently his major contribution to the organic movement.

According to Rodale, Sir Albert Howard ought to be regarded as the "father of organic farming." Among other things, Howard's book, *An Agricultural*

Testament, his so-called "Indore method" of composting developed while he was director of the Institute of Plant Industry at Indore, India, and his work as associate editor of *Organic Gardening and Farming* have earned him a hallowed position in the history of organic agriculture. In summary, Rodale believes that "the organic farming and gardening idea thrives as a continuation of the ideas of these three men."[9]

The late Dr. William Albrecht, long-time professor of soils and chairman of the Department of Soils at the University of Missouri, stands out as one of the earliest and most influential mentors of the movement. Although it is difficult to estimate the influence of Albrecht, his conventional academic credentials and symbols doubtless lent much needed legitimacy to the basic ideas of the movement.[10]

In addition to Schumacher, Rodale, and Albrecht, the ideology of such publishers as J.D. Belanger of *Countryside* magazine, Charles Walters, Jr., of *Acres, USA,* the editorial staff of *The Mother Earth News,* plus a number of lesser known but potentially influential publications, such as *The Journal of the New Alchemists,* must be included in the list of seers and sages who are contributing significantly to the ideology of the alternative agriculture movement.[11] A number of telephone conversations, personal interviews, and considerable correspondence with various members of the movement have also contributed to my understanding of its ideological character. Although it may not always be possible to give proper credit (some people asked not to be quoted), these sources have also influenced the following selected underlying ideological themes.

Probe the Earth and See Where Your Roots Are–Thoreau

Much of the ideology of the alternative agriculture movement can be summed up on the words of a well-known TV commercial: "You can't fool mother nature." Alternative agriculturalists believe that modern man has lost touch with nature, that he has become insensitive to nature's intricate, delicate, infinitely wise, and immutable laws. Consequently, man no longer sees "himself as a part of nature but as an outside force destined to dominate and conquer it. He even talks of the battle with nature, forgetting that, if he won the battle, he would find himself on the losing side."[12] Recognition of the centrality of this core belief is absolutely essential for a full understanding of the movement's overall ideology. For purposes of clarity and emphasis, however, the following analysis has been subdivided into various ideological subthemes.

Nature Is Capital. Although not all alternative agriculturalists would couch their objections to the squandering of natural resources in economic terms, they would strongly agree with Schumacher's assessment of the problem. He states that man's failure to perceive the difference between income and capital and to recognize the magnitude and importance of the capital which nature has provided (and which is being consumed at such a rapid rate) has created a tragic illusion—the "illusion of having solved the problem of production."[13] Schumacher uses fossil fuels to illustrate the difference between capital and income as well as to emphasize the importance of "natural capital." The following quote captures the essence of this central point:

First of all, and most obviously, there are the fossil fuels. No one, I am sure, will deny that we are treating them as income items although they are undeniably capital items. If we treated them as capital items, we should be concerned with conservation; we should do everything in our power to try and minimise their current rate of use; we might be saying, for instance, that the money obtained from the realisation of these assets must be placed into a special fund to be devoted exclusively to the evolution of production methods and patterns of living which do *not* depend on fossil fuels at all or depend on them only to a very slight extent. These and many other things we should be doing if we treated fossil fuels as capital and not as income. And we do not do any of them, but the exact contrary of every one of them: we are not in the least concerned with conservation; we are maximising, instead of minimising, the current rates of use; and, far from being interested in studying the possibilities of alternative methods of production and patterns of living . . . we happily talk of unlimited progress. . .[14]

This, more than anything else, in the view of alternative agriculturalists, places man on a collision course with nature.

Soil Is the Source of Life. Alternative agriculturalists place great stress upon the importance of soil quality and balance—soil with proper levels of organic matter, bacterial and biological activity, trace elements, and other nutrients. They believe that synthetic chemical fertilizers and pesticides reduce these levels and diminish the soil's natural fertility, thereby requiring ever-larger applications of artificial compounds. Moreover, they contend that food produced on artificially fertilized soil has less nutritive value than that which is organically grown. They believe that undesirable, toxic residues found in conventionally produced food contribute to increased rates of cancer and birth defects as well as other kinds of unfortunate or antisocial behavior such as crime, psychological depression, violence, hyperactivity, and a gradual decline in mental acuity. They contend, often strenuously, that we have seen only the tip of the iceberg and that continued reliance on "rescue chemistry" can only lead to even greater human suffering, the gradual erosion of soil quality, and ultimately the decline and fall of modern civilization.

The Organic Idea. Opponents of conventional agriculture insist that organic farming is the only workable, economically feasible, healthy, and sufficiently productive long-range solution to these and other problems. T.1ey believe also that time is on their side (assuming people survive long enough) and that eventually circumstances, such as prohibitively high synthetic fertilizer prices, will force a return to what they consider to be more ecologically and economically sound agricultural practices. What precisely is organic agriculture? What does the term *organic* mean to its practitioners and devotees?

Although "the central constructive activity of the organic grower is the making and using of compost," the organic idea involves far more than the simple act of building up the humus content of soil. According to Rodale, for example,

Organic farmers and gardeners not only wish to avoid the use of many pesticides that can cause damage to wildlife, and create toxic effects in a variety of ways but they also are very much concerned about the prevention of erosion, the adding of humus and other organic matter to soil to improve fertility, the preservation of small family farms, localized marketing of food, energy conservation, and proper nutrition. It is a rare organic grower who does not share those concerns, or pursue those activities.[15]

Thus, the organic concept reflects a number of separate but interrelated ideological goals. It is the combination of these goals which gives the organic movement such a powerful ideological base. The behavior of alternative agriculturalists, particularly organic farmers, cannot be fully grasped or appreciated without recognizing the breadth as well as the depth of their ideological commitment. Many people ask, Why would a farmer give up all synthetic fertilizers, as organic farming demands? Why stop using all pesticides, even those that seem to have a low toxicity for warm-blooded organisms? Most puzzling of all, why work so hard moving around large quantities or organic fertilizers and manure, when synthetic fertilizers are so much easier to handle? The answer lies in the total import of the organic ethic, without which organic farming will almost certainly appear irrational "if not downright crazy."[16] To those who understand this ethic and follow most of its principles, organic agriculture often becomes a way of life or even a semireligious experience. As one such practitioner said, "When I learned I could farm without chemicals, it made by soul feel good."[17]

Finally, alternative agriculturalists believe that consumers of organically grown food are aware of and subscribe to the organic concept. Rodale, for example, insists that "a great many people who buy organically grown foods are doing so for the purpose of *making a political statement. . . .*"[18] The same can be said for the manufacturers and suppliers of "natural" agricultural inputs as well as the wholesalers and retailers of organic foods. Although the commercial elements of the movement are motivated by economic gain, most appear to share and espouse the movement's basic ideology.

Earth Provides Enough to Satisfy Every Man's Need,
but Not for Every Man's Greed—Gandhi

If one accepts the basic proposition that "you can't fool mother nature," that many of earth's resources are, indeed, finite and fragile, and that man is simply one element in a delicate and vulnerable ecological system, then the Western philosophy of materialism becomes unacceptable. Alternative agriculturalists argue that Western materialism has no limiting principle, "while the environment in which it is placed is strictly limited." Thus, Schumacher concludes: "There can be 'growth' towards a limited objective, but there cannot be unlimited, generalized growth." Accepting this core proposition, many alternative agriculturalists appear wedded to what Schumacher views as the economics of peace and permanence—the antimaterialistic, nonviolent, ecologically sensitive, people-centered economics which applauds the work of organic farmers, conservationists, and cottage producers to name but a few.[19] The ideology of making-do-with-less or, as one observer put it, "living lightly on the earth,"[20] has helped spawn and sustain various elements of the alternative agriculture movement.

Some of the urban-to-rural migration of the 1970s was generated by this basic ideological orientation. Repulsed by the American economic system which it sees as unnecessarily wasteful and overly consumptive, the movement would, according to Reed,

have more people rely on their own personal resources and labor, especially for their food and shelter.... Labor saving devices like tractors are examined skeptically and used sparingly. Mule drawn equipment is reappearing. Toilets that convert wastes into compost and methane gas are being widely discussed.[21]

Organic fertilizers, biological pest control, and local marketing cooperatives are integral aspects of this so-called back-to-land agriculture.

There are thousands of traditional, well-established small farmers who reflect and proclaim this same basic ideology. Dick Lessig, for example, operator of a 100-acre farm in Hancock County, Ohio, is apparently more concerned about "his team of horses than the price of corn in Chicago."[22] Believing that one can make an adequate living on a small farm by keeping production costs to a minimum, Lessig is attracted to organic agriculture. He explains:

It's for two reasons, I guess, ... First of all, on a small farm, you can succeed only by keeping costs way down. You have to think about how not to spend cash. I use less chemicals and all the manure and natural fertility I can get because I think it means keeping more of the money I do make. But also, I'm convinced that the technology of bigness today is a step backwards. I believe that the old ways were far better for everyone, and I've done it both ways.... I can't get the yields organically yet that we were getting with chemicals, but I just couldn't enjoy farming chemically. If you are close to the soil, you have no trouble switching to organic methods once you see what anhydrous ammonia does to soil life.[23]

For many limited-resource farmers and some large operators, farming has not become a strictly commercial venture. Mining the soil is repugnant to their basic ideology, regardless of the economic benefits such practices usually produce. Being able to earn a decent though modest living while enjoying the simple pleasures long associated with country life is apparently more important to many farmers than continual economic growth and farm expansion. As Balanger points out, many farmers simply "*want* to be able to stand in a field and watch a hawk circle overhead.... Man is a delicate blend, of which economics is only a part."[24]

A number of research and advocacy alternative agriculture groups also appear motivated by the ideology of antimaterialism, of making-do-with-less, of treating the earth as a permanent resource. Here, the New Alchemy Institute is one of the most sophisticated, well-financed, and successful of such groups.[25] Promoting small, organic technology, the new alchemists are designing and testing

intensive food-growing methods that can be employed on a small scale and without recourse to the extensive mechanization and chemical consumption of modern agriculture. Their shared vision ... is one of a land of small, mostly self-sufficient communities in which most people live closer to nature and farther from the products, pressures and toxins of industry.... They refer basically to the quest for means of sustaining life at a comfortable level with minimal use of nonrenewable resources and with minimal mucking up of the environment.[26]

Believing that organic agriculture needs more science and less folklore, the new alchemists are perhaps uniquely committed to the scientific accumulation and testing of alternative agricultural methods. Thus, although they have adopted a different strategy and emphasize different practices, the new alchemists emerge as central figures in the ideology of alternative agriculture.

It's Time for a New Declaration of
Independence–Robert Rodale

The alternative agriculturalist's goal of making-do-with-less, of living lightly on the land, results not only from the ideology of conservation and antimaterialism but also from the felt need to achieve at least a modicum of personal autonomy and self-sufficiency. The specialization and interdependence of modern society are repugnant and threatening to many members of the movement. Rodale explains:

To be independent means that you have a basic liberty of existence. You are not tied to others when you are independent. You are able to support yourself, working with your own resources. The person who is truly independent will live well no matter what happens to the rest of society.[27]

Clearly, this basic ideological goal of greater individual and community independence has helped to foster and sustain various aspects and elements of the alternative agriculture movement. For example, local marketing cooperatives, a principal feature of organic ideology, frees people from large, impersonal, and interdependent marketing and distribution systems. Better health, a by-product, it is argued, of eating organically grown food, increases one's independence from a costly and sometimes indifferent health care system. Increased productivity, personal creativity, and fulfillment also results, supposedly, from small-scale, individual, neighborhood or community enterprises. Finally, it is contended that the use of organic fertilizers, biological pest controls, and increased human labor enables farmers and gardeners to produce good crops with little or no reliance upon the wasteful and increasingly unpredictable petrochemical industry. Alternate sources of energy are sought for the same reason. According to Rodale, "Whether you have a wood stove, a windmill, or solar panels on your roof, you are making a commitment to independence."[28] Rodale recently called for the creation of a Cabinet-level Department of Independence which would carry out a major research program in personal independence.

The Politics of the Alternative Agriculture Movement

Alternative agriculturalists express varying degrees of optimism about the possibilities of reorienting American agriculture in accordance with the broad ideological outlines of the movement. Predictions regarding the future of alternative agriculture range from mild statements of hope to positive, unqualified exclamations of absolute certainty; many feel that in time the movement will inevitably be successful. A complicated mixture of political, economic, social, and ideological variables will, of course, directly influence the course and character of the movement. The following analysis attempts to unravel and assess some of the major factors which bear upon the future of alternative agriculture.

The Organization of the Movement

Alternative agriculturalists are not well organized. Presently, there is no national umbrella organization capable of unifying or focusing the political objectives of the movement. Most of the organizations which do exist within the movement are apparently not typical political organizations at all in the traditional sense of interest group politics. That is, very little conventional lobbying activity is pursued. There are few, if any, Washington or state-based lobbies directly and specifically representing the ideological goals of alternative agriculturalists.[29] Indeed, many elements of the movement strongly oppose this kind of centralized organizational approach on ideological grounds. The adoption of traditional political forms would be in direct violation of the ideology of independence, individualism, localism, and above all smallness. The movement's relatively narrow range of specific governmental policy objectives contributes to the absence of traditional political activity.

Alternative and Emerging Organizations. The alternative agriculture movement is not, as some of its members contend, totally disorganized. There are a number of well-established and newly emergent organizational efforts within the movement. For instance, an elaborate networking system consisting of a variety of "newsletters, contact groups, and sourcebooks" facilitates informational exchanges and contributes to a sense of group identity and purpose. Isao Fujimoto contends that this elaborate networking system is an important "indicator of the growing popularity of eco-agriculture. . . ."[30] A sourcebook entitled *Farming*[31] contains a wealth of information relating to the various elements of this networking system. It is an excellent source for the names and addresses of alternative agriculture leaders, groups, publications, research findings, and activities.

The production and distribution aspects of the movement have also made important organizational gains in recent years. According to Rodale, there are now "172 organic gardening clubs, and about 13,000 members" active in the United States and Canada. Furthermore, "there are hundreds of food cooperatives in the U.S. handling largely organic foods." There are also some 22 regional organic farming groups active in 27 states.[32] These latter organizations help to "certify, inspect, market and distribute organically-produced crops in every area of the country."[33]

The wholesale and retail distribution system for organic foods has also grown notably in recent years. Prior to 1970 there apparently was no such system. Today, however, about 40 major distributors are servicing some 1500 retail outlets of organic foods. Evidently about an equal number of stores emphasize vitamins "but sell good food."[34]

Commercial enterprises engaged in the manufacture and sale of various kinds of alternative agriculture fertilizers, soil conditioners, compost starters, pesticides, and so on are also beginning to organize. Formed in 1975, the Association for Ecological Agriculture, Inc. (AEA) is essentially a trade association composed of manufacturers and suppliers of ecological agricultural inputs. Believing that the alternative agriculture movement is badly organized, the AEA is striving to become an umbrella organization for the disparate elements of the movement. To date, the organization has accomplished little.

Efforts to achieve at least a modicum of international organization within the alternative agriculture movement began in 1972. Although the International Federation of Organic Agriculture Movements (IFOAM) has been formally organized for four years, it has only recently begun to "reach out aggressively to serve as a communicator as well as a coordinator of organic farming developments."[35] In order to help accomplish this goal, IFOAM publishes a highly informative quarterly bulletin containing a variety of information on various developments pertinent to the alternative agriculture movement. There are English, French, and German editions. According to a recent bulletin, "the function of the Federation is to be a network for the diverse bodies concerned for the ecological development of agriculture in all nations." Membership in IFOAM is open to "research, development, education, media, and primary producer groups, practicing or advocating organic/biologic/ecologic agriculture...."[36] Individuals in such related fields as economics, nutrition, and ecology may also join. Despite the optimism of some members,[37] the fact remains that both IFOAM's budget and membership remain small (50 members in 17 nations). Whether IFOAM will be able to overcome the powerful centrifugal forces within the organization and develop into a visible and effective political force is a matter of conjecture.

How Big Is the Movement?

The networking system outlined above provides some indication of the movement's size. Millions of subscriptions to hundreds of alternative agricultural publications would appear to give the movement a substantial political base. (As mentioned previously, over 1 million people subscribe to *Organic Gardening and Farming* while approximately 1.5 million take *Prevention* magazine, another Rodale Press publication.) Although many people undoubtedly have multiple subscriptions to alternative agricultural publications, if simply buying and reading organic type literature qualifies one for group "membership," the size of the movement is indeed impressive.

Indicators of direct involvement in the movement are particularly important. In this regard, Rodale reports that there are approximately "15,000 organic farmers in the U.S. and the number is increasing. The number of organic gardeners runs into the millions."[38] Moreover, Charles Walters, Jr., editor and publisher of *Acres, USA,* believes that there are about 2 million acres being farmed more or less according to the principles of ecoagriculture as set forth in his publication, a figure which is "up considerably since two or three years ago." The number of private companies engaged in the manufacture and sale of various kinds of alternative farm production inputs is also increasing rapidly.[39] Likewise, as previously mentioned, the commercial distribution system for organic foods has experienced notable growth in this decade.

Viewed in isolation, these illustrative indicators of the size of the organic movement are reasonably impressive. When placed in the context of the overall United States food system, however, they appear at best to be marginally significant.

The Feasibility of Organic Agriculture

Until recently there was little reliable scientific evidence to support the feasibility of organic agriculture. In 1974, however, the Center for the Biology of Natural Systems at Washington University began a systematic study of the production, income, and energy use of 14 matched pairs of conventional and organic crop-livestock farms in the Midwest. The center, under the direction of Barry Commoner, has now analyzed the data for the 1974 and 1975 crop years. Preliminarily, the results of this investigation lend some credence to the feasibility of organic crop production in the United States.[40]

This is particularly true when viewed from the perspective of individual producers. Here, for instance, the "profitability of crop production per acre of cropland is comparable on the two groups of farms;..."[41] Although total output per acre of cropland was slightly higher for the conventional farms, the reduced input costs on the organic farms resulting from less use of expensive inorganic fertilizers accounted for the net income comparability. While the conventional farms had approximately 20 percent more cropland devoted to corn and soybeans (major cash crops in the Midwest), the organic farmers had relatively more acreage available for grazing and livestock production. Thus, on the key micro economic issues of per-acre yields, per-acre net income, and total farm net income, the organic producers compared quite well. This was especially true under the severe drought conditions of 1974. Finally, it should also be noted that the organic farmers required about 12 percent more labor but that the conventional group was 2.3 times more energy-intensive. Despite certain limitations of the Washington University study, it does provide some positive evidence regarding the feasibility of organic agriculture.

Policy Objectives

Given the diversity of the alternative agriculture movement, it should be noted that the following abbreviated catalogue of policy objectives represents only a partial overview of the movement's more pervasive policy objectives.

Some members of the movement place great stress upon the need for a greater research effort and commitment into organic agriculture and organic technology by the USDA, land-grant universities, and other related government agencies and departments. This may be the most pervasive policy objective within the movement. Many alternative agriculturalists believe that the agricultural research establishment has, as one man put it, simply "closed the books" on organic agriculture and related aspects of alternative agricultural production and technology. Even the efforts of the Extension Service to help small conventional farmers[42] do not address the specific needs of organic agriculturalists. Although major shifts in agricultural research priorities seem unlikely, alternative agriculturalists do report somewhat greater sympathy and support among mainline agricultural researchers than was true even a few years ago.

Alternative agricultural commercial farm suppliers view increased state product registrations as a major political objective. One of the principal purposes of the Association for Ecological Agriculture (AEA) is developing "ways and means for expeditious registration of 'eco-agricultural' products" by the state departments of agriculture.[43] Many feel that past difficulties in obtaining registrations have greatly diminished the sale and use of such products and directly impeded the movement. If, as many members of the movement insist, the proof of the pudding is in the eating, greater success in the area of product registrations would appear to be a prerequisite for the expansion of the movement. Farmers cannot adopt new methods of fertilization, pest control, and soil treatment if the manufacturers and distributors of these products are denied the opportunity to sell them.

State departments of agriculture predictably deny industry charges of harassment and unreasonable delays in their efforts to obtain state product registrations. The director of one state licensing agency told me that useful products are most welcome and that "organic people have a right to these things." Why then, it was asked, does industry claim it has difficulty obtaining registrations? The answer: "Because there are a lot of fly-by-night companies and some of these products are not worth a damn. . . . If they can prove that it works they can get certified." Agencies contend that their sole function is to protect farmers from the "wild claims" of unscrupulous companies.

Industry people see the issues quite differently. They believe that the states are playing God when they specify what is acceptable or valuable plant food. As one member of the movement vehemently insisted, "We don't know enough to write a law about fertilization!" Thus the major issue from the industry perspective is not simply whether the state agencies are willing to test alternative products, but rather the more basic issue of whether approved products ought to be required to meet state-mandated specifications for nitrogen, phosphorus and potash, NPK. (State law in this area varies greatly, but some states do require what is known as "product or grade registrations" where certain levels of NPK must be present in the laboratory analysis.) Furthermore, industry contends that it frequently takes far too long, sometimes several years, to get new products field-tested by the state departments. These extended delays impose an impossible economic burden upon the small, struggling companies that typically are attempting to develop these unconventional products. More complete knowledge of the politics of this issue area would undoubtedly shed considerable light upon the future of the alternative agriculture movement.

State certification of organic producers is being vigorously sought by some elements of the movement. Oregon (1974) and New Hampshire (1973) have such programs in place, while several other states are actively considering organic certification legislation. Bills calling for the creation of a national system of inspection and certification have been introduced in both houses of Congress.[44] Proponents of state and/or federal certification argue that such programs would eliminate fraudulent producers, reassure consumers, and enhance organic food sales. Opponents fear that unwarranted or unrealistic government regulations might actually hamper the movement. Some small growers simply object to paying registration fees.

Government recognition and protection of the organic concept and organic products,[45] stricter regulation of toxic chemical pesticides, policies designed to utilize urban sewage sludge by looping it back to the countryside for use as organic fertilizer, restrictions on chemical food additives and preservatives, and state programs which would promote direct farmer-to-consumer food distribution systems are also important policy issues. Although a detailed analysis of specific policy objectives falls far beyond the scope and purpose of this chapter, the foregoing indicates some of the movement's more pervasive policy goals.

Evidence of Elite Support

In general, elite interest in various alternative agriculture principles and policy objectives appears to be mounting. A brief overview of this growing interest and support follows.

Some universities and university-based researchers as well as various semi-official policy planning groups are becoming increasingly responsive to the alternative agriculture movement. The Center for the Biology of Natural Systems at Washington University, for example, is conducting a number of studies relating to several aspects of organic ideology.[46] Recently a University of Nebraska workshop explored a wide range of topics dealing with organic farming techniques.[47] A number of studies are underway at the University of Nebraska comparing conventional and organic crop production. The University of Maine has established formal advisory relations with the Maine Organic Farmers and Gardeners Association (MOFGA). The recent creation of a Small and Part-time Farmers Advisory Committee provides the MOFGA with direct and regular access to the dean of the College of Life Sciences and Agriculture. Dr. Robert Van Den Bosch, division chairman, Division of Biological Control, University of

California, Berkeley, is a strong supporter of organic technology, especially biological pest control. Dr. Van Den Bosch has written articles for *Organic Gardening and Farming* magazine. Dr. Ross Hume Hall, professor of bio-chemistry at the Health Sciences Center, McMaster University, Hamilton, Ontario, Canada, and the author of *Food for Nought*,[48] emerges as a strong voice for ecoagricultural methods. Dr. Rabindar Singh of the West Virginia University of Agricultural Experiment Station is doing research on declining levels of trace elements in conventionally grown food. Kansas State University has conducted similar research on the varying rates of iron content in organically and chemically fertilized spinach. The Alternative Agriculture Resources Project at the University of California at Davis is helping to set up a communicatons networking system among alternative agriculturalists.

Recently the Board on Agriculture and Renewable Resources of the National Academy of Sciences made a number of recommendations regarding food policy and research which coincide with organic ideology. It called for research focusing

on ways of decreasing dependence upon chemically synthesized nitrogen fertilizer, and on increasing the supply of biologically fixed nitrogen by forage and grain legumes and nitrogen-fixing associations of microorganisms with grasses, shurbs, trees, lichens; and marine organisms, and the design of new cropping systems.[49]

The report also recommended increased research on biological pest control and reduced energy use in food production.

Evidence of official government interest in various aspects of the alternative agriculture movement is revealed in a number of recent events. In 1976 the Community Services Administration provided over $3 million for the creation of the National Center for Appropriate Technology to be headquartered at Butte, Montana.[50] The General Accounting Office issued a report in 1975 which severely criticized the efforts of the USDA to help small farmers.[51] The Subcommittee on Family Farms and Rural Development of the House Committee on Agriculture held hearings in June 1976 on how to improve small-farm operations.[52] A December 1976 Senate subcommittee staff report severely criticized the inadequate regulation of chemical pesticides.[53] The 1974 USDA *Yearbook of Agriculture* formally acknowledged the existence of organic agriculture in a sometimes moderately supportive article devoted to the differences between organic and inorganic foods.[54] Finally, Secretary of Agriculture Robert Bergland recently suggested that alternatives to the heavy use of pesticides and other petroleum-based agricultural inputs must be found.[55]

Although purely illustrative, this abbreviated survey of elite support does give an indication of the range of university and government involvement with alternative agriculturalists. Members of the movement who have dealt with agricultural researchers over an extended period report a gradual improvement in relations as well as a more sympathetic attitude toward organically oriented research. More complete data are needed concerning elite support in other areas of the food policy subsystem such as conventional farm interest groups, the agriculture committees of Congress, the Extension Service, and the research components of the USDA. Knowledgeable alternative agriculturalists insist that a considerable amount of latent support exists within these institutions.

Some Concluding Thoughts on the Future of the Alternative Agriculture Movement

"What you have here is a slowly evolving technology." "It will be at least a generation before the USDA recognizes us." "We're off to a slow but sure start." As these statements indicate, alternative agriculturalists firmly believe that organic or ecologic agriculture is destined to play an increasingly important role in the future of American agriculture. While admitting that they now usually talk only to each other in "something of a fool's paradise," most alternative agriculturalists seem genuinely convinced that time and circumstances are on their side. As shown here, their efforts have already begun to bear fruit. And they definitely intend to "keep fighting the battle."

For the most part, the first phase of organic agriculture has involved those farmers and gardeners who "went organic" for a variety of ideological reasons— love of nature, nostalgia, concern for the environment, improved health, and the like. To the contrary, most of America's remaining 1.8 million conventional farmers continue to base production decisions mainly on economic considerations. The future of organic agriculture may depend more upon the future costs of chemically based, energy-intensive agricultural production than upon the political efforts of the alternative agriculture movement. Apparently, many farmers who are currently adopting various aspects of organic technology are doing so almost entirely for economic reasons, namely, the desire to minimize the increasing costs and uncertainties associated with conventional agriculture.[56]

Thus, ironically, the character of the fossil fuel industry which did so much to displace organic agriculture thirty years ago may one day be equally responsible for its rebirth. If so, alternative agriculturalists would have achieved their ideological and political objectives, but not because of their ideology or politics. For those dedicated and resourceful pioneers of the alternative agriculture movement there would, of course, be some satisfaction in being able to say: "We told you so."

Notes

1. Address by Don Paarlberg, Director of Agricultural Economics, USDA, at the National Public Policy Conference, Clymar, New York, September 11,

1975. According to Paarlberg, the agricultural establishment includes "the farm organizations, the agricultural committees of the Congress, the Department of Agriculture, and the Land Grant Colleges" (pp. 1 and 2).

2. Ibid., p. 12.

3. For a useful discussion of the character of these products, see Gene Logsdon, "Natural Fertilizers: How and Wat Are They?" in Ray Wolf (ed.), *Organic Farming: Yesterday's and Tomorrow's Agriculture* (Emmaus, Penn.: Rodale Press, 1977), pp. 164-172.

4. Simply defining the term *ideology* could become a major part of this chapter. Instead, for purposes of this analysis, the following definition has been selected. "Political, and much of social life, involves the use of power to achieve goals amidst changing circumstances. Central to this process are beliefs about the present nature of the world and the hope one has for its future. Such beliefs and hope, when integrated into a more or less coherent picture of (1) how the present social, economic, and political order operates, (2) why this is so and whether it is good or bad, and (3) what should be done about it, if anything, may be termed an 'ideology.' " Kenneth M. Dolbeare and Patricia Dolbeare, *American Ideologies: The Competing Political Beliefs of the 1970s* (Chicago: Markham Publishing Co., 1971), p. 3. This definition, with its emphasis upon beliefs and attitudes about the way the world is and the way it ought to be, is probably the most common and sensible characterization of ideology available. Here, for example, see T.W. Adorno, Else Frenkel-Brunswik, Daniel J. Levinson, and R. Nevitt Sanford, *The Authoritarian Personality* (New York: Harper and Row, Publishers, 1950), p. 2. For an interesting collection of the various historical interpretations of the meaning of ideology, see Robert E. Lane, *Political Ideology* (New York: The Free Press, 1962), pp. 13-14.

5. Robert E. Lane, *Political Ideology* (New York: The Free Press, 1962), p. 15.

6. For an excellent summary analysis of that heritage, see Donald Fleming, "Roots of the New Conservation Movement," in Donald Fleming and Bernard Bailyn (eds.), *Perspectives in American History,* vol. 6 (Cambridge, Mass.: Harvard University, Charles Warren Center for Studies in American History, 1972), pp. 7-91.

7. E.F. Schumacher, *Small Is Beautiful: Economics as if People Mattered* (New York: Harper and Row, Publishers, Inc., 1973).

8. For an interesting self-assessment of some of the philosophical and religious influences which affected Schumacher's ideology, see Sherman Goldman and Bill Tara, "An Interview with E.F. Schumacher: Changing Knowledge to Wisdom," *East West Journal* 6, no. 11 (November 1976):14-18.

9. Prepared statement of Robert Rodale in connection with public hearings of Federal Trade Commission, Washington, D.C., November 17, 1976, before William D. Dixon, presiding officer, regarding proposed TRR on Food Advertising, (16 CFR Part 437), as yet unpublished, pp. 14, 15, and 16.

10. For a representative sample of Albrecht's work, see William A. Albrecht, Charles Walters, Jr., (ed.), *The Albrecht Papers* (Raytown, Mo.: Acres, U.S.A., 1975).

11. The reader may find these addresses useful: *Acres, U.S.A.,* 10227 East 61st Street, Raytown, Missouri 64133. *Countryside,* 312 Portland Road, Highway 19 East, Waterloo, Wisconsin 53594. *The Journal of the New Alchemists,* The New Alchemy Institute, P.O. Box 432, Woods Hole, Massachusetts 02543. *Organic Gardening and Farming,* Organic Park, Emmaus, Penn. 18049.

12. Schumacher, *Small Is Beautiful,* p. 14.

13. Ibid.

14. Ibid., pp. 15-16.

15. Prepared statement of Robert Rodale, pp. 6 and 4.

16. Robert Rodale, "What Is Organic Farming?" *Organic Farming Yearbook of Agriculture* (Emmaus, Penn.: Rodale Press, Inc., 1975), p. 4.

17. Bryce Nelson, "Kicking a Farm Habit," *The New York Times*, January 24, 1974, p. 37.

18. Prepared statement of Robert Rodale, p. 5.

19. Schumacher, *Small Is Beautiful,* pp. 30, 33 and chap. 2.

20. Wade Green, "The New Alchemists," *The New York Times,* August 8, 1976, p. 12.

21. Ray Reed, "Back-to-Land Movement Seeks Self-Sufficiency," *The New York Times,* June 9, 1975, pp. 1 and 19.

22. Gene Logsdon, "The Quiet Farmers Agribusiness Ignores," *Organic Gardening and Farming,* 23, no. 12 (December 1976):49, 50.

23. Ibid., p. 50.

24. J.D. Belanger, "The Case for the Family Farm," (Waterloo, Wis.: Countryside Publications, 1976), p. 21.

25. For a brief statement of the purposes, goals, and activities of the institute as well as an annotated bibliography of the institute's journal, see "The 1976 Annotated Bibliography of New Alchemy Information," P.O. Box 432, Woods Hole, Massachusetts 02543. Copies are available upon request.

26. Green, "The New Alchemists," pp. 13 and 40.

27. Robert Rodale, "It's Time for a New Declaration of Independence," *Organic Gardening and Farming,* 23, no. 9 (September 1976):46.

28. Ibid., p. 49.

29. There are a number of organizations which support and lobby for some aspects of organic ideology. Among the more prominent of such organizations are: (1) Agribusiness Accountability Project, 1000 Wisconsin Avenue, N.W. Washington, D.C. 20007; (2) The Center for Science in the Public Interest, 1779 Church Street, N.W., Washington, D.C. 20036; (3) Center for the Study of Responsive Law, P.O. Box 19367, Washington, D.C. 20036; (4) Institute for Food and Development Policy, P.O. 40430, San Francisco, Calif., 94140;

(5) Rural America, Inc., 1346 Connecticut Avenue, N.W., Washington, D.C. 20036; (6) National Rural Center, 1200 18th Street N.W., Washington, D.C. 20036. The editors of Rodale Press, Emmaus, Penn. 18049, carry on the bulk of "lobbying" activity for organic farmers and gardeners. Even these efforts do not approach the organizational dimensions of conventional lobby groups. For a fairly complete listing of organizations concerned with food policy, see Catherine Lerza and Michael Jacobsen (eds.), *Food for People, Not for Profit* (New York: Ballantine Books, 1975), appendix 7.

30. Isao Fujimoto, "The Movement for an Ecological Agriculture and Its Social Implications," paper presented at Rural Sociological Society Meeting, New York, August 1976, p. 4.

31. *Farming,* sourcebook part I by the Alternative Agricultural Resources Project, Davis Citizen Action Press, Davis, Calif., June 1976.

32. Prepared statement of Robert Rodale, p. 18.

33. Letter from Jerome Goldstein, executive editor, *Organic Gardening and Farming,* Emmaus, Penn., November 15, 1976.

34. Letter from Frank Ford, Arrowsmith Mills, Inc., Hereford, Texas, January 3, 1977.

35. Letter from Goldstein.

36. International Federation of Organic Agriculture Movements, *Newsletter #17,* July 1976, p. 2.

37. Jerome Goldstein, "The World of Organic Agriculture Moves Ahead," *Organic Gardening and Farming,* 24, no. 1 (January 1977).

38. Prepared statement of Robert Rodale, p. 19.

39. Interview with Charles Walters, Jr., Raytown, Mo., December 28, 1976.

40. *Organic and Conventional Crop Production in the Corn Belt: A Comparison of Economic Performance and Energy Use for Selected Farms,* Center for the Biology of Natural Systems, Washington University, St. Louis, Mo., June, 1976.

41. Ibid., p. 30.

42. For example, see *Missouri Small Farm Program,* 1974 Report, University of Missouri at Columbia, Extension Division, MP 445.

43. Association for Ecological Agriculture, Inc., "Prospectus," Madison, Wisconsin, p. 3.

44. Prepared statement of M.C. Goldman in connection with public hearings of Federal Trade Commission, Washington, D.C., November 17, 1976, before William D. Dixon, presiding officer, regarding proposed TRR on Food Advertising, (16 CFR Part 437), as yet unpublished. Pages 5, 8, and 13-15.

45. Prepared statement of Robert Rodale.

46. Center for the Biology of Natural Systems, *Program 1975-1976,* Washington University, St. Louis, Mo.

47. *Organic Residues and By-Products in Crop and Animal Production,* Workshop, University of Nebraska Field Laboratory, Mead, Nebraska, December

10, 1975. Sponsored by Agricultural Experiment Station and Cooperative Extension Service.

48. Ross Hume Hall, *Food for Nought* (New York: Vintage Books, 1976).

49. *World Food and Nutrition Study; Enhancement of Food Production for the United States,* a report of the Board on Agriculture and Renewable Resources, Commission on Natural Resources, National Research Council, National Academy of Sciences, Washington, 1975, p. 15.

50. Proposal for the National Center for Appropriate Technology as funded by Community Services Administration, Washington, D.C., September 1976.

51. "Some Problems Impeding Economic Improvements of Small-Farm Operations: What the Department of Agriculture Could Do," report to the Congress by the Comptroller General of the United States, August 15, 1975.

52. U.S. House of Representatives, Committee on Agriculture, Subcommittee on Family Farms and Rural Development, *Upgrade Small Farmer Operations,* Hearings before Subcommittee, 94th Cong., 2d Sess., on H.R. 12917, June 10, 1976.

53. U.S. Senate, Committee on the Judiciary, *The Environmental Protection Agency and the Regulation of Pesticides,* Staff Report to the Subcommittee on Administrative Practice and Procedure, 94th Cong., 2d Sess., December 1976.

54. Ruth M. Leverton, "Organic, Inorganic: What They Mean," *Shoppers Guide: 1974 Yearbook of Agriculture,* U.S. Department of Agriculture (Washington: Government Printing Office, 1974), pp. 70-73.

55. Remarks by Secretary of Agriculture Robert Bergland to meeting of National Agricultural Chemicals Association, White Sulphur Springs, West Virginia, September 27, 1977.

56. Interview with Roger Blobaum, Agricultural Consultant, Creston, Iowa, December 1, 1976.

21 Social Research and Public Policy: The Case of American Agriculture

Philip Olson

Introduction

In the twentieth century, America has shown remarkable changes in the growth of technology, in the increasing complexity of large-scale organizations, in the social structure of daily life, and in the value systems of its peoples. We face today, in the last quarter of the century, the task of explaining the relations among these changes with an eye toward both understanding the characteristics of this era and actively dealing with those elements that emerge as undesirable.

The changes characteristic of this century are mirrored in the American system of agriculture. We have substantially solved the food supply problem for ourselves and are now exporting that knowledge along with our surpluses. We have created an impressive technology for food and fiber production. And we can observe that the production and distribution of food and fiber occur largely within the matrix of large-scale organizations, as have the creation and dissemination of the knowledge systems that contributed to solving the supply problems. The growth of large-scale organizations in agriculture is part of the changing social structure of modern society, as are the organization of family life away from the nuclear unit, the restructuring of community patterns toward metropolitan centers, and the occupational structure toward a managerial and white-collar majority. The changes in values are largely toward easier living, greater choices in consuming goods and services, greater tolerance of variation in behavior, and confidence in large organizations to solve problems.

In *The Active Society*, Etzioni characterizes our society as showing a

... continued increase in the efficiency of the technology of production which poses a growing challenge to the primacy of the values these means are supposed to serve. The post-modern period, the onset of which may be set at 1945, will witness either a greater threat to the status of these values by the surging technologies or a reassertion of their normative priority[1]

In effect, changes in our value and social system are a consequence of technological change. This thesis is a postmodern version of the culture lag theory put forth by William Ogburn in his work *Social Change,* in 1928, in which he stated that changes in the values and structure of society always lag behind technological change.[2]

This analysis of American agriculture takes the Ogburn and Etzioni thesis as a point of departure and develops it a step further: if our society has been capable of building systems of knowledge that have led to massive technological changes, then is not this same knowledge system capable of understanding, monitoring, and regulating the consequences of the technological changes on our social structure and value system? In this chapter I propose to explore the following question: *Why is it that our vast knowledge systems have not yet been successfully directed toward control of the changes (resulting from technological expansion) in the American social and value structures through the formulation and implementation of public policy?* In addressing this general question, I will focus on the case of agriculture to illustrate the issues.

James Hightower laid a foundation for the question I raised. In *Hard Tomatoes, Hard Times* he points out how USDA-sponsored research, particularly on agricultural technology, contributes substantially to the growth of agribusiness at the expense of the small farmer and, ironically, is funded by tax dollars allocated under the political banner of "Preserve Rural America."[3] Thus, government-sponsored (USDA) knowledge building has led to substantial improvements in agricultural production and resulted in the restructuring of the production system, the decline of farming opportunities for rural peoples, and the depletion of rural life. Where were the safeguards in the system to protect those adversely affected by this technological revolution? Where were the knowledge systems to identify these consequences before they happened? And where was the mechanism for getting this information to policy formulators in time for them to forestall these outcomes?

Policy Research

In order to bring to bear relevant knowledge systems for examining the consequences of technological change, there has arisen an explicit form of research called *policy research*. As Etzioni puts it, "Policy research is concerned with mapping alternative approaches and with specifying potential differences in the intention, effect, and cost of various programs."[4] And, "Policy research deals with values and seeks to clarify goals and the relations among them, as well as among goals and sets of means. . . . Policy research is inevitably *critical*."[5] Nolan and Hagen, in an article assessing policy research among rural sociologists, characterize social policy research as ". . . building issues into and drawing relevant implications from the research process. The researcher is thus taking an activist's role. . . . Social policy research requires an examination of the broad structural issues that affect numbers of people."[6] In addition, both Etzioni and Nolan and Hagen emphasize that the policy researcher must have contact with policy makers: ". . . knowledge generated by the research process must be viewed as a tool for utilization by decision-makers. . . ."[7] And, "A policy researcher must be able to interact effectively with politicians, bureaucrats, housewives, and minority leaders."[8]

Subsequently, we shall see that the failure by social scientists and the USDA to distinguish between policy and applied research and to pit applied research against basic research has contributed to failures in agriculture to address policy issues.

The Failure of Policy Research

The central question raised in this chapter is why social research has not been successful in affecting policy outcomes of technological advances. Specifically, this question is explored in the context of American agriculture. I have identified four factors that have contributed to this failure. Each plays a specific role, and together they form the major impediments to the effective utilization of information to shape public policy on food and fiber. These factors are (1) the American ideologies of pluralism and freedom, (2) the social structure of large-scale organizations that generates knowledge systems and formulates public policy, (3) the organization and ethos of social science research, and (4) the incredibly small proportion of public funds spent for social research.

The American Ideologies of Pluralism and Freedom

The American system has flourished under the belief that free enterprise and the consequent multiplication of competitive units were in the best interest of the society. Particularly, the production of knowledge has been looked upon as done best under conditions of complete freedom from constraint and direction. Such knowledge, produced rapidly, with no overarching design or goal, has led to technological advances that have transformed the entire social structure. The same factors that have led to these outcomes have, however, also led to the constraints on guiding the outcomes. Etzioni points out that ". . . the uses to which society puts new knowledge are not determined by the nature of the knowledge but depend on the structure and organization of the society itself. . . . Post-modern pluralistic societies seem to exhibit a historical tendency toward a slow increase in the societal guidance of knowledge."[9] Although social critics occasionally explore the implications of new technologies, they do not have the resources and technical staff for long-range study of the consequences. The ideology of pluralistic society is ". . . that society has to adjust to the societal implications of new knowledge . . . and those in power accepted societal adjustment to rather than guidance of technological change."[10]

It is a further belief in our society that the elected politician is responsible to the public for social policy, not the creators of knowledge. Thus, the academics and intellectuals of the society, even if they "know" more than elected officials, are curbed from having a direct role in decision making.

The Social Structure of Large-Scale Organizations

Large-scale organizations such as the USDA generate knowledge systems that are capable of both modifying and regulating the changes in our society in such diverse areas as food production, community development, farm management, homemaking, and youth activities. Why has it not happened that policy issues were explored within USDA? The answer lies partly in the nature of large-scale organizations and how they generate knowledge and how decisions get made.

A principal issue is the vast separation between those making decisions for the organization and the army of technologists, data processors, and creators of "intelligence" within the organization. Each operates with his or her own priorities of what is important. As Wilensky points out, ". . . dedicated specialists have always pushed their specialties. . . . Experts who move into policy circles typically provide analytical advice defining major alternatives in a situation of great uncertainty. Top executives typically incorporate analytical judgements, value judgements, practical experience, and intuition into policy decisions."[11] And ". . . whatever the uses of electronic data processing . . . and whatever the expansion of applied research . . . there remains a great shortage of generalized policy advice."[12]

Central factors of the organizational failure to generate and use its own sources of "intelligence" in dealing with policy are (1) the structure of the organization, which requires specialization of tasks, and organizational separation that leads to internal rivalry and ineffective communication upward to decision makers, and (2) operating doctrines within the organization that categorize "intelligence" into "facts" and "interpretation," "technical detail" and "general outcomes."[13] As a consequence,

. . . the alert executive is everywhere forced to bypass the regular machinery and seek firsthand exposure to intelligence sources in and out of the organization. In matters delicate and urgent, more imaginative administrative leaders typically move to points along the organization's boundaries: looking toward the bottom, they rely on internal communications specialists such as education directors and auditors; looking outward they rely on . . . press officers, lobbyists, mediators. They talk to reporters and researchers . . . they establish study commissions or review boards comprised entirely of outsiders . . . they assemble *ad hoc* committees, kitchen cabinets, general advisors, personal representatives. . . . These unofficial intelligence agents . . . may constitute the most important and reliable source of organizational intelligence.[14]

In this model, policy is the outgrowth of a selective style of information gathering by the top administrator, rather than a deliberate organizational posture.

Among those organizations that engage in more systematic policy research—there are some in both the government and private sectors—Van deVall found that projects with external researchers took longer to complete than those done within the organization and had a greater time lag between completion of the research and policy implementation.[15]

The Organization and Ethos of Social Science Research

Public policy science falls largely to the social scientists in our society—they are those trained to know the intricacies of social, economic, and political systems. Yet, social scientists are on a different path—leading toward intellectual power. Their allies are the scientific community, their heirs are their students, and their benefactors are the public and corporate world. Only a few cross the line into the public policy arena. They are constrained to cross because the ethic of scientific neutrality filters their image of the political process. (Elsewhere I have pointed out, however, that what masquerades as neutrality is often merely a commitment to one's ideologies.[16])

Many who do cross the line of scholarly research do so in the applied dimension, believing it okay to solve practical problems with known knowledge. This posture is characteristic of experiment station researchers in both the life and social sciences. This is viewed by many as policy research, i.e., dealing with problem solving. Indeed, there is almost no distinction made in USDA between applied and policy research. Even the Pound report, in its critique of USDA research, nowhere addresses the need for policy research.

In his statement on policy research, Etzioni makes a clear distinction between applied and policy research:

Applied research accepts specific assignments from clients and tries to serve their needs largely in their terms. . . . Policy research ought not to take on specific assignments but to concern itself with the problems of the social unit to which it relates, . . . [and] . . . applied research deals with means, taking the goals for granted. Policy research deals with values and seeks to clarify goals and the relations among them, as well as among goals and sets of means.[17]

In the social sciences, applied research has grown into a respectable aspect of professionalism, but this has not generally included policy research. Those who engage in research frequently think in terms of usefulness, i.e., ". . . whether research findings conceivable could be used at some time, perhaps unknown to the author, for shaping legislative or practical concerns."[18] This is not, however, policy research.

Rural sociology, one of the few areas within the agricultural sciences that could engage in policy research, is focused on applying sociology to the study of rural life and to the solutions to rural problems; yet rural sociologists are not in strategic locations to make policy inputs. Ford reports that in 1972 and only 25 rural sociologists were in federal government agencies and fewer than that in state agencies.[19]

Nolan and Hagen, building upon an article by Sewell,[20] note that of the articles published in *Rural Sociology* since it began in 1936, 33 percent were policy-related in the 1936-1945 period, in the 1946-1955 period the percentage declined to 17 percent and dropped to 8 percent during the 1956-1965 period and 6 percent in 1966-1974.[21]

The significance of these trends lies in the finding of Nolan and Hagen that the principal direction of rural sociological research is toward "individualistic and social psychological" studies ... "which excludes the possibility of confronting broad social structural issues which many argue are at the core of good social policy research."[22]

The factors prompting this redirection of research effort are that "... rural sociologists appear to have been drawn into defining problems and gathering data in such a way that the probabilities of being 'scientific' are maximized but relevance for policy is minimized."[23]

The most perceptive and revealing analysis of rural sociology is offered by James Copp, long-time USDA employee and rural sociologist in his 1972 presidential address before the Rural Sociological Society. He confesses that, after reviewing the research programs in most of the major universities conducting rural studies, "if most of the research which rural sociologists were doing in 1969 and 1970 were to have some how disappeared, the world would have noticed little loss."[24] He identifies this failure to study "relevant" and policy-related social problems as rooted in the availability of funds. "As a result of my survey, I come to the conclusion that rural sociologists really were not the masters of the phenomena of rural society."[25] In other words, the larger concerns of USDA were guiding rural social research, determining what ought to be studied. Copp concludes: "... in our sustenance relationship with USDA and the experiment states we have sacrificed some of our independence and been less incisive than we might have been."[26]

Within sociology, James Cowhig points out, respectability goes to those making "significant contributions to the theory and methods of the discipline."[27] This means that basic research takes precedence over applied and policy research.

Cowhig, himself an employee of a federal research granting agency, the National Science Foundation (NSF), points out that federal research grants are unlikely to support policy research because peer review of proposals leads to an emphasis on professional standards and not policy relevance; the time lag in funding makes impossible the use of results in policy formulation and implementation; the relatively low level of funding of projects limits them to local or regional relevancy whereas policy research almost always requires national data; and since most grants go to academics who are heavily engaged in teaching and academic life, there are long delays in completing funded research.

The Proportion of Public Funds for Social Research

Hightower makes the important point that although the social research currently sponsored by USDA is of generally poor quality, there are no plans to upgrade it or add more money. He reports that USDA plans to raise the proportion of program funds to "raise the level of living of rural people" from 2 percent in 1965 to 3 percent in 1977.[28] NSF reports that the social and psychological sciences received only 11 percent of federal basic research monies in universities in 1974, rising from only 8 percent in 1964. Since most policy research comes from the social sciences, it is clear that until more money is put into this area, policy research must continue to hold a low-priority place in our society—continuing evidence of the gap Etzioni points out in our system between producing technology and assessing its consequences.

Conclusions

The producers of knowledge in our society are weighted toward technological advances. "Intelligence" about how to structure and guide these advances is not being generated or, when it is, is not instrumental in affecting public policy. This point is acknowledged in a recent paper that claims professional social scientists have had less impact on our society than Hightower's journalistic crusade against USDA.[29] It is not often that academics and researchers can shape federal spending and thus policy. It is important to note, however, that the Pound report played a crucial role in the congressional House Committee on Science and Technology in September 1975, when Glenn Pound and others testified on behalf of the recommendations of his report. The House committee report[30] indicates that the report was influential in the committee's recommendations.

The dilemma facing American agriculture is the strain within the organization itself. The research person is oriented toward scientific respectability, meaning emphasis on basic research. (The Pound report mirrors this point of view.) Yet the organization—USDA—strains to meet political demands—more answers to technical questions, more applied research. It is difficult to imagine that, under these conditions, policy research will emerge as a focal point for the USDA.

Nevertheless, it needs to be said that if our society is to survive the onslaught of technology, it must have policy studies, notably in our system of agriculture.

In the building of such policy studies, their chance for success can be enhanced if the four points in this chapter identified with the failure of policy research are heeded.

1. Government leaders, including USDA administrators, need to declare their intent to establish powerful policy research programs, thereby eschewing the public ideology that all knowledge is produced in a laissez-faire mode.
2. With an understanding of how large-scale organizations circumvent the orderly flow of information upward, there can be established deliberate mechanisms for overcoming the impediments. And following Van deVall's research, internal policy researchers need to be recruited, rather than contracting for policy research in academic settings.
3. Special programs to train policy researchers and then recruit them into USDA positions will help attract social scientists away from an already saturated academic marketplace and thereby avoid the conflict of academic respectability versus the organizational needs of USDA.
4. Increasing the level of funding of social science research, both basic and policy-oriented, will go a long way toward alleviating the relative paucity of knowledge available to us that is necessary for the policy scientist.

The accomplishment of these four objectives will take the concerted efforts of both administrators and scientists and their willingness to avoid the self-rationalizations that typically stand in the way of change.

Notes

1. Amitai Etzioni, *The Active Society* (New York: The Free Press, 1968), p. vii.
2. William F. Ogburn, *Social Change* (New York: Viking Press, 1928).
3. James Hightower, *Hard Tomatoes, Hard Times* (Cambridge, Mass.: Schenkman Publishing Co., 1972).
4. Amitai Etzioni, "Policy Research," *The American Sociologist* 6 (June 1971):8.
5. Ibid., p. 9.
6. Michael Nolan and Robert Hagen, "Rural Sociological Research, 1966-1974: Implications for Social Policy," *Rural Sociology* 40 (Winter 1975):437.
7. Ibid., p. 437.
8. Etzioni, "Policy Research," p. 10.
9. Etzioni, *The Active Society,* p. 211.
10. Ibid., p. 208.
11. Harold Wilensky, *Organizational Intelligence: Knowledge and Policy in Government and Industry* (New York: Basic Books, 1967), p. 183.
12. Ibid., p. 182.
13. Ibid., pp. 174-177.
14. Ibid., p. 180.

15. Mark Van deVall, "A Theoretical Framework for Applied Social Research," *International Journal of Mental Health* 2 (1973):6-25; and "Utilization and Methodology of Applied Social Research," *Journal of Applied Behavioral Science* 11 (1973):14-38.

16. Philip Olson, "Rural American Community Studies: The Survival of Public Ideology," *Human Organization* 23 (Winter 1964):342-350.

17. Etzioni, "Policy Research," pp. 8-9.

18. Nolan and Hagen, "Rural Sociological Research, 1966-1974," p. 437.

19. Thomas Ford, "Toward Meeting the Social Responsibilities of Rural Sociology," *Rural Sociology* 38 (Winter 1973):380.

20. William Sewell, "Rural Sociology Research, 1936-1965," *Rural Sociology* 30 (December 1965):428-451.

21. Nolan and Hagen, "Rural Sociological Research, 1966-1974," p. 437.

22. Ibid., p. 443.

23. Ibid., p. 444.

24. James Copp, "Rural Sociology and Rural Development," *Rural Sociology* 37 (December 1972):515-533.

25. Ibid., p. 521.

26. Ibid., p. 526.

27. James Cowhig, "Federal Grant-Supported Social Research and 'Relevance': Some Reservations," *The American Sociologist* 6 (June 1971):66.

28. Hightower, *Hard Tomatoes, Hard Times,* p. 67.

29. Michael Nolan and John Galliher, "Rural Sociological Research and Social Policy: Hard Data, Hard Times," *Rural Sociology* 38 (Winter 1973):491-499.

30. U.S. House of Representatives, *Special Oversight Review of Agricultural Research and Development,* report by the Subcommittee on Science, Research, and Technology, of the Committee on Science and Technology (Washington: Government Printing Office, 1976).

Indexes

Index of Names

Index of Subjects

About the Contributors

Jeffrey M. Berry is assistant professor of political science at Tufts University. He recently authored *Lobbying for the People* and was co-author of *To Enact a Law*. Articles have appeared in *Polity* and the *Harvard Journal on Legislation.*

J.D. Esseks is associate professor of political science at Northern Illinois University. This article marks a research departure for an African scholar who has previously published in such journals as *Western Political Quarterly* and *Journal of Politics.*

James L. Guth is assistant professor of political science at Furman University. His research has focused almost exclusively on agricultural policy and his publications have appeared in the Journal of *Political Science, Agricultural History,* and *Ripon Forum.*

Joseph Hajda is associate professor of political science at Kansas State University. He has authored several agricultural related articles and recently co-edited *The Future of Agriculture in the Soviet Union and Eastern Europe.* He has served in the Office of the Secretary of Agriculture, in the White House Office of the Special Representative for Trade Negotiations, and as a member of several agricultural trade missions.

Charles M. Hardin is professor emeritus of political science at the University of California-Davis. He is a prolific scholar on agricultural policy, having written the classic, *Politics of Agriculture* and other studies of agricultural policy-making, farm program structure, and agricultural education.

Jonathan Lurie is associate dean of the Graduate School and associate professor of history at Rutgers University-Newark. His articles appear in *Agricultural History, Rutgers Law Review,* and *American Journal of Legal History.* His forthcoming book is on the Chicago Board of Trade as a case study in administrative law.

Jan E. Mabie is associate professor of political science and public administration at Georgia College. He has journal articles on Congress and bureaucracy.

Ardith Maney is assistant professor of political science at Iowa State University. She has recently become active in agricultural policy studies.

Alex F. McCalla is professor of agricultural economics and former dean of the University of California-Davis. His research has been published in the *American*

Journal of Agricultural Economics, Canadian Journal of Agricultural Economics, Review of Economical Statistics, and *Agricultural History.*

Kenneth John Meier is assistant director of the Bureau of Governmental Research and assistant professor of political science at the University of Oklahoma. He has published articles on representative bureaucracy, affirmative action, regulatory policy, budgeting and voting behavior. He is author of the forthcoming *Bureaucracy and Politics.*

Heather Johnston Nicholson is assistant professor of political science, Program in Science, Technology and Public Policy at Purdue University. She is co-author of *Agriculture, Food and Human Values.* Another of her articles on agricultural research is published in *Minerva.*

Philip Olson is professor of sociology and former chairman at the University of Missouri-Kansas City. He has authored articles in *American Communities Tomorrow, Human Organization,* and the *American Sociological Review.* His most recent book was *The Study of Modern Society.*

Isidro D. Ortiz is acting assistant professor of Chicano studies and political science at the University of California-Santa Barbara. He is presently involved in an extensive analysis of farm labor politics.

Don Paarlberg is professor emeritus of agricultural economics at Purdue University. He formerly served in several subcabinet positions at USDA under three different secretaries of agriculture and has authored books and articles on farm policy.

William C. Payne is deputy chief of the Program Planning and Evaluation, Office of Equal Opportunity, U.S. Department of Agriculture. He previously monitored USDA as a staff member for the U.S. Civil Rights Commission.

John G. Peters is assistant professor of political science at the University of Nebraska-Lincoln. While his research now focuses on agriculture, he has also done extensive research on legislative reform and political corruption. His work appears in the *American Political Science Review* and other journals.

Laurellen Porter is associate professor of political science at Indiana State University. Her research interests focus on congressional change as well as economic policy.

John B. Richard is professor of political science and former chairman at the University of Wyoming. A state politics and public administration specialist, he has published in the *Public Administration Review, Western Political Quarterly,* and other journals. He is also the author of *Government and Politics in Wyoming.*

Alan S. Walter is an agricultural economist with the Commodity Economics Division, Economic Research Service, U.S. Department of Agriculture. He was on detail to the Congressional Budget Office from December, 1976 through May, 1977.

Charles W. Wiggins is professor of political science at Iowa State University. Research and publication interests focus on state politics, legislative behavior, and interest groups. He has published in most of the professional political science journals and authored *The Iowa Legislator* as well as a monograph series on regional state government.

Ivan Garth Youngberg is professor and chairman of political science at Southeast Missouri State College. He has authored several papers on agriculture policy and previously published in the *Policy Studies Journal* as well as other professional journals.

About the Editors

William P. Browne is associate professor of political science at Central Michigan University. His publications on interest groups, bureaucracy, and local government appear in such journals as *Ethnicity, Public Administration Review* and *Western Political Quarterly*. He also authored the forthcoming *Politics and the Bureaucracy*.

Don F. Hadwiger is professor of political science at Iowa State University. He has authored a number of books and journal articles on food, agriculture, and rural development policy.

DATE DUE

MAY 2 0 '80			
JUN 18 '80			
OCT 21 '80			
DEC 11 '80			
NOV 3 '81			
2 1981